FOOD, FARMING, AND THE COMMON MARKET

KEY

—— National Boundaries

········· Regional Boundaries

L **LUXEMBOURG**

S SAARLAND

V VALLE D'AOSTA

0   100   200
M
0   100   200   300
KM

SCHLESWIG HOLSTEIN

HAMBURG

BREMEN

The Hague

NEDERLAND

NIEDERSACHSEN

BELGIQUE

Brussels

NORDRHEIN-WESTFALEN

Bonn

NORD

L

HESSEN

RHEINLAND PFALZ

S

BASSE-NORMANDIE

HAUTE

PICARDIE

BRETAGNE

PAYS DE LA LOIRE

Paris

RÉGION PARISIENNE

CHAMPAGNE

LORRAINE

ALSACE

BADEN-WÜRTTEM-BERG

BAYERN

CENTRE

BOURGOGNE

FRANCHE COMTÉ

POITOU CHARENTE

LIMOUSIN

AUVERGNE

RHÔNE-ALPES

AQUITAINE

MIDI-PYRÉNÉES

LANGUEDOC

PROVENCE CÔTE D'AZUR

PIEDMONT

LIGURIA

LOMBARDIA

TRENTINO ALTO ADIGE

FRIULI VENEZIA GIULIA

VENETO

EMILIA-ROMAGNA

TOSCANA

MARCHE

UMBRIA

ABRUZZI

CORSE

Rome

L A Z I O

MOLISE

CAMPANIA

PUGLIA

SARDEGNA

BASILICATA

CALABRIA

SICILIA

Regions of the European Economic Community

FOOD, FARMING,
AND
THE COMMON MARKET

MICHAEL BUTTERWICK
AND
EDMUND NEVILLE ROLFE

London
OXFORD UNIVERSITY PRESS
NEW YORK   TORONTO
1968

Oxford University Press, Ely House, London W.1

GLASGOW NEW YORK TORONTO MELBOURNE WELLINGTON
CAPE TOWN SALISBURY IBADAN NAIROBI LUSAKA ADDIS ABABA
BOMBAY CALCUTTA MADRAS KARACHI LAHORE DACCA
KUALA LUMPUR HONG KONG TOKYO

© Oxford University Press 1968

Printed in Great Britain

CONTENTS

TABLES

MAPS

ACKNOWLEDGEMENTS

Thanks are due to a very large number of people on both sides of the Channel for help given to us in the course of writing this book. Information and advice have always been readily forthcoming, often at short notice, from the Commission of the European Economic Community, from the Ministries of Agriculture of the United Kingdom and of the member countries, from the Statistical Office of the Communities, from the National Farmers' Union and farmers' organizations in the Community, from the National Union of Agricultural Workers, from University and other agricultural economic research institutions in a number of countries, as well as from individual members of the grain, feed compounding, and meat trades, the dairy, poultry, sugar-refining, agricultural machinery, and fertilizer industries, and of Agricultural Co-operatives here and on the Continent.

We are especially grateful to Herr Hans-Broder Krohn, of the Directorate-General for Agriculture in the EEC Commission, for his support and interest, and for putting his time and that of so many of his staff at our disposal. We have also received invaluable help from Mr. Derek Prag and the staff of the London Information Office of the European Communities, and, at the Brussels end, from Herr Ernst Freisberg of the Agricultural Section of the Community's Information Services. No thanks can be too great to Miss Valerie Williams, the Librarian at the London office, and her assistant Mrs. Hall, for submitting so patiently to our constant inquiries.

We also thank Mr. George Ford, Agricultural Counsellor at the United Kingdom Delegation to the European Communities in Brussels, for his help over the past eighteen months.

Last and not least our gratitude is due to Mr. Kenneth Clark and Mr. Frank Taylor of the Oxford University Agricultural Economic Research Institute for preparing the Tables and Maps.

INTRODUCTION

The United Kingdom has now made two attempts to become a member of the European Economic Community. Government policy is still directed towards obtaining membership, provided suitable terms can be obtained, at the earliest possible date. In this it receives support in general from the two Opposition parties. The second attempt, which was formally launched in July 1967, has, like the first, been blocked, at least for the time being, by opposition from France. On both occasions the UK agreed to accept the principles of the common agricultural policy.

The main purpose of this book is to describe the differences between the UK and the EEC on agricultural policy and to assess the effects on the UK of making the changes that will be necessary to come into line with the Community. In setting out to achieve this purpose we faced a very obvious difficulty. The EEC's common agricultural policy is still in a state of evolution and so, though to a lesser extent, is policy in the UK. Nevertheless, the Community is within sight of achieving uniform prices and common regulations for all the major agricultural products. While some changes will certainly occur between now and publication this seemed as good a moment as any to bring out a book of this kind. We have also been able to make the necessary adjustments resulting from the sterling devaluation of November 1967. For a number of products this has substantially improved the prospects for UK farmers inside the EEC.

The general objective of the book is to bring together, for the benefit of interested people in the UK and the Community, information about food and farm policy, farming, and the ancillary trades and industries, here and in the EEC. The book is divided into two more or less self-contained sections. Part I gives a general picture of the situation on both sides of the Channel. It analyses the main differences in agricultural policy and trade which would have to be resolved during the course of any future negotiations, pre-negotiations, period of association, transition, or whatever formulas were eventually agreed upon as a preliminary to assumption by the UK of full membership of the Community. Part I also considers briefly the impact of membership on each of the factors of production in the UK.

In Part II, on the other hand, the issues for each of the main temperate farm products are discussed separately. Each chapter contains sections on the existing situation, as regards policy and production, in the UK and in the EEC, and another on the effects for UK policy and production of entering the EEC. The length of each chapter is to some extent governed by the quality of the available information. There is considerable disparity between the present six member countries in this respect. That space somewhat disproportionate to their share of gross agricultural output should have been allotted to eggs is due to the particularly difficult and uncertain conditions likely to be experienced by the majority of producers both in the UK and in the EEC during the next few years. An Appendix summarizes the general issues, from the point of view of food and farming, for the UK's three fellow applicants for membership. The existence of these issues, so far as new applicants are concerned, was recognized by the Commission of the EEC in its report to the Council of 29 September 1967.

Any calling into question of the essential features of this [common agricultural] policy upon the accession of new members is therefore ruled out. In the course of the future implementation and further development of the agricultural policy, the Community might, however, consider certain adjustments which might have to be made in order to allow both for the new factual situation resulting from enlargement and for a number of interests or specific problems peculiar to the new Member States for which there was agreement that Community solutions were necessary.[1]

The statistical material in Part II is arranged mainly so as to give a picture of comparative production in the Six and in the four applicant countries, indicating general orders of magnitude only. We have preferred not to burden the text with extensive statistical tables. Up-to-date figures of annual output are regularly published by the Statistical Office of the European Community, and are available for the other countries in national statistical publications. During the course of 1968 first results of the stratified random sample survey of nearly 2 mn. holdings carried out in the Community in the late autumn of 1966 should in addition give detailed and uniform information on the structure of production and of the agricultural population, much of which is at present either unreliable or non-existent. Except where specially noted, figures quoted in the text are from official sources. Tons, unless otherwise stated, are long tons in the UK and metric tons in the EEC. Appendix L lists some conversion factors.

In aiming at our main objective, of providing a useful reference book, we have had to reach a compromise between considerations of space and of readability. No attempt has been made, for instance, to analyse every major EEC regulation down to the last detail. But we hope that completeness will at least have been sacrificed to clarity, even if somebody's favourite subject is bound to have been skimped. We are aware, for instance, that the complicated procedures involved in the importation, processing, and re-export in processed form of cereal and livestock products have received summary treatment.

We have also had it in mind that a book of this kind would help to guide the reader through the agricultural issues which would be presented if, or when, actual negotiations over the terms of UK membership of the EEC were to begin. Even if such negotiations do not commence in the near future we hope that the book will provide material to illuminate the debate about how far the UK government should proceed in adapting its existing

---

[1] *Opinion on the Applications for Membership received from the United Kingdom, Ireland, Denmark and Norway*, Commission of the European Communities, Brussels, 29 September 1967.

farm policy towards the common agricultural policy. If the French government is finally persuaded by its partners to agree to the fixing of an eventual date for British accession, the intervening period of transition or association will inevitably involve such a process of adaptation. The benefit to the exchequer of replacing deficiency payments by import levies, at any rate until these have to be remitted to a Community Fund; the incentive that levies could give to import-saving increases in output at home of, amongst other things, wheat, beef, and dairy products; the advantage of being able to spread the impact of higher food prices over a relatively long waiting period; these are all factors which are bound in any case to weigh heavily with any British government determined in the long run to get into the EEC.

In the meantime the common agricultural policy itself will not be standing still. Although uniform prices for all major products will be in force throughout the Community by 1 July 1968, the common regulations for milk and for beef and veal are still in course of last-minute revision and are unlikely to have been finalized much before they become applicable on 1 April. The threat of mounting butter surpluses, totalling about 150,000 tons for the Community, makes the interlocking of the milk and beef regulations a particularly delicate operation, politically as well as economically.[2] With surpluses of other products besides butter and soft wheat in the offing, the EEC authorities have become increasingly aware that achievement of uniform prices and marketing arrangements provide a very partial solution to problems of an agricultural common market. Working out a successful common structural policy will be even harder. Under Article 39 of the Treaty of Rome the Six are committed to taking special account of 'the social structure' of agriculture. This has been taken to mean preserving the family farm unit. As a principal objective it is not easy to reconcile with the economic and technical realities of agricultural production and marketing in developed economies, particularly where farm units are of such small average size as in the Community.

A further stage yet to be reached in the agricultural common market is the establishment of uniform veterinary, plant health, and food standard regulations. These negotiations, in which the UK among other non-members has taken part as an observer, have made very slow progress. Member governments are understandably disinclined to surrender too easily a number of serviceable pretexts still available for closing their frontiers to imports of farm produce. These are also spheres of influence where national civil servants and local authorities can be relied upon to

---

[2] 30 per cent of cows in the Community are in herds of under 5 cows. In Germany, it is estimated that of the 900,000 cows in such herds one-third are owned by part-time farmers. The so-called 'postman's cow' has a potential annual output of 40,000 tons of butter. It would be unfair to blame it all on the postmen; in 1962 the railwaymen-farmers' journal is said to have had a circulation of 190,000. Premiums for giving up production have been suggested as a possible solution, but this might merely provoke a switch to part-time pig-keeping instead. Another 300,000 cows in small herds of not more than 7 or 8 cows provide an important source of income for farmers in mountain areas of France and Italy. Even if half of these could be induced to raise their calves for beef the milk position would be eased.

resist change, outside interference, and reduction of their own powers, with vigour and tenacity.

Finally, even if farmers receive uniform prices throughout the Community but continue to bear different costs in different countries the common agricultural market is still incomplete. The achievement of uniform product prices should therefore act as a catalyst to harmonization of transport and tax policies, both urgent items on the EEC agenda. Agriculture also provides a precedent for the pattern of Community action in both these fields: first, harmonization of *systems* (cf. the common marketing regulations mainly agreed between 1962 and 1965), then a gradual reconciliation of national *rates* (cf. target prices) from a relatively wide *fourchette* to complete uniformity. In the field of taxation a common value-added tax system will have been adopted by all six countries by the end of 1969. It will then remain to make uniform by the end of a second stage, preferably brief, the rate at which the tax is levied. Transport policy and freight rates will probably be treated in two stages in the same way.

What follows, then, is an account of the present situation for food and farming in the United Kingdom and in the European Economic Community, how it has evolved, and the direction in which it is moving. We hope to have provided in convenient form information which will help the assessment of what measures might be taken on this side of the Channel to adapt conditions of farm production to those appropriate in an enlarged Community.

Oxford.
February 1968

PART I

Reconciling Agricultural Policies

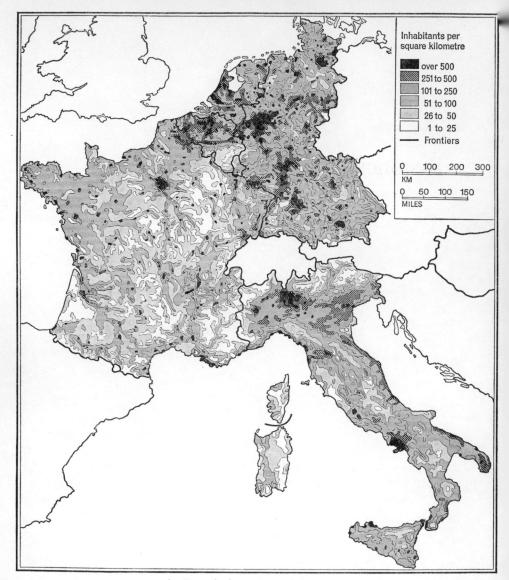

1. Population map of the EEC.

(Source: Information Office of the Communities)

TOWNS AND CONURBATIONS OF OVER 300,000 INHABITANTS IN EEC AND APPLICANT COUNTRIES

Data: 1965, unless stated, in '000s.

*London	7,949	*Lyons	886	The Hague	593	Bochum	357
*Paris	7,369[1]	Amsterdam	862	Bremen	592	Bari	335
Rome	2,514	Cologne	854	Hanover	559	Coventry	330
*Manchester	2,457	*Newcastle	851	Duisburg	490	*Toulouse	329[1]
*Birmingham	2,393	Genoa	848	Sheffield	489	*Nantes	328[1]
Berlin, W.	2,202	*Marseilles	807[1]	Bologna	481	Mannheim	327
Hamburg	1,857	*Lille-Roubaix	771[1]	Nuremberg	472	*Rouen	325[1]
*Glasgow	1,789	Rotterdam	728	*Bordeaux	462[1]	Nottingham	311
*Leeds	1,726	Essen	727	Florence	454	*Nice	310[1]
Milan	1,673	Düsseldorf	700	*Liège	443	*Strasbourg	302[1]
*Liverpool	1,381	Frankfurt/Main	691	Bristol	431	Hull	300
Copenhagen	1,370[2]	*Antwerp	657	Wuppertal	423		
Naples	1,236	Dortmund	656	Belfast	407	* Conurbations	
Munich	1,210	Palermo	634	Catania	396	[1] 1962	
Turin	1,107	Stuttgart	633	Gelsenkirchen	374	[2] 1964	
*Brussels	1,066	*Dublin	595	Venice	364		

1. The Making of the Common Agricultural Policy, 1958–1968

In 1958 farming was occupying fifteen million people in the six signatory countries of the Treaty of Rome, over 20 per cent of the total working population. Given the impact that this must have on an economic community it is hardly surprising that the Treaty explicitly provided for a common agricultural policy. Previous concepts of a united Europe, notably those in which the United Kingdom had been involved as a possible participant, during the fifties were inclined to have less ambitious plans for agriculture. The Six, however, with an eye to the distorting effects on costs and wages of sharp differences in farm prices between member countries of an industrial common market, were convinced of the need to eliminate the differences in agricultural support policy which gave rise to them. In the event a mere nine out of the Treaty's 248 articles laid the modest base on which over the intervening ten years has been erected a complex structure of regulations. In order to understand the importance attached in 1968 by the European Economic Community to acceptance by new applicants of its Common Agricultural Policy without major modifications it is worth having a brief look at the main events of this complicated building operation and at the very disparate materials which the architects had at their disposal.

The creation of an agricultural community involved reconciling both climatic and geographical conditions and official attitudes that were widely dissimilar. The first cut across national frontiers, but the latter narrowly defined them. The Community may be roughly divided into three types of geographical region,[1] shared by no means equally between the six member countries. About 45 per cent of the land surface consists of lowlands below the 650-foot contour, mostly fertile. A broad semi-circular belt stretches across the west and north from the Pyrenees to the frontier of East Germany. There is the Po basin in northern Italy, and, around the Mediterranean, from the Pyrenees to the Adriatic, a series of coastal plains, some stretching far inland like the Rhône Valley, others sandwiched between the mountains and the sea. The second type of region, between 650 and 1,600 feet above sea level, covers just over a quarter of the land area, including much of central and eastern France, central and eastern areas of the Federal Republic, and parts of central Italy. Most of

---

[1] See J. Bourrinet, *Le problème agricole dans l'intégration européene* (Montpellier, 1964), pp. 40 *et seq.*

this is suitable for livestock rearing, and much of it is also used for cereal growing. Thirdly, almost 30 per cent of the EEC's land area is hill and mountain: the Alps, the Pyrenees, the Massif Central, the Vosges and Jura, and the Appenines. The farms in these areas, unsuited to modern methods of husbandry, present major social and economic problems. Half of the surface of this type of region lies within the frontiers of Italy, and a third is in France. France, on the other hand, enjoys by far the largest share of the lowland area—55 per cent—with Germany having 20 per cent and Italy only 15 per cent. The whole of the Netherlands and most of Belgium lie within this generally fertile area, but Luxemburg is entirely within the second, upland, type of region, facing it with agricultural problems whose exceptional treatment is the subject of a Protocol to the Treaty. Finally, the considerable variations in mean annual temperature and rainfall, and particularly in its distribution over the year, should not be overlooked. A mean temperature of 17·3° C. (63° F.) in Palermo may be compared with one of 7·3° C. (45° F.) on the Danish border. Flushing and Lecce (in the heel of Italy) both have the same average annual rainfall —650 mm. (25·5 inches). At Flushing half of it falls between April and September, in Lecce less than a third. In Lecce it is concentrated in 72 days of the year, in Flushing it is spread over 118 days.[2]

Since the war national support policies for agriculture mostly developed in a somewhat *ad hoc* fashion in Western Europe, with varying stress being laid in different countries and at different times, according to the current political and economic climate, on long-term measures to improve farm structure and marketing and on short-term adjustments to prices. In Germany, despite the increasing attention given in the annual Green Plan during the fifties to land consolidation and other measures of structural improvement, as well as generous price support, production was unable to keep pace with rising demand, so that the country was only 60 per cent self-sufficient by the end of the decade compared with 75 per cent at the beginning. Four Import and Storage Boards, for cereals, sugar, milk and milk products, and oilseed rape, administered a system of import taxes and quotas and direct farm subsidies designed to adjust the prices of imports to the level of the guaranteed producer prices for the commodities which they administered.

Besides import duties and quotas, the most permanent feature of French agricultural policy since the war has been the complete control of cereal marketing by ONIC,[3] an official agency dating from 1936 on which government, farmers, and grain trade are all represented. From 1953, after the end of the post-war phase of encouraging production at any price, products other than cereals such as meat and milk received selective encouragement on a year-to-year basis. The trial between 1957 and 1960 of long-term target prices for most major products, fixed three or four

[2] *Major agricultural regions of the EEC*, in OECD, Food and Agriculture Series No. 27, 1960.

[3] *Office National Interprofessionel pour les Céréales*. The extension of the term 'profession' to occupations other than those to which it is at present narrowly limited in English usage seems a likely, and welcome, result of joining the EEC.

years ahead but also tied to the cost of inputs by a complicated system of indexing, had to be abandoned as a failure. The agencies responsible for administering these non-cereal schemes, mostly with 'professional' participation as well, were eventually taken under the wing of the FORMA (*Fonds d'Orientation et de Régularisation des Marchés Agricoles*) set up, with government finance, under the *Loi d'Orientation Agricole* of 1960. This law and its *Loi Complémentaire* of 1962, mark a fundamental attempt to drag French agriculture into the second half of the twentieth century and equip it, structurally and technically, to make good the opportunities presented by the Common Market.

Improving structure and infra-structure has been a feature of agricultural policy since the middle fifties in Italy, where only the price of wheat, and that by ancient tradition, received direct government support. Minimum import prices were maintained for butter, and for beef and veal. Olive oil production was aided in years of poor harvests. Prices of tobacco and sugar-beet were fixed, but not subsidized. The post-war land reform, carried out from mainly political motives, created large numbers of small-holdings many of which are not economically viable today, particularly where there is no irrigation. Neither the authors of the reform nor those of subsequent Agricultural Plans can be entirely blamed for failing to foresee the industrial development which revolutionized the Italian economy after 1955. In trying to raise farm incomes, especially those in the south, they saw the problem set permanently in a context of mainly subsistence agriculture and widespread under-employment relieved only by migration abroad. All the same, far too little attention was given to organizing markets for the extra production which official policy was even then busy encouraging. It was an omission only now being made good under pressure of the need to export.

Netherlands farmers, in contrast to those of Italy, have a long tradition of both co-operation and exporting. They also received considerable government support in the form of guaranteed prices for cereals, sugar-beet, potatoes for starch, and milk. Levies were raised on imported feed grains and milk products received export subsidies. Egg exporters were also given rebates to compensate for the higher cost of imported feed. Basically, guaranteed prices were fixed in accordance with officially analysed production costs, but in effect they were also adjusted to guide output away from surplus products. Besides price support an extensive programme of structural reform, including a graduated pension scheme for farmers voluntarily giving up their holdings for amalgamation, has been in operation for the past ten years. Dutch farms being particularly small and fragmented, this has helped to give practical effect to the notion of the 'well-managed holding justifiable from a social and economic point of view' which has been the basic criterion of official policy.

In Belgium, on the other hand, structural policy has been belated and half-hearted, the problem of fragmentation being especially complicated by the prevalence of leasehold. Support for farmers was therefore mainly through price policy, target (but not firm guaranteed) prices being set for wheat, milk, butter, eggs, beef, and pigmeat. An Agricultural Fund intervened with export and other subsidies, including some on inputs. There was a consumer subsidy for milk. Luxemburg was the only country of the Six to have a system of deficiency payments, equivalent to about 17 per cent of the value of gross agricultural output.

None of the policies pursued by the six signatories of the Treaty of Rome up to 1961 can be said to have been more than partially successful in solving the problem of either farm incomes or farm structure, or of encouraging notably high levels of productivity. Except in the Netherlands, where incomes from agriculture were reckoned in 1958 to be just over three-quarters of those in other sectors, in most of the member countries they were something over half, and in Italy as low as 38 per cent.[4] Two-thirds of all holdings in the Six were still under 25 acres at the end of the fifties, and each of the 6·5 mn. holdings consisted on average of some six separate plots. In Germany the average was eleven plots. Although labour productivity in the Netherlands was relatively high, 11 per cent of the labour force being occupied in farming in 1959 and accounting for 10·1 per cent of GNP, in Italy the corresponding proportions were 30 and 18·7, in France 27 and 12·5,[5] and in Germany 15 and 8·0.

The six governments made understandably slow progress at first in putting into effect their determination to set agricultural policy above national interests.[6] A conference convened at Stresa, in July 1958, under the chairmanship of Dr. Sicco Mansholt, former Netherlands minister of agriculture and the member of the EEC Commission especially charged with agricultural policy, had a clear mandate under Article 43 of the Treaty. Its purpose was to analyse, within the considerable limitations of the statistical information then available, the existing situation and current policies of each member country, and to make recommendations for a future common policy. Both the analysis and the subsequent discussion revealed a sharp confrontation of national points of view: the French laying special emphasis on organized markets, the Germans on structural reform as a means of raising farm incomes, the Italians on liberalizing trade and abolishing subsidies, the Dutch showing themselves fiercely anti-autarkic, and the Belgians generally conciliatory. The conference did, however, throw up a number of major conclusions, providing a *point de départ* for the Community philosophy which the Commission's officials, through all the ups and down of the past ten years, have developed and strengthened. It is worth summarizing at the outset, in order to understand what makes the CAP tick, the objectives which the officials of ministries and farmers' organizations laid down at Stresa:

   (i) to increase trade in agricultural produce between member countries and with third countries and eliminate all quantitative restrictions;

[4] Stresa Conference working paper, quoted by Bourrinet, *op. cit.*, p. 124.   [5] 1954.
[6] For a detailed description of the course of the Community negotiations from 1958 to 1962 see Bourrinet, *op. cit.*, pp. 140 *et seq.*

(ii) to maintain a close correlation between structural and market policies;

(iii) to achieve a balance between supply and demand, avoiding encouragement of surpluses, and giving scope to the comparative advantage of each region;

(iv) to eliminate all subsidies tending to distort competition between one country or region and another;

(v) to improve the rate of return on capital and labour;

(vi) to preserve the family structure of farming;

(vii) to encourage rural industrialization so as to draw away surplus labour and eliminate marginal farms, and to give special aid to geographically disadvantaged regions.

As will be readily evident to the reader, not all these objectives can be at all times reconciled one with another. But, within the limits of the art of the possible, politics and philosophy have gone hand in hand.

It was left to the Commission to translate these resolutions into draft regulations. Constitutional procedure under the Treaty requires the submission of these to the Assembly of the Community.[7] Although this was done at the beginning of 1960, approval was not complete until June. As a result of further discussion by the Economic and Social Committee,[8] the Commission agreed to bring matters such as agricultural education, social security for farmers and farmworkers, grants for transfer out of agriculture, and rural housing, under the CAP. The Treaty of Rome clearly envisaged a three-stage progress towards a common agricultural market. The first exploratory stage was to last not longer than three years. A second stage, during which national policies and prices would be gradually aligned and merged in common regulations, was to be completed not later than 1 January 1970, the date set for the end of the Treaty's transitional period for the alignment of industrial tariffs. The third stage would be the completely integrated organization for all agricultural produce within the common external frontier of the Community. Except that Article 44 allowed for the maintenance of minimum import prices between member countries during the second phase at a level calculated not to discourage the development of intra-Community trade, the Treaty gave no indication at all of the mechanism to be adopted. By the end of 1960, however, the variable levy had been accepted in principle by the Council of Ministers as the means of adjusting current external market prices to internal target prices, whether between

[7] The assent of the Assembly (or European Parliament, as it has been re-named) consisting of 142 members of the national legislatures, is required to approve the Commission's proposals. It may amend them, but has no power to initiate policy or to legislate. Use is made of parliamentary questions to obtain information from the Commission.

[8] An advisory body whose members mainly represent employers' associations and trades unions of the member countries. It may formally approve the Commission's proposals or suggest amendments (*avis*) or merely state majority and minority views (*rapport*). The main work on agriculture is done by its appropriate sub-committee of members (*section spécialisée*) in the presence of representatives of the Commission, of the secretariat of the Council, and occasionally of the permanent delegations of the member countries.

individual member countries or between third countries and the Community as a whole. In this way EEC producers would be protected from competition from lower prices prevailing on world markets outside. The prices of imports would be raised automatically by the appropriate customs levy to threshold levels fixed close to the internal target prices.[9] The alternative method of the deficiency payment was not found to be acceptable on two main grounds: its high cost, and the difficulty of administering a system involving claims by some six million farmers, most of whom would be poorly educated and many illiterate. Two other considerations, though not explicitly stated, must have weighed in favour of the proposed 'free market' system. It would provide a more effective lever for moving out of agriculture the vast labour surplus. Deficiency payments however much hedged about by standard quantities and other qualifications, involve a greater degree of firm price guarantee than does the Community system. In such a situation political pressures resulting in 'feather-bedding' price levels might have been even harder to resist. Secondly, in none of the six countries did there exist a tradition of cheap food for the consumer. There was therefore no particular incentive suddenly to start providing him with it at world prices by introducing deficiency payments as part of the CAP.

Despite this agreement in principle about levies little further progress was made during 1961 in getting the Six to surrender their tried national systems and patterns of trade. The Germans were reluctant to reduce their meat imports from South America and continued to maintain health regulations against those from France. The Italians accused the French of dumping wine. French farmers began to see their hopes dashed of an easy outlet for their surpluses. The Dutch continued to look mainly to their overseas trade. It is ironic that one of the longest of the Treaty's agricultural clauses made detailed provision for the conclusion of long-term contracts between the signatories during the initial period. So little were they *en rapport* at the time that only one was ever made, for a rather paltry amount of 650,000 tons of cereals supplied by France to Germany. Although in June 1961 M. Debré, the French prime minister, was saying that without a common agricultural policy there could be no common market and no Europe, it was not until 18 December that the pressure of events forced the Council of Ministers into action. With the three-year time limit for the preparatory period due to expire at the end of the month, and the United Kingdom's recent application to join as a further spur, the Council embarked on the celebrated marathon and package deal that was to become the prototype for several more, and no doubt for others still to come. So far at no other time has it been found necessary officially to stop the clock: the decisions, eventually reached at 5.30 a.m. on 14 January 1962, had to be made effective from midnight on 31 December 1961 to comply with the Treaty.

[9] A summary, in tabular form, of the main protective measures and arrangements for regulating internal markets for each commodity is given in Appendix A.

Six years afterwards the agreement initiating a common policy for cereals, pigmeat, eggs, poultry meat, fruit and vegetables, and wine, and laying down the broad principles for financing it, which was hammered out by the Council in the course of 17 days, and nearly as many nights, of sessions, looks quite small beer compared with the unified market for these and almost as many other products again which is completed on 1 July 1968. But in spite of later hazards the first step was undoubtedly the hardest one. Until it was taken no specifically Community policy could emerge. Once it had been taken, however many compromises might be necessary or temporary exceptions and allowances made, there was no going back to separate national policies. The second instalment of regulations, covering the rest of the main products, left hanging in mid-air when negotiations with the UK were broken off in January 1963, was not agreed until nearly two years after the first, in December 1963, following a second, though somewhat shorter, marathon.

The main effect of these new policies was to eliminate distortions to fair competition due to national subsidies and import quotas and establish common standards of quality for the commodities covered by the regulations and for their numerous by-products. During the first two years of the CAP, 1962/63 and 1963/64, relatively slow progress was made in reconciling the wide divergence of prices which had previously existed. Leaving Luxemburg out of account, where prices were generally the highest in the Community, the spread was in most cases widest between Germany and France, with the other three member countries somewhere in between.[10] In 1960/61 the lowest national wheat price in the EEC was 72 per cent of the highest, the lowest barley price 63 per cent, egg price (the Netherlands) 62 per cent, and milk and sugar-beet prices 80 per cent each. These wide differences were not fully reflected in the *fourchette* of member country target prices fixed for cereals and cereal conversion products (eggs, pigmeat, and poultry meat) for 1962/63 under the new regulations. Progress in ironing them out was nevertheless slow, necessitating the raising of substantial levies between the countries. The Commission therefore proposed early in 1964 that the Community should proceed at one stage to the harmonization of cereal prices (and thus to those of conversion products as well) for the 1964/65 harvest year. Cereal prices being, as had always been recognized, the key to the CAP, such a step would have notably accelerated the whole pace of European integration. Its effects would be felt far beyond agriculture itself, making a unilateral devaluation of its currency, for instance, by any member country a great deal more difficult. Although in the day-to-day business of the Commission common prices are customarily discussed, for convenience, in terms of a particular national currency, the Deutsch Mark, formal decisions concerning them are expressed in terms of the neutral 'unit of account', equivalent in value to the United States gold dollar. The dissociation of the harmonized farm prices from national frontiers is thus underlined.

[10] Bourrinet, *op. cit.*, p. 207.

Although the principle of accelerating price unification was agreeable to member governments, the so-called Mansholt proposals were considered too precipitate. The unified prices for cereals eventually agreed upon, after the customary extended bargaining, in December 1964 were not to come into force until 1 July 1967. As a *quid pro quo* for accepting the key soft wheat price of DM425 per ton the German government, which was under strong political pressure from the farm lobby to hold out for DM450 or more, secured the payment out of Community funds between 1967 and 1970 of compensatory lump sums to German farmers. The justification for this subsidy was the bringing forward of the date of the unified market from the one laid down in the Treaty. Italy on the other hand was compensated for the loss which would be caused to its livestock producers by the rise to them of the price of feed grains. Besides similar lump sums, special lower minimum import prices were to be allowed till 1972, and the importance to Italy's agricultural economy of horticultural products was to be recognized by a complete redrafting of the common fruit and vegetables regulation to allow for market support out of Community funds. Further, Italy's contribution to the Fund during 1965/66 and 1966/67 would be limited to a ceiling of 18 per cent and 22 per cent respectively. As a logical consequence of these decisions the Commission was requested by the Council of Ministers to submit to it proposals for the financing of the CAP not only for the two years still to run before the beginning of the unified market, but, more important, for the unified market itself.

Emboldened by the success of the three marathons of December 1961, December 1963, and December 1964 the Commission, in giving its reply to this request in March 1965, wrapped up in its package a number of controversial issues. Apart from the details of the future working of the Agricultural Fund, which are discussed below,[11] it was proposed that as a logical extension of the harmonization of agricultural prices, all intra-Community duties on industrial goods should be abolished on 1 July 1967, thus bringing forward by two and a half years the end of the transition period in all its aspects. Further, the entire proceeds not only of the agricultural levies but of the common external tariff on industrial goods should also accrue to the Community budget. In view of the likely cost of the CAP this also had some logic. Finally, the Commission proposed that owing to the enormous financial responsibility which such an arrangement would place upon it, the European Parliament should be given wider powers of supervision of the Commission's stewardship. As is well known, the Commission's proposed package proved wholly unacceptable to President de Gaulle, and resulted in the withdrawal of the French from the Council of Ministers at the end of June without even arrangements for the interim financing of the CAP from 1 July having been agreed. It was implied that the Commission had exceeded its brief and had been acting *ultra vires* in making these proposals. The Commission, however, relied on the sense of Article 201 of the Treaty, which begins: 'The Commission

[11] See pp. 12 *et seq.*

shall study the conditions under which the financial contributions of Member States provided for in Article 200 may be replaced by other resources of the Community itself, in particular by revenue accruing from the common customs tariff when the latter has been definitely introduced. For this purpose, the Commission shall submit proposals to the Council.'

The settlement reached on the working of the Fund after the return of the French to the Council table nearly a year later is described below.[12] The Luxemburg agreement, so called from the 'neutral' *venue* of the first full Council meeting held after the breach in May 1966, advanced the date of the full customs union by eighteen months only, to 1 July 1968. The Commission's *risqué* proposal about the additional powers of the Assembly was tactfully forgotten. Despite the cost to the Commission in influence and self-confidence of the 1965/66 crisis it could not be deprived of the exclusive power given it under the Treaty of initiating proposals for regulations, an initiative not enjoyed by the Council of Ministers itself. The Council may issue directives defining principles of common policy, but these have no legally binding force. Its agreement is, however, required to the regulations, which are the Community's law and which are issued in the Council's name. In effect the Council seldom rejects out of hand the Commission's draft regulations on major topics though it quite often amends them. Since the day-to-day working of the CAP also involves large numbers of regulations of a technical nature, often the result of decisions having to be taken at short notice, the Commission is empowered to issue these without prior reference to the Council, which only meets, on average, once a month.[13] The Commission may, of course, be required by the Council to justify its actions *a posteriori*. Disagreements on this kind of issue between Commission and Council are, however, virtually excluded by means of the system of Management Committees (*comités de gestion*). These operate for each of the products for which a market regulation is in force. They have the same national representation and voting powers as the Council of Ministers except that their chairmen, who have no vote, are members of the Commission, which also provides the secretariat. Their members, being all officials of the ministries of agriculture of the member states, provide a vital link between governments (which have, after all, to carry out the regulations) and the Commission in the day-to-day application of the CAP. This is an important check, from the Council's point of view, on the executive powers of the Commission. The Committees are, however, prevented by the voting arrangements from completely hamstringing the Commission's administration. A majority of at least 12 out of the 17 votes is required to enable a Committee to stop any action by the Commission and have it referred back, within a month, to the Council, which may then, by a similar qualified majority, oblige the

[12] See p. 13.
[13] Consisting, when agricultural questions are to be discussed, of either the foreign ministers, finance ministers, or ministers of agriculture of the member countries, with the chair occupied in rotation by each member country.

Commission to withdraw the measure. Therefore as long as the Commission can carry with it at least one of the major member countries (with four votes) and either Belgium or the Netherlands (with two votes each) on any Committee, giving at least six votes in favour of its action and only eleven against, its wishes cannot be frustrated. To a liberal parliamentarian these checks may seem little more than an elaborate bureaucratic conspiracy. The existence of the Committee is certainly a restriction on the Commission's supranational role.

We have given this brief historical account of the origins and development of the CAP in order to stress how far apart the Six were when they started out on their journey into the common agricultural market and what substantial sacrifices of principle and self-interest, not by any means shared equally, will have been made by the time the transition period laid down by the Treaty has run its full course on 1 January 1970. The last great test to be undergone before then concerns the permanent method to be adopted of financing the CAP. A look at how this problem has developed since 1962 will help to clarify the points at issue.

So far paying for the CAP has proceeded by a series of compromises about the share to be contributed out of national budgets. Agricultural support falls under two main headings: price guarantees, and what, for want of a better word to translate the French word *orientation*, has come to be known officially as guidance. Under the first heading are the costs of (a) official intervention to support the market, either by purchase for storage or transformation (e.g. de-naturing of wheat for stockfeed, melting down of butter into cooking fat, distilling of sugar) for subsequent re-sale on domestic or third country markets, and of (b) restitutions or subsidies paid on exports of Community produce to enable them to be sold at lower world market prices. Guidance covers the cost of all types of aid out of Community funds towards structural improvements of production and marketing.

For 1962/63 the costs of the CAP were met entirely out of national budgets according to a scale of contributions, or key, laid down in Article 200 of the Treaty for the Community's budget (which covers its administrative costs). This scale (Germany, France, and Italy, 28 per cent each; Belgium and the Netherlands 7·9 per cent each; and Luxemburg 0·2 per cent) was also used as a basis for contributions to the Agricultural Fund, which was set up as a result of the January 1962 marathon. Article 40 envisaged a Fund or Funds, but in the event separate financing of individual commodities was rejected in favour of a central European Agricultural Guidance and Guarantee Fund, generally known as FEOGA (*Fonds Européen d'Orientation et de Garantie Agricole*). The Fund is divided into two distinctly managed Guidance and Guarantee Sections. For 1963/64 90 per cent of the Guarantee Section's expenditure was to be met from contributions assessed according to the key, and the remaining 10 per cent in proportion to each member country's share of the Community's net imports. For 1964/65 these proportions were modified to

80 per cent and 20 per cent respectively. The French withdrawal from the Council of Ministers left the question of financing FEOGA hanging in mid-air. It was not until May 1966, almost the end of the 1965/66 accounting year, that the Luxemburg settlement fixed a new scale of contributions to the Guarantee Section for that year and for 1966/67 (see Table 3). Italy's share for 1965/66 having been limited to 18 per cent at the time of the December 1964 marathon, Germany agreed to exceed, for that year only, the ceiling of 31 per cent already placed on its contribution under an earlier arrangement, and France for the first time accepted the largest share. For the remaining two and a half years to the end of the transition period, from 1 July 1967 to 31 December 1969, when the Fund would be directly financing the whole of Community expenditure on guarantees for the first time (see below), contributions were to be assessed, according to the Luxemburg settlement, on an entirely fresh basis. A variable element consists of 90 per cent of each country's receipts from levies and customs duties on agricultural produce raised at the common external frontier. This should cover about half the expenditure of the Guarantee Section of the Fund. The balance is to be found according to a fixed scale per cent: France 32, Germany 31·2, Italy 20·3, Netherlands 8·2, Belgium 8·1 and Luxemburg 0·2.

During each of the first four years the financing of export restitutions (to make up the difference between world market prices and internal target prices) accounted for about 80 per cent of drawings from FEOGA for guarantee purposes, the high proportion devoted to cereals in the first two years falling fairly rapidly once other commodities were brought under the CAP. In 1965/66 export refunds on milk and milk products already amounted to $70 mn., compared with $104 mn. on cereals. To this must be added internal market support for butter costing $28 mn. and for cereals (mainly for denaturing) costing $16 mn. These figures do not of course represent the full amounts actually paid to farmers in the Community by way of price support for these products. In 1965/66 the proportion of guarantee payments being shouldered by FEOGA was still only six-tenths. Rising by stages from one-sixth in 1962/63 the Fund's responsibility finally extended to 100 per cent[14] of payments from 1 July 1967 on the establishment of the unified markets for cereals, pigmeat, eggs, and poultry meat.

It will be evident that, owing to the considerable variations in self-sufficiency between one member country and another, individual contributions to and drawings from the Guarantee Section of FEOGA have never balanced very closely and are never likely to. A glance at Table 3 will show the preponderant benefit accruing to France in the early years of the Fund's operation.[15] Given France's position as a net exporter it is

[14] There is an upper ceiling of $60 mn. a year for market support costs of fruit and vegetables (of which Italy is alloted $40 mn.) up to 1969.

[15] Owing to delays in auditing, national claims payments by FEOGA have normally been a year or more in arrears. At the unified market stage, however, settlements are to be made several times a year.

always likely to remain the principal beneficiary. Market support for products other than cereals, notably butter, cheese, pigmeat, fruit and vegetables, and olive oil has, however, considerably redressed the balance in favour of the other countries. Narrowing of the price ratio between wheat and feed grains may help to reduce French wheat surpluses whose export has to be subsidized by FEOGA. The long wrangles which have gone on within the Council of Ministers over the years about the contribution scales to the Fund are easily understandable, each member feeling that in one way or another his treasury was being asked to make an uneven sacrifice. Heated arguments such as whether restitutions should be refunded to national exchequers on the basis of gross or net exports are now mainly of historical interest. Since 1 July 1967 they have been calculated on the basis of gross exports, the rate at which they are payable being either the full or partial levy rate currently applicable, according to the nature and destination of the exports. Rates of restitution are agreed between the Commission and the appropriate Management Committee.

Financing of the Guidance Section of FEOGA has been much simpler. In the first place expenditure was from the outset fixed annually at one third of the expenditure of the Guarantee Section, and the 1965 Luxemburg agreement subsequently established an upper ceiling of $285 mn. National contributions have been fixed according to the percentage scale prevailing for the Guarantee Section at the time. Capital grants from the Guidance Section are allotted up to a maximum of 25 per cent (in Italy and Luxemburg up to 45 per cent in certain cases) of the total cost of approved investment projects, on condition that the individuals, co-operatives, or firms benefiting from the grants contribute at least 30 per cent (which may be in the form of borrowing), and that some part of the balance is found by the sponsoring member government. Applications, which cannot be entertained for work already started, must be made by the proposed beneficiary or his agent, such as a bank, through his ministry of agriculture or competent institution. Payments out of the Fund are made through the same intermediaries. Although in the first three years applications were forwarded to FEOGA on the initiative of member countries, from October 1967 only projects have been acceptable which fall within the Community's official common three-year programmes (1967–69). The $672 mn. which it is estimated will accrue to the Guidance Section during this period will be divided up under ten major headings in three main groups: programmes designed to increase productivity, particularly that of labour; those promoting improved marketing of horticultural and milk products; and those combining improvement of both productivity and marketing (for meat, wine, olive oil and generally backward regions). The first group of programmes comprises land consolidation, irrigation, drainage, and development of woodlands as part of structural improvement.

Since the amount of funds available for a given year to the Guidance Section is only known after the drawing up of the Guarantee Section's accounts, allocations have to be made in arrears. As will be seen from Table 2 the delay between the submission of applications to national ministries and their actual approval by FEOGA can be hardly less than two years. This must considerably lessen the value to individual farmers of the Fund as a source of aid. In any case its contribution to investments in EEC agriculture will remain a fairly modest one. It has been estimated by the Commission that by 1970 all forms of structural investment in agriculture in the Six will amount to $11,000 mn. With a ceiling of $285 mn. and normal participation of 25 per cent, the Guidance Section would by then be assisting about $1,100 mn. worth of investment, or 10 per cent of the total.

Apportionment of grants between member countries is supposed to be on an 'equitable and harmonious basis'. That amounts paid in and drawn out by each country were at first roughly equal is said to have been a coincidence. In any case, unlike the disbursements of the Guarantee Section, those of the Guidance Section are made to individual organizations and not to national treasuries. Pressures within the Council of Ministers and the relevant Management Committee (*Comité des Structures*)[16] are therefore less. For the first two years funds were allocated fairly evenly between marketing schemes and those promoting structural improvements on the land and in marketing. For 1965/66 a greater stress was evident on marketing, $25 mn. out of $42 mn. going for schemes of this kind, $24 mn. to raising productivity, and the balance to schemes of a mixed purpose. In addition a special grant of $45 mn. for production and marketing of olive oil, fruit and vegetables, and $15 mn. for tobacco, was allotted to Italy to be spent up to the end of 1969. Table 1 gives an idea of the variety of undertakings which are eligible for aid.

We have examined at some length the part played by finance in the evolution of the CAP, since it is a question about which a good deal more will be heard. The importance of FEOGA as a focus for progress in harmonizing other national policies, fiscal, monetary, transport, and social, makes the ultimate decision about its future after 1969 a particularly vital one for the Community. The Fund has been described as 'un facteur d'intégration implacable'.[17] The solution adopted will be essentially a political one, hammered out in the Council. With President de Gaulle still on the scene it is unlikely to resemble closely the Commission's full-blooded supranational proposals of 1965. Whatever happens 100 per cent of the agricultural levies will, under Regulation 25 which governs FEOGA, be payable into the Fund from the end of the transition period onwards. This might cover 50 per cent of its needs. The negotiations will concern the balance. Should this continue to be found from national budgets according to some fixed scale, or from all or part of the customs duties on industrial

---

[16] Day-to-day contact between the Commission and national fiscal administrations is maintained through the Fund's other Management Committee, that for the Guarantee Section, the *Comité du Fonds*.

[17] Bernard Robert, *Le financement de la politique agricole commune* (EEC, Brussels, September 1965).

imports into the Community? Under the Commission's earlier proposals a progressively larger share of these duties would, between 1967 and 1973, have been put at its disposal. One of the weak points of the Commission's case in 1965 was that the full amount of duties accruing to the Community budget after 1972 would probably have provided a larger revenue than was necessary. The Commission proposed, rather lamely, that any surplus should simply be handed back again to member countries. It seems probable that when the Commission presents to the Council its draft regulation for the Fund's future, which under the Treaty it is required to do, a modified version of the 1965 proposal on customs duties will be included. Not all the Six have an equal interest in surrendering the full amount of duties collected at their frontiers, as will be evident from the preponderant part played in the Community's trade with third countries by Antwerp, Rotterdam, Amsterdam, and German North Sea ports.

The situation is further complicated by the fact that the Treaty of Rome could, in theory at least, have been superseded by 1969 by a new treaty confirming the fusion of the three European Communities, the EEC, the European Coal and Steel Community and Euratom. The fusion of their Executives has already made some progress since 1967. The new Commission, temporarily enlarged to eleven members, should submit its proposals for a new treaty within two years. This must inevitably involve the important question of financing. It is interesting in this connection to note the greater autonomy under the Treaty of Luxemburg of the High Authority of the ECSC, which levies taxes on the coal and steel industry that do not pass through national treasuries at all. Thus a decision on the future of FEOGA could have all the makings of a really jumbo-size package deal. It is hardly surprising that some people in the Community do not want any new members joining in this super-marathon.

Overshadowing these political issues is the rapidly mounting overall cost of agricultural support. Even with the expenditure of the Guidance Section pegged at $285 mn., this is expected to reach $1,640 mn. by 1970. The liability of the Guarantee Section for dairy produce alone will by then, according to the Commission's latest estimates, exceed $800 mn.[18] There is a dilemma central to financing the CAP. High levels of price support involve high rates of levy, but the surpluses to which the high prices give rise impose a growing burden of expenditure on the Fund. In the long run a diminishing volume of imports will tend to reduce its revenue as well. Lowering target prices, on the other hand (granted this were politically acceptable), would result in a lower rate of levy on a somewhat higher volume of imports. This might make the Guarantee Section marginally more self-financing. It would also lead inevitably to heavier calls on the Guidance Section, farmers' loss of income having to be offset by more intensive structural reforms. It seems in any case likely that its present ceiling will have to be raised after 1969. Either way, high or low, levies alone will be increasingly inadequate to finance FEOGA, in a Community of Six at any rate.

[18] *Rapport de la Commission au Conseil sur la situation économique du secteur laitier dans la Communauté* (Brussels, January 1968), p. 18.

TABLE 1. SCHEMES GRANT AIDED UNDER GUIDANCE SECTION OF FEOGA, 1964/65 ACCOUNTING YEAR

Nature of scheme	Germany	France	Italy	Netherlands	BLEU
Marketing/processing					
milk	10	–	1	–	11
milk powder	1	–	–	–	1
butter	4	–	–	–	–
cheese	1	–	–	–	–
beef/veal	2	13a	4	–	–
pigmeat	1	1	1	–	–
eggs	1	1	2	2	–
poultry	1	1	–	5	–
fruit/vegetables	4	–	17	3	3
potatoes	–	–	–	–	1
hops	–	–	–	–	1
sugar	–	–	1	–	–
wine	6	–	17	–	–
olive oil	–	–	16	–	–
tobacco	–	–	2	–	–
Buildings					
cattle	–	–	7	–	1
pigs	1	–	1	–	1
grain/seeds	6	–	1	5	–
refrigeration	–	–	3	–	–
Roads	–	–	–	–	2
Electrification	–	–	2	–	–
Irrigation (incl. spray)	4	–	3	–	–
Drainage/water supply	6	–	–	2	–
Afforestation/windbreaks	–	–	2	–	–
Renovation of hill pastures	–	1	–	–	–
Land reclamation	–	–	–	–	2
Consolidation of holdings	5	–	1	4	4
Compound feed plants	–	7	5	–	–
General storage for co-ops	–	1	2	–	–
Machinery co-op	–	–	1	–	–
General markets	–	1	1	1	–
Research/education					
food preservation	–	–	–	1	–
cattle breeding	–	–	7	–	–
plant breeding	–	–	2	–	–
machinery	–	–	1	–	–
general	–	1	1	–	–

a Includes general abattoirs.

Source: *Information Memorandum*, EEC, Brussels, August 1967.

TABLE 2. FEOGA: EXPENDITURE

A. GUIDANCE SECTION

Accounting year	No. of applications	Value $ mn.	Closing date	Schemes agreed (by countries)							Value $ mn.	Date agreed
				G	F	I	N	B	L	Total		
1962/63	138a	51	July 64	9	10	27	8	4	1	57	9·1	Oct. 65
1963/64	103b	23·3	Oct. 64	21	21	40	8	6	–	97	17·3	July 66
1964/65	362c	72·9	Oct. 65	59	33	119	20	20	3	254	41·6	July 67
1965/66	d	d	Oct. 66								80·0e	

a Plus 46 rejected as not fulfilling conditions. b Plus 29 rejected as not fulfilling conditions. c Plus 69 rejected as not fulfilling conditions. d Not yet available. e Estimate of funds available.

Source: *Information Memorandum*. EEC, Brussels, October 1965, August 1966, August 1967.

B. GUARANTEE SECTION

Accounting year	1962/63		1963/64		1964/65		1965/66		1966/67	
	$000	per cent	$000	per cent	$000a	per cent	$000a	per cent	$000a	per cent
Grains	27·958	97·3	49·022	96·7	126·814	74·2	120·356	51·0	136·509	36·9
Pigmeat	50	0·2	nil	nil	7·665	4·5	14·434	6·1	15·289	4·1
Eggs	551	1·9	968	1·9	1·210	0·7	1·150	0·5	711	0·2
Poultry meat	164	0·6	700	1·4	1·250	0·7	2·105	0·9	2·872	0·8
Dairy products	—	—	—	—	25·217	14·8	98·027	41·5	131·664	35·6
Rice	—	—	—	—	769	0·4	47	··	577	0·1
Vegetable oils and fats	—	—	—	—	8·000	4·7	nil	nil	79·160	21·4
Fruit and vegetables	—	—	—	—	—	—	—	—	60	··
Sugar	—	—	—	—	—	—	—	—	3·400	0·9
Total	28·723	100·0	50·690	100·0	170·925	100·0	236·119	100·0	370·242	100·0

a estimated .. negligible — not subject to market regulations.

Source: Agricultural Information Division, EEC, Brussels.

TABLE 3. FEOGA, GUARANTEE SECTION: CONTRIBUTIONS AND EXPENDITURE

Accounting year	1962/63		1963/64		1964/55		1965/66		1966/67		1967/68 1968/69
Proportion of total cost of guarantees financed by FEOGA	one sixth		one third		one half		six tenths		seven tenths		ten tenths
Assessment of national contributions	according to the 'key' (Article 200 §1 of Treaty)		90 per cent by the 'key'; 10 per cent by net imports		80 per cent by the key; 20 per cent by net imports		according to agreed scale		according to agreed scale		90 per cent of all levies; balance to agreed scale[a]
	Contributions *as per cent of total*	Drawings *as per cent of total*	Contributions *as per cent of total*	Drawings *as per cent of total*	Contributions[b] *as per cent of total*	Drawings *as per cent of total*	Contributions[b] *as per cent of total*	Drawings[b] *as per cent of total*	Contributions[b] *as per cent of total*	Drawings[b] *as per cent of total*	
Germany (FR)	28·0	6·3	28·2	4·8	29·3	4·0	31·67	6·76	30·83	7·37	
France	28·0	86·0	25·6	85·3	24·3	67·0	32·58	59·96	29·26	41·62	
Italy	28·0	3·3	28·6	1·3	28·0	6·6	18·00	2·01	22·00	25·95	
Netherlands	7·9	3·4	9·3	7·8	9·7	21·0	9·58	26·84	9·74	20·23	
Belgium	7·9	} 1·1	7·9	} 0·7	8·5	} 1·4	7·95	4·40	7·95	4·80	
Luxemburg	0·2		0·2		0·2		0·22	0·03	0·22	0·03	
	100·0	100·0	100·0	100·0	100·0	100·0	100·00	100·00	100·00	100·00	

a Germany, 32·2; France, 32·0; Italy, 20·3; Netherlands, 8·2; Belgium, 8·1; Luxemburg, 0·2.
b Estimated.
Source: *News of the Common Agricultural Policy*, Agricultural Information Division, Brussels, *passim*.

C

2. Developments in Post-war Agricultural Policy in the United Kingdom

What principles, if any, have guided post-war agricultural policy in the UK? In 1945 the newly established Nuffield Foundation decided it was the right moment for careful study to be made of these principles. It was a time when farming enjoyed considerable goodwill following the remarkable wartime expansion which seemed to have saved the nation from starvation. The Nuffield Foundation therefore set up a Committee under the chairmanship of Professor Engledow of Cambridge University to examine the state of agriculture from the economic, scientific and social points of view and to deduce principles. The difficulty of so doing is illustrated by the fact that ten years later nothing had been published and in the end the hotchpotch of material that the Committee had collected was handed over to Mr. (now Professor) H. T. Williams, who finally published a book based on it in 1960.[1] This book fulfils some useful purpose in bringing together many of the main arguments, economic, social, and strategic, which can be used to build up a set of principles for agricultural policy, but unfortunately (and no doubt mainly due to the long gap between starting and finishing the study) the principles that emerged are neither clear nor firm.

The Act which has mainly influenced government post-war agricultural policy, at least until very recently, is the Agriculture Act 1947. The preamble to the Act lays down that government policy is 'to promote a stable and efficient industry capable of producing such part of the nation's food as in the national interest it is desirable to produce in the UK and to produce it at minimum prices consistent with proper remuneration and living conditions for farmers and workers in agriculture and with an adequate return on capital invested'. No doubt the purpose of the Nuffield Foundation Committee's work was to attempt to throw some light on the 'national interest' in relation to the level of agricultural production, to define what constituted 'proper remuneration' and to produce criteria for 'adequate return on capital invested'.

The particular significance of the 1947 Act was that through it the government accepted a far more positive role in relation to farming than ever before in peacetime. A clear responsibility was taken for the level

[1] *Principles for British Agricultural Policy*, a study sponsored by the Nuffield Foundation. Edited by H. T. Williams (O.U.P., 1960).

of farm incomes and farm output. The Act put an end to *laissez-faire* in agricultural policy which, with the exception of a number of protective measures taken in the thirties, had prevailed in the UK in peacetime for over a hundred years.

By increasing the extent of state intervention in agriculture the UK was following the lead of most other countries. Support for farming and government intervention in agricultural trade is general throughout the world. Even in North America, the cradle of free enterprise, Federal and State governments play a role in almost every part of agriculture, by tariffs and export subsidies, through special grants and credits, by means of irrigation schemes and rural electrification, and of course through price policy. The reasons for this remarkable degree of state intervention in an industry in the private sector are partly economic and partly political. They have been described elsewhere,[2] and detailed examination of the argument lies outside the scope of this book. Briefly, the basic economic arguments are threefold. First, farmers, left to themselves, are slow to adjust their output to falling prices caused by a slackening of demand or an excess of supply, and indeed often increase output in these circumstances in an attempt to maintain their incomes. Second, consumers do not, in general, significantly increase their total purchases of food if prices fall; in other words demand is rather price inelastic. And third, without special assistance, farmers and farm workers are slow to move from agriculture into other occupations even if they are underemployed where they are and could obtain better incomes elsewhere. The political reasons for state intervention are, of course, related to the importance of the farm vote. Even in the UK which has a quite unusually small (and declining) percentage of its working population in agriculture, farmers are still able to exert some political pressure.

To 'promote a stable . . . agriculture' involves insulating farmers' prices and hence their incomes from the effects of free, and often fluctuating, market prices. There are three principal methods of doing this. The government can guarantee a certain price to farmers for any commodity, allow them to sell it on the free market and then make a direct payment to them consisting of the difference between the guaranteed price and the market price. This is a deficiency payment. Second, the domestic market can be kept at an artificially high level by putting quotas on imports, banning them, making imports difficult through health regulations or special quality standards, or by imposing tariffs or variable import levies tied to a threshold price. The last, which is the general EEC system, has already been described. The other main method, which is really only appropriate to an exporting country, consists of a government intervention agency purchasing supplies in the market, and thus pushing up prices, and selling what it has bought on export markets at lower prices either

---

[2] See in particular Peter Self and H. Storing *The State and the Farmer* (George Allen & Unwin, 1962), and G. McCrone *The Economics of Subsidising Agriculture*, University of Glasgow Social and Economic Studies (George Allen & Unwin, 1962).

direct or via merchants. Much the same effect is produced by awarding export subsidies to the trade, as this withdraws from the market supplies which would have a depressing effect on prices. Most countries which are major exporters of agricultural products manage their export markets in one of these ways.

The methods used for agricultural support in the UK are generally referred to as its 'system' of farm support. The word will be used here though it is misleading as the variety of methods used and the multiplicity of grants, introduced for a particular purpose in response to a particular political need, can scarcely be called a system. The UK is the only country other than Luxemburg which has made any very extensive use of deficiency payments. During the past ten years an average of about £150 mn. annually has been paid out to farmers in this way (see Appendix G). Why have deficiency payments been preferred? The answer is simple. The lower a country's degree of self-sufficiency the more advantageous this method becomes. To the UK with its very large imports of a number of foods it has proved attractive to allow imports to enter more or less freely and make up to farmers the difference between market prices, as formed by imported supplies, and guaranteed prices. For commodities in which the bulk of supplies is home-produced, farmers' incomes can be more easily supported by frontier controls on imports leading to higher market realizations. The basic difference is that deficiency payments are paid from the exchequer whereas the cost of supporting farmers through levies, etc., falls on consumers in the form of higher food prices. As the UK has become increasingly self-sufficient since the war the arguments in favour of deficiency payments have weakened.

A much more important objection to deficiency payments may be that their annual cost cannot be calculated in advance. A fall in world prices increases the cost per ton of making up the guaranteed prices. If domestic production increases there are more tons on which the deficiency payments have to be paid. A fall in world market prices presents the government with the problem of having to choose between the benefit to consumers and to the balance of payments of enjoying these low prices and the additional burden to the Exchequer of having to pay more in deficiency payments. Recent government policy has been to prefer stable prices. In 1961/62 the government was presented with a bill of £225 mn. for deficiency payments alone (£343 mn. being the total cost of support) and since then deficiency payments have become less and less open-ended. Standard quantities, the amounts agreed at each Annual Review on which the full guaranteed price will be paid, limit the commitment to a stated tonnage. Agreements with overseas suppliers linked with minimum import prices keep prices stable and prevent a collapse in the market. The objection to standard quantities is that their impact on average prices, which fall as the standard quantity is surpassed, cannot have an immediate influence on decisions of producers, none of whom individually can push the average price closer to the guaranteed price by cutting output. The agricultural industry accepted the idea of standard quantities without much protest. This was surprising as they are an effective weapon for a government that wants to check output and at the same time trim treasury liability.

The second objective of the 1947 Act was the promotion of an 'efficient agriculture'. This has been achieved in two ways. Farm prices and incomes have been kept under fairly severe restraint. While one of the objectives of this policy has been to save money on support costs, equally important has been the aim to maintain incentives for farmers to improve their efficiency. Many farmers run their businesses so as to get a certain more or less defined income rather than maximize profits. If this income can be obtained easily a wasteful use of resources may result. The farmer in these circumstances may employ more men than he needs, or buy an expensive piece of machinery that will be under-utilized. To keep farm prices and incomes under close control as well as to 'persuade' the industry into increasing its efficiency has been a policy of successive governments since the war. Every year farm costs (labour, rent, machinery, fertilizers, and so on) rise and at every Annual Review the farmers' unions ask that the industry should recoup these increases through higher prices for farm produce. In most years—not surprisingly the exceptions have often coincided with elections—farmers are given less than they ask for and told to absorb some of the increased costs themselves. Some may be able to do this and still preserve their incomes, by means of a more economic allocation of their resources. Others cannot. The central problem, therefore, of the UK's post-war agricultural policy has been to assess how far price policy can be pressed in the interests of efficiency, while still preserving 'proper remuneration' and 'adequate return on capital'.

The second way in which efficiency has been encouraged has been through some of the production grants. There are about twenty of these special grants, the total cost of which has recently been averaging a little over £100 mn. a year. Some of them, particularly the calf subsidy, are barely distinguishable from additional payments under the implementation of price guarantees. Some, like the various hill farming subsidies, are for special areas and are as much social as economic. But others were designed specifically to improve efficiency, the original aim being largely educational. The ploughing grant was introduced to encourage ley farming, the fertilizer grant to draw attention to the economic benefits obtainable by applying fertilizers, the field drainage grant to stimulate improvement of the vast areas of agricultural land in the UK that would benefit from drainage, and grants under the Farm Improvement Scheme to draw capital into farming for the construction of labour-saving buildings and thus enable farmers the more easily to release labour to other occupations. Under the last scheme nearly £100 mn. has now been paid out since the grants became available a little over ten years ago. Grants under this scheme, and a few others of a capital nature, are not treated as a part of farm income from the point of view of the Annual Review. One of the few subsidies that have not yet been used in the UK is that of cheap credit.

With the exception of a small subsidy injected through an interest-free reserve fund into mortgage loans from the Agricultural Mortgage Corporation (currently worth about 0·5 per cent), the UK farmer borrows at market rates.

Has post-war policy produced 'proper remuneration' for farmers? Not surprisingly their unions claim that it has not, and point to the way that rising costs have prevented them from keeping up with increased incomes in other sectors. For instance, the average earnings of farm workers have more than doubled over the past fifteen years while the incomes of their employers and of self-employed farmers rose by only about 40 per cent. In assessing the adequacy of farming incomes there are two particular difficulties. First, while a nominal deduction is made from gross income representing rent for the whole national farm, in order to arrive at farm net income, the latter includes return on tenants' capital as well as reward for managerial skill and farmers' own labour. The second difficulty is to know with what other occupations farmers should be compared so far as incomes are concerned. Further, income comparisons between farming and other professions ultimately involve considerations which are not quantifiable. To give only one example of this: as life becomes more and more hectic, cities crowded and roads jammed with traffic, should an increasing premium be put on the comparative privacy associated with most farmers' lives, to say nothing of the access they have to more intangible benefits of the land, such as ownership and fresh air. Probably the only satisfactory way of assessing 'adequate remuneration' is to look at the economic performance of the farming industry, for instance at gross capital formation which has shown a fairly steadily rising trend over the past ten years and is now about 50 per cent higher in real terms, or at net output which at least until the last two or three years has risen fairly steadily ever since the end of the war. Many outside factors influence the level of agricultural land prices, but the fact that they have more than doubled over the past ten years does not indicate an unduly depressed industry. Finally, there are still plenty of people wanting to take up farming either as managers or independent farmers, and this provides additional firmness to the land market.

The last few years have seen a number of new developments in agricultural policy. In this respect Labour governments have been more positive in reformulating policy. This is not altogether surprising. The Conservative Party's roots are still too close to farming and landownership to permit it to make new assessments at all readily. Three main changes have been introduced recently.

First it is now recognized that there are a large number of farmers who, in the words of a surprisingly plain-spoken White Paper,[3] 'however hard they work, and however well they manage their businesses, just cannot hope to get a decent living from their farms'. For these farmers, estimated to number something like 100,000, the government subsequently intro-

[3] *The Development of Agriculture*, Cmnd. 2738 (H.M.S.O., August 1965).

duced legislation (in the Agriculture Act 1967) to provide grants to assist farm amalgamations, to encourage co-operation, and to make special provisions for retirement. A Central Council for Agricultural Co-operation was established to administer a large number of government grants. The particular importance of this White Paper and subsequent developments was the recognition now given to the fact that the UK has a structural problem in agriculture, for which the government has a responsibility, and whose solution it can assist through grants, pension schemes, retraining programmes, and the like. Previously the UK had no structural policy for agriculture, the single previous attempt to influence structure (a pilot scheme at Yetminster in Somerset in 1950) having proved abortive.

Second, the Labour government has tended to lay more emphasis on the import-saving role of domestic agriculture, whereas Conservative governments showed more concern about the effects of increased home output on the sales of the UK's traditional suppliers of agricultural produce, mainly Commonwealth countries. Shortly before the 1964 election the Labour Party carried out some studies on import-saving measures, including the possibility of agricultural expansion. While no crash programme for agriculture seemed appropriate during the foreign exchange difficulties following 1964, the new government was inclined to welcome increases in net output on import-saving grounds. Unfortunately at this time net output tended to level off. The index of agricultural net output in the UK (average 1954/55–1956/57 = 100) which had risen to 137 in 1964/65 from 127 in the previous year, fell to 136 (provisional) in 1965/66 and to 135 (forecast) in 1966/67. This tendency for net output to level off has been a strong influence on recent government policy and largely determined the fairly generous awards of the 1967 Annual Review.[4]

The third change in agricultural policy is connected with the use of planning. The post-war Annual Review procedure has been frequently criticized as being conducive to the making of short-term decisions based on the experiences of the past year. There was no declaration of long-term government policy. In particular nobody knew what the optimum output of each agricultural product would be in five or ten years' time. The sections on agriculture in the 1964 National Plan are on the whole clear and well-constructed. In an otherwise rather discredited document they remain a valid declaration of the government's medium-term intentions for agriculture.

We have commented in some detail elsewhere[5] on the uses and limitations of planning in agriculture. Our general conclusion is that it is a worthwhile exercise valuable as much for its side effects on the agricultural industry as for the benefits it should have in clarifying government policy. A National Economic Development Council, representing the main agricultural interests and the relevant government departments, has begun

---

[4] *Annual Review White Paper 1967*, Cmnd. 3229 (H.M.S.O., March 1967), p. 31.
[5] M. W. Butterwick and E. Neville Rolfe, 'Planning in Agriculture: the French experience', *The Three Banks Review*, March 1965.

making periodical reports to the Council. But it is much too early to tell what effects embryonic planning of this kind might have on UK agricultural policy in the long run.

Finally it is worth noting current attitudes at the time of writing (October 1967) to the general question of what is the most appropriate agricultural support system for the UK. Both the opposition parties now favour a gradual move towards the use of variable levies and a phasing out of deficiency payments. The government still ostensibly favours deficiency payments, the present Minister (Mr. Peart) being a particularly strong advocate of their continuation. As part of a more open-minded approach to EEC and other current topics, the farmers' unions' attitude to a possible change in the system is much less dogmatic than at the time of the 1960 White Paper (discussed in Chapter 4); but understandably the unions prefer to reserve their position. Many leading farmers and writers on agricultural subjects also favour a change. The specialized farming press frequently carries articles critical of the high degree of dependence of agriculture on treasury grants.[6] A switch in the support system would now receive a more widespread welcome than three or four years ago.

[6] A typical example is an article by Clifford Selly in the *Farmer and Stockbreeder*, 4 July 1967, entitled 'Living with big brother' in which he observes that 'the gradual enmeshment of agriculture in the State machine would have astonished previous generations of farmers'.

3. Impact of the United Kingdom adopting the Common Agricultural Policy

(i) EFFECTS ON THE BALANCE OF PAYMENTS AND RETAIL FOOD PRICES

How much will adoption of the common agricultural policy cost the UK in foreign exchange? How much more will people have to pay for food? From the UK's point of view these two questions are as important as any others that arise from the possibility of the UK becoming a member of the EEC. In the first negotiations a few attempts were made to answer them but they came late in the day and suffered from the real difficulty that some of the EEC prices were unknown at the time. As part of the rather different circumstances of the second attempt, which are described in Chapter 4, more detailed estimates have been made to provide the answers. They include those of the Ministry of Agriculture, the National Farmers' Union, Mr. T. K. Warley for a Chatham House–PEP Study[1] and Unilever Ltd. for the CBI report, *Britain and Europe*.[2] Adjustments must be made to these estimates following the sterling devaluation of November 1967. But in general we do not intend to add to these a new set of calculations. There are two reasons for this. First we believe it to be more important to describe the ingredients of the calculations and in particular to show which of the elements can be quantified accurately, which can be estimated with fair confidence and which are not much more than guesses. And secondly, bearing in mind that different assumptions are used and the figures differently presented, there is no fundamental disagreement between those who have made calculations of this kind, including ourselves.

The balance of payments

Imports of food and feeding stuffs make up about 30 per cent of the UK's total import bill. As foreign exchange crises have so dominated the UK's economic circumstances since the Second World War it is at first sight surprising that more studies have not been made about what further contribution home agriculture could make to the balance of payments, leading possibly to a clear-cut policy on this issue. The description in

[1] T. K. Warley, *Agriculture: the Cost of Joining the Common Market* (Chatham House and PEP, London, April 1967).
[2] Confederation of British Industry, London, December 1966.

Chapter 2 of the course of agricultural policy since the war will have shown that a constant view on the merits or otherwise of agricultural expansion has been notably lacking. After allowing for tropical products such as tea and coffee, spices and some fruits, hard wheat which cannot be grown in the UK, cane sugar for which special factors apply, and some partly seasonal commodities like New Zealand lamb and Australian apples and pears, there are perhaps about £500 mn. of agricultural imports for which home production could theoretically be substituted. The main items are feeding stuffs, dairy produce, and meat. There has been no decisive view as to whether increased domestic output of these products should be welcomed. Before turning to the possible agricultural effects of EEC membership on the UK's balance of payments, it is worth examining why this has been the case.

The first part of the evaluation of domestic agriculture's contribution to the UK's balance of payments is fairly straightforward. It involves deducting from gross agricultural output the cost of imported inputs. The most important of these are feeding stuffs, raw materials for the fertilizer industry, and farm machinery. In 1965/66 the cost of these imports totalled about £220 mn., and this sum obviously has to be deducted from gross output to arrive at agriculture's net contribution. Unfortunately from this point the arguments become less well-founded on facts. Proponents of domestic agricultural expansion point to the UK's dominating position in the world market for a number of foods and suggest that a slight reduction in her import requirements brought about by an expansion of home supplies might lead to a worthwhile reduction of the unit cost of the remaining imports. Opponents suggest that any reduction of the foreign exchange earnings of countries supplying the UK with agricultural products would be reflected in losses in UK exports. Some work has been done on the reciprocity effects between the UK's imports and the demand for its exports.[3] The principal difficulty of applying the results of this work to government trade policy is that the reciprocity effects are not likely to be constant over a very long period. In other words there is the danger, which applies to most economic analysis, of locating an effect from statistical evidence, incorporating it as a factor in government policy and then finding that other circumstances have altered and that the reciprocity effect is altogether different.

In arguments over the merits of agricultural expansion in the UK on balance of payment grounds many different viewpoints have been expressed. Out-and-out free traders have no use for any form of domestic protection. Others like to see every square yard of country used for food production at whatever cost and to the exclusion of any other purpose—roads, houses, airports or even National Parks. Between these extremes there is plenty of room for more modest disagreement, but this has not polarized between the political parties. The Conservatives, apparently more

---

[3] For instance Lynden Moore, 'Factors Affecting the Demand for British Exports', *Bulletin of the Oxford University Institute of Economics and Statistics*, Vol. 26, No. 4, November 1964.

cautious about expansion (to judge from a number of rather negative Review awards particularly in the sixties and their introduction of standard quantities), brought in minimum import prices associated with 'gentlemen's agreements' with overseas suppliers which appeared to be sacrificing balance of payments' benefits in the interests of savings on deficiency payments. The Labour Party, which through its Plan and subsequent Annual Reviews seems more committed to agricultural expansion and greater self-sufficiency in food, has maintained a generally moderate price policy despite recent evidence of declining net farm output.

Left to itself, that is to say without the issue of EEC membership, government policy in the UK, whichever party was in power, would be likely to remain neutral, or at most lukewarm, to domestic agriculture's role as an important further contributor to the balance of payments. Conservatives would change, or at least greatly modify the support system, using threshold prices implemented by variable levies to bring up market prices, thus saving on deficiency payments. In itself this makes no difference so far as the balance of payments is concerned, except that if food becomes more expensive, slightly less of it will be demanded and slightly less imported. If home market prices are raised through the application of levies on imported foods the national economy still gets the benefit of world prices although consumers are paying higher food prices in order to support domestic farmers. This is a most important point. It is not the adoption of the EEC-type farm support system that affects the UK's balance of payments but joining the EEC itself.

In what ways will the balance of payments be affected? Let us start with the debit side. Levies will be raised on imports of food and feeding stuffs from third countries and these will of course be in sterling, which will have to be remitted to Brussels (90 per cent now and, in principle, after 1969 *in toto*) at a cost in foreign exchange. To estimate from a static viewpoint what these levies would amount to presents no problem, but such an estimation is of no value. It ignores switching that would take place between supplies from third countries and supplies from the EEC; it ignores the effects of changes in UK agricultural production under EEC prices; and it ignores the changes in consumer spending on food that would follow from, for instance, a doubling of the price of butter. Unfortunately none of these are quantifiable at all precisely. There are further difficulties. For the only two commodities for which special arrangements are realistically negotiable, sugar and butter, both the levies per ton and the total yield from the levies are potentially very high. A negotiated transition for these two products might include arrangements which would reduce the cost of remitting levies on them to Brussels. Estimations of possible switching of purchases from third countries to member countries are extremely hazardous. It is not merely a question of comparing Community surpluses with UK deficits. Maize, for instance, in which both the existing EEC and the UK are deficient, could be bought by the UK either from third countries, as at present, or from France which should be capable very soon of exporting large quantities. Apart from any quality differences the source of these UK imports will depend on technical questions, such as the relationship between levies and restitutions, which could hardly be included in the negotiations for entry. Of course in calculating the overall effect on the UK's balance of payments it makes little difference if it buys French maize at EEC prices, or US maize at world prices and then remits the whole of the levy to Brussels. But the view taken on this kind of problem influences the attitude adopted by negotiators to the question of the scale of contributions to FEOGA over and above the payment of the levies.

Forecasts of the direct contributions which the UK might have to make to FEOGA are hazardous. As Chapter 1 has shown, the Fund's expenditure is for three main purposes: intervention in domestic markets, restitutions on exports, and structural reforms. Only expenditure on the last can be readily controlled, as it is at present limited to £120 mn. The Commission's present estimate is that total expenditure in 1970 (for a Community of Six) will reach £700 mn. including the £120 mn. for Guidance. As the UK's levy contributions to FEOGA are unlikely to be less than £150 mn., or nearly 30 per cent of the Fund's projected expenditure on guarantees for a Community of Six it seems improbable that direct contributions will have to be very large. Obviously the object of the UK negotiators is either to limit the total UK contribution or to decide the appropriate proportionate contribution. One of the biggest difficulties of forecasting FEOGA's requirements, and therefore possible contributions to it, consists of assessing how much of the enlarged Community's farm surplus would move to the UK (no cost to the Fund for restitutions) and how much would have to be subsidized into non-EEC markets.

On the credit side of this balance of payments calculation there are two main elements, additional receipts from exports and payments made by the Fund for intervention and structural improvements. UK exports of agricultural products under the CAP would be likely to be higher in volume. Total output would rise and products most stimulated by price increases would include meat and grains, for which export markets could fairly readily be obtained. But far more important than any increase in volume would be the higher prices which would be obtained. As a member of the EEC the UK would sell her agricultural exports either to fellow members at EEC prices or on the world market with export restitutions. Calculations of how much benefit these might produce are little more than guesswork. Restitutions and additional receipts from higher prices on grain exports might be worth over £20 mn. a year.

Nobody expects the UK to get much from the Guidance Section of the Fund. Perhaps a nominal £5 mn. might be obtained. A somewhat larger sum might be paid for market intervention. T. K. Warley, making what he describes as an inspired guess, suggests a total of £20 mn. for these two. Even if one adds another £20 mn. to this, representing restitution payments on British agricultural exports, giving a total drawback from the Fund of

£40 mn., the UK would still remain by far the largest net contributor to the Fund.

Unilever estimated that the adverse effect on the balance of payments in 1975 might amount to £65 mn. Warley, nobly acknowledging that he had used the arts of the clairvoyant as well as of the econometrician, came up with a figure for the immediate future of £212 mn. These two lie at either end of the bracket suggested by the government. Devaluation has since raised threshold prices in terms of sterling, but the adverse effect of this might be more than compensated by a lower volume of imports due to higher producer prices and reduced consumption. A rounded figure of £200 mn. gives a fair indication of the possible effect on the UK's balance of payments if reasonable provisions affecting FEOGA were agreed to.

Retail food prices

Mercifully the arguments concerned with the effects of adopting the CAP on the UK's retail food prices and cost of living are somewhat less tortuous. Wholesale prices would become EEC wholesale prices, which can be guessed at sufficiently well for these purposes. Their exact future level will of course depend on how far target prices are achieved. These prices can be applied to present UK prices. To calculate from here the effect on consumers' total food expenditure involves two difficulties. The first is to know whether food manufacturers and distributors would put their usual percentage mark up on the higher wholesale prices. There would be no good case for doing so as their costs would be unchanged with the exception of a small increase in the cost of financing their stocks. The second difficulty, already mentioned, is to estimate with any reliability how big an effect higher prices of, for instance, sugar and butter, or lower prices for some fruits and vegetables. would have on expenditure. The Ministry of Agriculture after making some informed guesses about possible changes in consumption patterns following alterations in relative food prices, forecast that the increase in the cost of food to the UK consumer 'might lie within the range of between 10 and 14 per cent'. As expenditure on food currently accounts for about a quarter of total consumer expenditure this is equivalent to a rise of between $2\frac{1}{2}$ and $3\frac{1}{2}$ per cent in the cost of living. The CBI study looking ahead to 1975 which necessitated a rather more sophisticated technique, arrived at an estimate only slightly lower than the Ministry's, which can, however, be regarded as acceptable. These estimates were all pre-devaluation.

The increase in consumer expenditure on food, about £600 mn. to £800 mn. a year, is possibly the biggest disadvantage of all for the UK in the calculations concerning EEC membership. Offsetting this increase is, of course, the saving in the cost of agricultural support. All the deficiency payments and most of the production grants will no longer be required, a saving to the exchequer and taxpayer of up to £200 mn. a year. As has been frequently suggested this sum, at the very least, could be available to cushion the effects of higher food prices on those least able to pay them.

Family allowances would be increased to bring them more into line with those paid in some EEC countries and pensions would have to rise. The problem of how a transition period could be used to shield consumers from the effects of more expensive food prices is discussed in Chapter 4.

(ii) EFFECTS ON THE PATTERN OF UK TRADE IN AGRICULTURAL PRODUCTS[4]

Virtually all the UK's imports of foods and feeding stuffs will be affected if it adopts the CAP. These imports, which cost about £1,500 mn. a year, cover a very wide range of products and originate from many countries. (Imports from EEC countries, mainly grains, preserved meats, cheese and fresh fruit are relatively small.[5]) Although analysing individual effects might appear to be a rather unmanageable task, it is not in fact difficult to pick out the more important commodities and the food exporting countries which will be most affected by UK membership of the EEC.

Chapter 2 contains some observations about government policy towards agricultural trade and notes the tendency for the UK to become increasingly self-sufficient. In some products self-sufficiency is now complete or virtually so. These include barley and oats, eggs and poultry meat, liquid and condensed milk, pork and potatoes. The main products for which imports still make up a big proportion of total UK supplies are shown below. It will be seen that since the War there has also been an increase in self-sufficiency in most of these products.

TABLE 4.   UK: SELECTED COMMODITIES, IMPORTS AS PER CENT OF TOTAL SUPPLIES

	Average 1934–38	1966 (provisional)
Wheat	77	55
Maize	100	100
Beef and veal	51	27
Mutton and lamb	64	54
Bacon and ham	68	64
Sugar	82	71
Butter	91	93
Cheese	76	57

Source: Ministry of Agriculture, Fisheries and Food.

About two and a half million of the 4·3 mn. tons of wheat imported by the UK consists of hard North American wheats which should not be greatly affected by the UK joining the EEC, the quantity of hard wheat produced in the EEC being very small. The only important supplier of soft wheat is Australia which shipped about half a million tons to the UK in

[4] Parts of this section appeared in an article entitled 'Terms for Australia and New Zealand' by Michael Butterwick in the *Three Banks Review*, December 1967.
[5] See Appendix D.

1966, a trade it would be likely to lose if the UK adopts the CAP (see below). There may be some shifts in UK imports of maize, French being substituted for American, but what the United States, much the largest supplier, loses in the UK market it will probably pick up in other EEC countries. The principal suppliers of beef and veal are Argentina (10 per cent of total supplies) Australia and Ireland (which together provide about 6 per cent). Some of this trade may be at risk, but the danger to the first three comes from increased home production stimulated by EEC farm-gate prices, rather than from competition in the UK from meat produced on the Continent. Altogether it seems most unlikely that beef and veal exports to the UK will be much affected. Most probably the same applies to mutton and lamb in which New Zealand has the largest stake (46 per cent of total UK supplies and nearly 90 per cent of UK imports). Bacon imports are controlled by market-sharing agreements. Much the largest supplier, accounting for three-quarters of total imports is Denmark which is hoping to join the EEC at the same time as the UK. Sugar, the subject of a binding eight-year Agreement, is a separate issue. The future of this Agreement once the UK were in the EEC is discussed at length in Chapter 12. At least until the outstanding term of the Agreement runs out the trade of Commonwealth sugar suppliers should not be damaged. Of the main commodities, therefore, only dairy produce presents any great problem, and of this butter is the paramount difficulty. In 1966 New Zealand supplied 165,000 tons (35 per cent of total UK supplies and 37 per cent of UK imports) and Australia 79,000 tons ($16\frac{1}{2}$ per cent of total supplies and $17\frac{1}{2}$ per cent of UK imports). The effects of UK membership of the EEC on the agricultural trade of these two countries is potentially very great. We shall therefore describe in some detail how this trade is made up and how it may be affected.

Australia

After generations as Australia's leading trade partner the UK has recently been overtaken by Japan as its biggest export customer. By a Trade Agreement signed in 1957[6] the UK agreed to give various degrees of preference in exchange for preferences (mostly $7\frac{1}{2}$ per cent) which it obtained in the Australian market. The Agreement has been modified in the case of butter for which Australia no longer has a preference of 15s. 0d. per cwt, but otherwise it still applies, being now terminable at six months' notice. The 1957 Agreement must be viewed in the context of many years of close trading links between the two countries fostered by the preferences which began to be established soon after the First World War. Apart from agreement over the level of preference the 1957 Trade Agreement set up a system of annual consultations between the two countries which particularly applies, under Article 6, to wheat and flour. In addition to the quota arrangements for butter, which have already been mentioned, there has been a separate Meat Agreement, which lapsed in September

[6] Cmnd. 91 (H.M.S.O., February 1957).

1967, and Australia is, of course, a signatory to the Commonwealth Sugar Agreement. The last is the only long-term agreement between Australia and the UK which cannot be cancelled, but Australia has always maintained that the absence of any other Agreement of a long-term nature should not be taken to mean that the preferences were not intended to remain in being indefinitely.

Australian exports to the UK in 1965/66 totalled A$473 mn., equivalent to 17 per cent of its total exports. The main agricultural items were wool, beef and veal, sugar, mutton and lamb, wheat, butter and cheese, and fruits (fresh, canned, and dried). With the exception of wool, which is Australia's leading export (about 30 per cent of total exports), all of these would be at risk if the UK joined the EEC. Wool is treated at present by the Community as an industrial product and bears no tariff. The UK, which in 1965/66 took about 10 per cent of Australian wool exports, has recently become a less important customer, being far outdistanced by Japan. This trend may well continue but UK membership of the EEC will make no direct difference to it. The following Table analyses the position for the other main agricultural products, which together make up nearly half of Australia's exports to the UK.

TABLE 5. AUSTRALIA: PRINCIPAL EXPORTS TO THE UK AFFECTED BY THE UK ADOPTING THE COMMON AGRICULTURAL POLICY

Commodity	Present UK regime	EEC regime	Exports 1965–66 A$ mn.	As per cent of total Australian exports of the commodity
Beef and veal	Free 20% pref. boned	CAP and CET	54·6	28
Sugar	CSA pref. price	CAP	43·8	47
Mutton and lamb	Free	20% CET	5·1	11
Wheat	Free	CAP	32·5	12
Butter	Quota (pref. suspended)	CAP	38·9	78
Cheese	Free pref. 15%	CAP and 23% CET	4·0	30
Fruits fresh apples and pears	Free with pref.	8% CET	15·9	43
canned fruit	Free pref. 12⅝%	25% CET (average)	24·6	65
dried fruit	Free with pref.	8% CET	12·0	45
		Total value	231·4	

Source: Commonwealth of Australia Federal Trade Statistics.

How badly affected would these exports be if the EEC system were substituted for the present UK regime? It has already been indicated that the prospects for the world beef trade look favourable. The EEC system consisting of a common external tariff plus variable levies would be likely to stimulate home production. If Australia loses some volume of trade it should receive some compensation through higher prices. Sugar may be a very serious problem in eight years, but at least it is not such an immediate difficulty. An international sugar agreement should be concluded within this period. Failing this the consequences for Australia's sugar industry could be serious. As long as the EEC has no common regulation for mutton and lamb Australian exports to the UK should continue at about the current level. The prospects for UK suppliers if market regulations are introduced to take the place of, or supplement, the present EEC tariff, are described later in connection with New Zealand, whose trade is a great deal more important than Australia's. As has already been stated most of the wheat exports would be lost. While this appears to be serious, it is fair to say that the UK has anyway been declining in importance as an importer of Australian wheat (taking 22 per cent in 1959/60, 12 per cent in 1965/66 and only about 6 per cent in 1966/67) and that this trend is likely to continue as home production expands. Article 6 of the 1957 Agreement is no more than a 'best endeavours' clause and the UK is already taking considerably less than the quantity mentioned in the Agreement.

The remainder, dairy products and fruits, present much the worst difficulties. As a result of reduced demand for butter due to the very considerable price increase, a probable increase in the UK's own production, and substitution of EEC-produced butter (including that of new members joining at the same time as the UK) for third countries' exports, the market available to Australia in the UK would be much reduced. If New Zealand is given a special arrangement for its butter the market would be much more drastically reduced, and for this small quantity Australia would be competing on equal terms with other exporters of dairy products. While Japan is now importing large quantities of Australian butter it is difficult to see where Australia could sell some 70,000 tons if it is effectively shut out of the UK market.

While some preference is given to Australian apples and pears under the present UK regime, and a reverse preference would be applied if the EEC system were adopted, a more important protection is provided by Australia's different production season. Unfortunately modern storage techniques are tending to erode the value of this protection. Australia would certainly lose some trade in fresh fruit if the UK joined the EEC, but it is liable to do so anyway in the face of greater competition from both home and EEC producers. The effects on canned fruit exports would be much more disastrous. With the loss of its preference Australia would have difficulty in competing with the United States, a much larger producer. Besides, the common external tariff should enable canners in Italy and

D

France to obtain a big share of the UK market. Australia would lose most of this trade. Dried fruits might be almost as badly affected as both Australia's main competitors, Greece and Turkey, have association agreements with the EEC and would therefore enjoy preference in the UK market.

Faced with these probable effects on its exports to the UK it is hardly surprising that Australia has consistently been unwilling, on economic as well as on political grounds, to see the UK take up membership of the EEC. From the time of the first negotiations when Sir Alan Westerman of the Australian Department of Trade presented to the UK/EEC conference a very comprehensive statement of the Australian position, the Australian view has been that failing special arrangements, its trade, mostly in agricultural products, would be very seriously affected. In presenting its case to the UK Australia has issued constant reminders of the UK's commitment to safeguard essential Commonwealth interests, and has so far held to the view that *all* its exports are essential.

This view is a long way from anything that one hears in the Community. Typical reactions, for instance, from the Commission would include relating the total given in the Table above to all exports and showing that it consists of less than 9 per cent. Of the more vulnerable commodities exports to the UK of butter are 1·4 per cent of all Australian exports and of canned and dried fruits respectively 0·9 per cent and 0·5 per cent. Further, the Community would argue that if a new member joins a customs union some trade switching to the benefit of the other members is anyway to be expected.

In due course Australia may, of course, have to narrow down its requirements. Apart from the Commonwealth Sugar Agreement, in which Australia is only one among many, the UK should attempt to obtain for Australia, as part of the UK entry negotiations at least three concessions: first a transition period, which might be three to four years during which time the Australian preferences in the UK would be phased out (and also presumably the UK preferences in Australia) and the reverse preferences phased in; second a part, even if only a small one, of whatever is arranged for New Zealand over butter (see below); and third a special trade agreement to provide access for a limited period, beyond the transition period, for canned and dried fruits. The transition period is fully discussed in Chapter 4. Its benefits for Australia are obviously very limited. The other two concessions are worth pressing for, but neither can be regarded as a 'sticking point' for the UK negotiators. Indeed, one of the harsher aspects of any UK application to join the EEC is that it can expect to get little or nothing for Australia.

New Zealand

In as much as the commodities concerned—butter and cheese, meat, and fruits—are the same, the problems raised for New Zealand exports by the possibility of the UK joining EEC are not dissimilar to those of Australia. But there are important differences between the two. The rather small significance of each of the 'at risk' commodities to total Australian exports has already been mentioned. In the case of New Zealand the significance is very much greater. In 1966 butter exports made up 13·2 per cent of total exports, cheese 5·4 per cent, meat (mostly mutton and lamb 26·2) and fresh fruit (apples) about 1 per cent. All together the 'at risk' commodities which at present are being exported to the UK compose about one-third of New Zealand's total exports. The position is illustrated by the following Table.

TABLE 6. NEW ZEALAND: PRINCIPAL EXPORTS TO THE UK AFFECTED BY THE UK ADOPTING THE COMMON AGRICULTURAL POLICY

Commodity	Present UK regime	EEC regime	Exports 1965–66 £ mn.	As per cent of total New Zealand exports of each commodity
Beef and veal	Free 20% pref. boned	CAP and CET	6·7	25·0
Mutton and lamb	Free	20% CET	49·9	82·5
Butter	Freeª (quota and pref. suspended)	CAP	46·8	85·9
Cheese	Free pref. 15%	CAP and 23% CET	16·1	78·5
Fresh fruit (mostly apples)	Free with pref.	8% CET	2·0	55·4
		Total value	£121·5 mn.	

ª Governed by 1966 Trade Agreement.
Source: New Zealand Government Trade Statistics.

The Table shows that the New Zealand problem can really be confined to its two well-known exports, mutton and lamb and dairy produce (particularly butter). The 20 per cent tariff on mutton and lamb if applied to the UK along with the prices and regulations covering other meat, would cause very little disturbance to either home producers or New Zealand exports. The new price relationship between the various meat products would not be unfavourable to mutton and lamb, home producers (with the possible exception of hill farmers) would be adequately compensated for their loss of a guaranteed price and deficiency payments (even to offset a loss on returns from wool), and free entry of New Zealand produce would continue subject to the payment of the duty. New Zealand might even gain a little on both price and volume. This satisfactory state of affairs might be disturbed if mutton and lamb regulations were made by the EEC so as to bring them into the usual CAP system of target and threshold prices and variable levies. Not only would this system, to judge from its application to other commodities, be likely to be more restrictive to third countries' exports than a tariff, but by maintaining price relationships between the various meats it could also be used to prevent any favourable price development for mutton and lamb. In other words if prices of EEC produced beef became depressed it might be possible to strengthen the market by raising the threshold price for mutton and lamb. In spite of this the prospects for New Zealand lamb if the UK adopts the CAP are not too unfavourable.

The same cannot be said for New Zealand butter. As this is by far the most difficult problem affecting UK agricultural trade raised by the possibility of joining the EEC it is worth examining the background to the current position. The 1959 Trade Agreement between the two countries guaranteed a right of access for butter (among other products) with preference until 31 May 1967. Owing to the very low prices that it obtained in the UK market with this system New Zealand in 1962 agreed to waive both free access and the preference in exchange for the application of a quota system on all suppliers. This arrangement worked out well enough until 1966 when New Zealand, faced with renewed UK interest in the EEC, made a new Trade Agreement.[7] Under this Agreement the UK, while reiterating the principle of unrestricted imports of New Zealand butter, in fact obtained permission to regulate them, the quantity for New Zealand being agreed at 170,000 tons a year plus 'reasonable opportunity . . . to share in any growth in imports of butter into the UK'. The Agreement ends on 30 September 1972 on which date the 1959 Agreement can also be completely terminated subject to giving six months' notice. Until then New Zealand's position is protected, the period corresponding, of course, to the UK government's estimation in 1966 of what might turn out to be the transition period for entry into the EEC.

Summer stocks of butter in the EEC are running at or just above the level of total New Zealand exports in 1966, 190,000 tons, nearly 90 per cent of which went to the UK. For reasons which have already been given the prospects for third countries' exports of butter to the UK under the CAP are very poor. The significance of this trade to total New Zealand exports and its importance in relation to gross national product (5 per cent) have been recognized on many occasions by the UK, in the 1961–63 negotiations by the existing member countries, and in October 1967 by the Commission in its report on the UK application. None of these have gone very far beyond stating that there is a problem over New Zealand's butter exports and that this comes into a different category from any other commodity.

What can be done for New Zealand? Before trying to answer this, it is important to distinguish between the short-term and long-term problems. So far as the former is concerned a few inspired guesses can be made. Over a short transition period UK consumption might fall by perhaps 20

[7] Cmnd. 3170 (H.M.S.O., December 1966).

per cent or about 100,000 tons and home production rise by about 50,000 tons. Increased purchases of butter produced by other EEC members might amount to a further 50,000 tons. After allowing for these (which, once again, are no better than guesses) the amount left for all third countries is only about 100,000 to 150,000 tons, less than New Zealand's own exports to the UK. This is bad enough, but the long-term problem of how to contain mounting EEC surpluses of dairy produce in the future is even worse. In other words, while the prospects for exports of New Zealand dairy produce for a period up to about 1975 are by no means favourable, the outlook for ten to fifteen years seems even less happy.

Any solution involves a combination of price and access. New Zealand would prefer as much access as possible in order to get rid of the whole quantity, whereas the EEC would prefer very limited access accompanied by compensation through higher prices or direct payments. As a result of the higher EEC prices and in spite of the levy system, some price compensation should anyway be obtained. On the whole the simplest solution would be to allow New Zealand to sell a certain quantity (100,000 tons might be appropriate) over a period (perhaps fifteen years with a phase-out at the end) at the full EEC price. An arrangement of this kind would mean that New Zealand's foreign exchange earnings from butter after 30 September 1972 would be rather higher than before, thus giving it some assistance in the adjustments to its farming industry which in the long-term are inevitable if the UK joins the EEC. Price and access (and in the last resort supplementary compensation in cash) can be juggled in innumerable ways to provide results similar to this, which must be regarded as the minimum which the UK could accept on behalf of New Zealand if it joined the EEC.

(iii) THE COST OF FARM INPUTS

(a) FARMERS AND THE LAND

If the most significant post-war development in agriculture in both the UK and the EEC countries has been the great upsurge of production, the reduction in the farm population is almost equally remarkable. In France the agricultural labour force has fallen by 3·5 mn., in Germany by 1·5 mn. and in the UK by about 0·5 mn. since 1950. The reduction on this scale in the labour force of a major industry is made still more remarkable by the fact that it occurred while agriculture was enjoying a period of reasonable prosperity. France was also absorbing refugees from North Africa and Germany those from the East, many of whom were resettled in farming.

The trend continues and it is interesting to speculate how much further it could go. The average size of farm is still small in both the UK and the Community. Setting aside 'factory-farms' based on the intensive conversion of purchased feed into livestock products, and horticultural enterprises, the smallest viable farm will very soon be not less than about 120 acres, roughly the same as the present *average* size of farm enterprise in the UK and about four times the average in EEC. It has been estimated that there are some 220,000 full-time farmers in the UK. Government policy, as expressed in the White Papers *The Future of Agriculture* and *The Development of Agriculture* and in the 1967 Agriculture Act, calls for a reduction in this number, but to what extent is not specified. To estimate how many independent farmers are required to run the agricultural industry would involve assessment of the managerial demands of every farming area of the country compared with the supply of managerial talent now and in the future. This is an impossible task. But at least it can be said that, both in the UK and in the EEC, the industry could certainly be run by very many fewer entrepreneurs without danger of loss of efficiency. In the UK between 2,000 and 3,000 farmers are believed to be ceasing full-time operations every year. Of those remaining the 42,000 largest businesses account for about half of total output.

Co-operation among farmers

Agricultural co-operation is not what most people would imagine it to be. It does not consist, except to a minor degree, of farmers pooling their land, labour, machinery, or livestock and undertaking communal activity. This is the form that co-operation takes in Communist countries, such as East Germany, where the farmers were persuaded to pool all or most of their resources, methods being used to persuade them which would not be tolerable in a Western democracy. In the East German *Genossenschaften*, which typically farm about 1,000 to 2,000 acres, co-operation is complete except that the formerly independent farmers usually retain some nominal legal interest in the land. Co-operation of this kind on a voluntary basis either in the EEC or the UK is still very rare. Instead co-operation is normally limited to certain specified activities and of these the bulk purchasing of members' requirements and the joint selling of members' produce are much the most common.

To say that agricultural co-operation in Western Europe has limited objectives is not to deny its power. In all EEC countries and in the UK agriculture is still the biggest industry and the control that the co-operative movement has over its buying and selling gives it great economic and political importance. In the Netherlands, for instance, the two co-operative groupings are strongly centralized, well organized and professionally managed. In France the co-operatives dominate the marketing of most farm products, being particularly strong in cereals. The movement is almost as well entrenched in the other EEC countries.

In the UK agricultural co-operation has recently celebrated its first centenary. The progress of the movement has been by no means unchecked. Between the wars turnover in several years became quite small, under £10 mn. a year, and frequent reorganizations proved necessary. Since 1945, however, turnover has increased very rapidly from £36 mn. a year to the current level of over £300 mn. a year. This rise is partly accounted for by the growth in farm incomes and prices but the co-operatives have also gained a bigger share of the total market at the expense of the private trade. There are now over 400,000 members, but this figure makes no allowance for membership by a farmer of more than one society, which is fairly common. It is estimated that UK farm co-operatives now supply about 20 per cent of farmers' requirements excluding machinery. The chief problem for the future growth of co-operatives in the UK concerns finance. In most EEC countries there exist not only grants and interest subsidies favouring co-operatives but also a co-operative credit system, the funds of which are available to provide credits for co-operatives. There is no such system in the UK, where co-operatives depend for finance on their members' share capital and loans and on ordinary commercial borrowing. The problem is described in a recent report[8] prepared for the movement's central body, the Agricultural Co-operative Association.

Current government policy in the UK is directed towards assisting agricultural co-operation. In the words of the White Paper *The Development of Agriculture*, 'The Government believe that the time has come to make a major effort to encourage agricultural co-operation, particularly among the smaller farmers'. As a rough estimate it is thought that about 100,000 farmers could benefit from co-operation, who might otherwise have to go out of business. A number of new grants have been established to help co-operatives and a new body, the Central Council for Agricultural and Horticultural Co-operation, set up to administer the grants and take an active role in promoting co-operative activities. It is far too early to make any assessment of the Council's work or to judge whether the schemes will, as is hoped, enable farmers to become more competitive and to improve their incomes, thus lessening their dependence upon government subsidies.

Structural reform

In all member countries national policies have for many years been directed towards the improvement of the structure of agriculture. This takes two forms, reducing the number of farmers so that those who remain have large enough holdings to provide a reasonable income, and improving the structure of individual holdings through consolidation of scattered fields, providing water and electricity, making farm roads, assisting with the relocation of farm houses and buildings, and so on. Vast sums of public money have been spent on these schemes. For instance, in Germany a major part of the Federal expenditure on agriculture has been spent in this way, and the Land governments have also given financial assistance. Much remains to be done. Nevertheless, despite these consolidation measures, there is still an average of eleven separate parcels of land per holding. Even in the Netherlands, which has the best farm structure in the EEC, the average is still nearly four. The basic reason for this state of affairs, the absence of primogeniture, is well-known. In areas where consolidation has taken place, however, it is now usually obligatory either

8 *Financing Agricultural Co-operatives* (Maxwell Stamp Associates Ltd., April 1967).

for the principal heir to buy out his co-heirs in cash in order to prevent a renewed division of the land, or for the inherited property to be sold as a single lot and the proceeds shared between all the heirs.

The costs of consolidation vary greatly from area to area. A rough guide is provided by the experience of France, where the administrative costs of consolidation (*remembrement*) have been running at about £5 per acre. The State pays this in full and, in addition, contributes 60 per cent of the cost of *travaux connexes* (new roads, ditching, the removal of hedges and banks etc.) which is usually about £10 to £15 per acre. The slow progress of *remembrement* caused the French government in 1960 to set up new organizations to assist structural reform. These are the so-called SAFERs, semi-public Land Improvement and Rural Resettlement Companies, whose activities, being unique in Western Europe, deserve to be described in some detail. SAFERs now cover practically the whole of France, though the extent of their activity varies. The 1960 Law obliges all prospective sales of farm land to be notified to the local SAFER, which has two months to decide whether to intervene. If the land is in an area where the SAFER is interested in carrying out structural improvement it can buy by friendly agreement or exercise a right of pre-emption (which operates against all but sitting tenants). In the latter case the price can either be that originally asked by the vendor or a 'fair price' assessed by the SAFER, against which the vendor can appeal to arbitration. Or he can go to public auction, where the SAFER must compete against other bidders. In practice most farms have been acquired by agreement and the pre-emption rights are mostly useful as a known weapon of last resort. Intervention takes place usually when land is being sold to a purchaser outside the commune or neighbouring commune; or to a large local farmer when the long-term social advantage might rather lie in amalgam-ating the land with another fairly small farm; or to someone who is not a genuine farmer and who is not prepared to let the land in question to a tenant approved by the SAFER. Intervention has recently been taking place in about 10 per cent of sales.

The SAFER may hold the land for up to five years, during which im-provements (often quite extensive land reclamation) can be made, and an interim tenant, with no statutory protection, installed. Increasingly, however, SAFERs already have local purchasers in mind, usually younger forward-looking farmers on the look-out for more land who will be in touch with the SAFER's local officials, and in these cases improvements take place after the re-sale of the land. The SAFERs, which derive their main income from a government subsidy of 2 per cent on turnover, also receive grants of 60 per cent of the cost of improvements. Disposal of the land they have acquired presents no great problems. The economic and social objectives of their activities are fairly clear. In practice there is usually no great difficulty in choosing to whom to sell, particularly as they sell at the market price. It is rare to find a locality where there are two or more purchasers who have adequate finance to buy (not less than 40 per cent of the purchase price must be deposited) and to farm the land, are about the right age, have farming experience, and already possess neighbouring farms which would benefit equally from the addition of the land which the SAFER has to offer.[9]

The more vigorous attitude to structural reform shown by the SAFERs is reflected also in EEC's regional policy towards remote and difficult agricultural areas. These exist in all member countries, the more intractable being the south of Italy, much of the west of France and the south-east of Germany. Description of regional policy to assist the infrastructure of these areas through industrialization, attraction of tourism, improvement of transport facilities and so on, lies outside the scope of this book. Some of the measures have now become the responsibility of the Guidance Section of FEOGA whose activities have been described in an earlier chapter.

The UK, since the single abortive attempt (at Yetminster in Somerset) to put into practice the structural reform clauses of the 1947 Act, had no positive structural policy for agriculture for twenty years. The 1967 Act, mentioned earlier in this chapter, introduced new grants to promote amalgamations. Possibly these may accelerate the progress of structural reform. It is, however, notable that when, not long ago, the Agricultural Executive Committee of a southern county investigated the situation of small farms of between 30 and 150 acres in a number of 'problem districts' of the county, its members reached the conclusion that size of the farms was not a major contributory cause to low incomes. On a random sample of farms of between 50 and 100 acres (the size group with the lowest gross output per acre, the poorest stocking rate and the lowest return on capital) farmers' age, educational background and efficiency of management were found to be more significant factors than size or fragmentation.

Farming unions

It is hardly surprising that farmers everywhere combine together for collective action. The peculiarity of farmers' unions is that their objects are more directly political than those of most other unions. In the case of farming the bargaining of greatest importance is done with the government rather than with other organizations, such as workers' unions, engaged in the agricultural industry. Even with the decline of the farm population, unions representing farmers still have considerable political influence. In the EEC, the German *Bauernverband* with its very close contacts with both the Federal and Land governments is probably the strongest. The farmers' unions in the UK, particularly the National Farmers' Union of

---

[9] Two different types of action are also being taken in Germany. *Flurbereinigung* corresponds rather closely to *remembrement*. *Aussiedlung* has an affinity with some of the work of the SAFERs. Under this system a number of farmers, usually the most go-ahead ones, are moved out of congested village communities to new isolated farmsteads on enlarged and consolidated holdings. These often lie on the periphery of the district to which the village forms the centre, the land closer in being left to some of the smaller, and often part-time, farmers who continue to occupy the old farmsteads in the village. Others are encouraged to give up farming and lease their land to the farmers who have been resettled, thus enabling them to increase their scale of operations.

England and Wales, which takes an acknowledged lead, consider themselves just as politically influential, although the proportion of the electorate which they represent is extremely small—only about 1 per cent. The part played by the NFU in the development of the UK's relationship with the EEC is described in the next chapter.[10]

At this point the most interesting feature of the activities of farming unions is their role in Brussels, where the national unions have established an organization, COPA,[11] specifically to maintain contact with the Commission and influence the Community's agricultural policy. Influence is applied in two different ways. First, through unofficial though not necessarily informal meetings with Dr. Mansholt and others in the Commission COPA is able to give its views on general trends in policy. These meetings, which take place about half a dozen times a year, were particularly useful when the fundamental principles of the common agricultural policy were being established. Dr. Mansholt has consciously provided access to COPA as well as to other organizations representing agricultural interests. Second, COPA has members sitting on the Consultative Committees which are formed after the regulations for any product have been agreed. While it is possible for the chairmen of these Committees to take the initiative in calling meetings, the more normal procedure is for the Commission to send out a *demande d'avis* to the appropriate committee asking for its views on certain specific subjects, questions of prices and incomes being excluded.

The role of the Consultative Committees is rather limited. Most of the initiative for the choice of subjects lies with the Commission, which also provides the secretariat and even has discretion as to whether the minutes of meetings should be published. The Committees' views often have to be given in a hurry as the Council is waiting to give a decision on a proposal from the Commission. Discussion of anything remotely political is prevented. While the meetings of these Committees are sometimes quite useful, unions representing farmers in EEC member countries are realistic if they calculate that influence on policy is still applied most effectively *via* their governments in the Council of Ministers, the Permanent Delegations, or the Management Committees. The Community has consistently avoided having to formulate agricultural policy through the bargaining processes which, from time to time, have occurred in the UK Annual Review. Now that the main lines of policy have been decided, increasing opportunity may be given to COPA to give effective expression to the interests of its members. But it will not be consulted about farm prices. In the EEC these affect consumers just as directly as farmers. Therefore, it is argued, farmers are not entitled to any privileged hearing from the Commission.

(b) LABOUR

There are many complications in making international comparisons

---

[10] See also Self and Storing, *The State and the Farmer.*
[11] *Comité des Organisations Professionelles Agricoles.*

between the numbers, pay, and conditions of work of farm workers. For instance the distinction is not always clear between hired labour on farms and family workers who are paid a regular wage. It is often difficult to put a value on fringe benefits like free housing or produce, which can amount to a significant proportion of total receipts. Variations exist between hours of work, overtime conditions, and length of paid holidays.[12] Much of the statistical material on these and other questions has to be treated with caution. The notably weak unionization of farm workers throughout Western Europe has inhibited the collection of reliable statistics.

Two important features of the employment of farm workers are common to both the UK and all EEC countries. First, farm workers are poorly paid in comparison with other workers. Here again it is easy to mislead by trying to be too precise. Not only is there the difficulty over non-cash benefits. The problem of which other categories of workers should be compared with farm workers, who cover a very wide range of abilities, from non-skilled men performing simple manual tasks to specialists responsible for the care of valuable livestock and expensive machinery. Second, there has been a steady and marked movement of workers out of agriculture which, since the war, has been the principal source of new employment for industrial and service occupations.

The United Kingdom

There are about 400,000 full-time farm workers in the UK. Numbers have been declining recently by about 3 per cent each year. A minimum statutory wage is set for the whole country by the Agricultural Wages Board. In February 1968 this wage was £11. 11s. 0d. for a 44-hour week for men over 20. Many farm workers, however, are paid over the minimum, and in addition overtime is frequently worked at peak periods, so that actual earnings average a little under £15 a week. Cowmen and others with special responsibilities may earn up to about £20 a week apart from the value of a free house, free milk, and sometimes other benefits.

Less than half the farm workers in the UK belong to a union. The two unions serving their interests, the National Union of Agricultural Workers and the agricultural section of the Transport and General Workers' Union find it difficult to obtain a large membership in a widely scattered industry consisting of many businesses employing in some cases only one or two workers. In agriculture personal loyalties between farmer and worker are often very strong. Increasingly farmers are tending to introduce incentive schemes including bonuses related to annual profits. To workers enjoying such schemes the activities of the unions, which are greatly concerned with improving minimum wages, may seem of limited interest except as providing a standard to which their own earnings can be compared.

Apart from wages the chief union activities have been concerned with improving conditions of work, particularly better safety regulations, and

---

[12] Many of these are noted in *Aperçu de la situation en matière de durée du travail et de salaires dans l'agriculture à la date du 15/12/65* (EEC, Brussels, March 1967).

with the well-known issue of the tied cottage. The majority of farm workers live in houses belonging to their employers, the occupation of which is a condition of their employment. The service tenancy can be terminated as soon as the employment comes to an end. The justification of the system is that farmers, particularly those in remote areas, must be able to depend on being able to house their workers close to where they work. The objection to it, with which many farmers sympathize, is that the occupation and retention of a home should not be dependent on holding down a particular job.

Nowadays this intractable problem has become less severe. The rundown in the agricultural labour force has taken some of the pressure off rural housing. The Courts generally delay the application of eviction orders so that occupants of tied cottages have time to find somewhere else to live. This has produced a more equal balance of power between employer and worker on the housing issue. Finally, the publicity given by the unions to the problem of tied cottages seems to have induced a more liberal public attitude as a result of which most farmers would now hesitate before trying to turn a worker out of a tied cottage without helping him with reasonable notice.

The EEC

By contrast with the UK, farmers in all EEC countries greatly outnumber farm workers. In some small-farming areas such as southern Germany, and parts of Belgium and France, non-family hired workers are very rare indeed. There is no statutory control of wages, which instead are the subject of collective bargaining. Those employers who steer clear of wage bargaining are able to undercut the normal rate in areas where there is a surplus of agricultural labour. For this reason the evidence on comparative hourly rates provided by Table 7 below must be treated with some reserve.

In some parts of the Community summer overtime is avoided by working shorter hours in the winter and averaging out. Paid holidays are longer than in the UK. In Italy for instance, farm workers get three weeks' holiday in addition to seventeen public holidays. Nor is any comparison based on a common consumer price index altogether satisfactory. Nevertheless the Table shows the high hourly earnings of farm workers in Denmark, the Netherlands, and Belgium, compared with the UK, and the very low earnings of French farm workers.

These low earnings must in large part be due to poor unionization. Only in the Netherlands and Germany (and to a lesser extent Belgium) are the farm workers at all well organized. In France and Italy a strong centralized union is completely lacking. The unions, such as they are, are linked together in the European Land Workers' Federation, one of the regional groupings of the farm workers' international organization, the International Federation of Plantation, Agricultural, and Allied Workers. There is also a small branch confined to EEC countries.

TABLE 7. HOURLY INCOME OF FARM WORKERS IN EUROPE
(*DM per hour*)

	Wages		Wages plus family allowances for 2 children	
	1957	*1965*	*1957*	*1965*
Denmark	1·96	3·78	2·04	3·77
UK	1·86	2·36	1·96	2·46
Belgium	1·79	3·13	2·15	3·77
Netherlands	1·52	2·86	1·74	3·19
Germany	1·35	2·86	1·35	3·05
France	1·52	1·74	1·85	2·21

As above, adjusted to a common consumer price index

Denmark	2·18	3·93	2·27	4·22
UK	2·04	2·44	2·15	2·54
Belgium	1·67	3·23	2·01	3·85
Netherlands	1·74	3·59	2·00	4·01
Germany	1·35	2·86	1·35	3·05
France	1·18	1·73	1·73	2·20

Source: National Union of Agricultural Workers based on research by Dr. Theodor Berg-
mann, Germany.

The United Kingdom as a member of the EEC

Farm workers would not be immediately affected by UK membership. The unions have expressed fears as to the future of the Agricultural Wages Board, but these are without foundation. On a longer view the NUAW has been concerned with the general effects of EEC entry on the prosperity of agriculture in the UK. The union, which in spite of its small number of registered members (about 115,000 in 1967) has produced several leading trade unionists, has adopted a cautious but more open-minded approach than the farmers' unions. Like the NFU the organizations representing farm workers have also been interested in regional effects in the UK of the adoption of the common agricultural policy: the question, for instance, of whether there will be a quicker run-down of farm labour in livestock areas than in cereal-growing areas as a result of changing levels of profitability. Migration of workers presents another interesting field for conjecture. At present foreign farm workers may enter the UK (on a permit which has to be applied for by the employer) provided that there are no British workers available to take on the job. Theoretically the foreign worker has to stay in agriculture for four years, but in practice he often leaves to go into industry before this minimum period has elapsed. Permits are virtually never refused and over the last few years the number issued has averaged roughly 1,000 a year.

Bearing in mind social, linguistic, and cultural barriers it is difficult to believe that the end of restrictions on migration of farm workers will cause the present trickle to increase very significantly. There is at present a migration of farm workers from Italy into southern Germany and France, apart from seasonal migration, but the move is, for many reasons, an easier one than to the UK. Besides, wages paid in Germany are at least as high as in the UK. Any increase of the movement of foreign workers into Britain may well be balanced by emigration of British farm workers looking for a sunnier climate. But on neither side is the increase likely to amount to much.

(c) CREDIT

A farmer borrows money, or attempts to borrow it, for much the same reasons as anyone else. In the case of short-term credit his requirements are usually based on the need to finance a production cycle, often seasonal, or to tide over a temporary set-back in an otherwise sound business, or to provide a bridging loan while awaiting long-term finance. He starts looking for long-term credit when the savings (including inherited savings) which he is prepared to put into the farm business are less than the amount which he considers he can profitably invest at prevailing interest rates. In this a farmer is responding like any other businessman. There are, however, three important respects in which agriculture's needs for long-term credit can be distinguished from those of other industries.

First, farming is characterized by relatively poor ability to accumulate capital through its own retained profits. For reasons which are well known, farm incomes in the West have tended to remain below non-farm incomes. In these circumstances the farm business is unlikely to leave much residue for capital expansion after family needs have been provided for. In the UK, where primogeniture has been the normal form of inheritance, farm savings have often been preserved from generation to generation with beneficial effects on farm structure. But elsewhere in Western Europe farm savings have had to be divided, by law or custom, among a number of inheritors, giving rise either to fragmentation or a farm deprived of capital through the need to pay off other members of the family.

This weakness in accumulating capital has been associated in recent years with a greatly increased demand for it. The reduction in the numbers of farmers, far more pronounced on the Continent than in the UK, has contributed to the demand, as farmers going into other occupations take their farm capital with them. So has the dramatic increase in farm land values. But by far the biggest factor has been the technological advances which farmers, deprived of hired labour by the demands of other industries and squeezed on their incomes, have turned to and adopted remarkably quickly. New farm machinery and dairy and other equipment have been required, and with them the buildings to house machinery, bigger livestock numbers (with larger forage requirements), and increased grain production. All these investments have to be financed.

The third characteristic which distinguishes agriculture from other industries is the difficulty that farmers often encounter (without special assistance) in raising finance from outside sources. In general the capital market is not able to provide long-term equity capital for agriculture. Farmers are sometimes remote from banking centres. Their accounts are often in a form which does not readily provide the sort of information which lending institutions prefer. Even in Western Europe where government powers are frequently available to prevent large price fluctuations, farming is still regarded as a somewhat risky business, at the mercy of the weather and of crop and livestock diseases. All these still count against agriculture's credit-worthiness in competition with other potential borrowers.

The United Kingdom

The principal sources for lending to farming in the UK consist of private lenders, mostly relatives of farmers, the banks and the Agricultural Mortgage Corporation (AMC). Some estimates have been made of the first but these are really no better than informed guesses. The clearing banks report separately their loans to agriculture, which now amount to over £500 mn. This figure includes farmers' borrowing on private account and also merchants' borrowing. The AMC's outstanding loans in mid-1967 were about £90 mn. These loans are all secured on first mortgages of agricultural property.

The clearing banks in the UK have always adopted a rather ambivalent attitude to agricultural credit. For seasonal lending there is no problem. But many loans which start off on a short-term, or even seasonal, basis, often turn out in practice to be long-term loans. Farmers, especially owner-occupiers, are rated as good customers by the banks. Many hold substantial credit accounts with the banks, the industry as a whole being probably a net lender to the banks. Their stake in the AMC, which they own in conjunction with the Bank of England, encourages the banks to put activity in the direction of the AMC, which has much expanded its business in recent years. Despite this expansion the Corporation's lending still only amounts to a few pounds per acre of agricultural land in England and Wales (there is a separate lending organization in Scotland).

A special problem in the sphere of agricultural credit in the UK is presented by the co-operatives, which find it difficult to raise the medium and long-term credit necessary for their expanded business. The report by Maxwell Stamp Associates Ltd. which was mentioned earlier in this chapter recommended the setting up of a new financial organization specially designed to provide credit for co-operatives, with the benefit of a government reserve fund and state-subsidized interest rates. These recommendations are now being considered by the Central Council for Agricultural and Horticultural Co-operation.

The EEC

In the Netherlands, which has the most comprehensive farm credit system, the first co-operative banks were established as a result of the initiative of farmers' organizations after the agricultural depression of the nineties. The banks soon after (1898) formed two national organizations which correspond, like the two main trading co-operatives, CEBECO and CIV, with the religious and geographical divisions of the country. The two groups, the *Cooperatieve Centrale Raiffeisen-Bank* based on Utrecht and the *Cooperatieve Centrale Boerenleenbank* with headquarters in Eindhoven, compete against each other in the centre of the country but each enjoys exclusive territory in the extreme north or south. These central banks have about 1,300 local co-operative agricultural credit banks affiliated to them with a total of some 2,200 branches. There are only a handful of agricultural credit banks which are not affiliated.

Most of these local co-operative banks have only a very small salaried staff, usually a cashier and one or two clerks. The management is in the hands of a managing board, consisting often of three people, who are responsible for considering loan applications, setting rates of interest, and deciding any policy issues for the cashier. They are in turn responsible to a supervisory board which reports to the general meeting of the members of the co-operative. Members of these boards, usually distinguished local farmers, do not receive any remuneration.

Over 80 per cent of deposits at these banks consist of savings accounts, payable either on demand or at very short notice. Membership of the bank, which involves the acceptance of unlimited liability is open to anyone living or carrying on business in the bank's area. Frequently depositors become members of the bank but it is not compulsory. On the other hand the banks normally insist on borrowers taking up membership, the Utrecht organization being the more strict on this point. Loans are made both to agriculture, including co-operatives, and to other activities.

Loans to farmers are of varying terms with many different types of security. Most are long-term and over 80 per cent are secured by mortgage. The normal practice is to advance up to two-thirds of the value of the farm offered as collateral. The proportion can be increased up to 90 per cent of the value provided reinsurance cover is taken, the cost of which falls on the borrower. This reinsurance can be of two kinds: through using the government's Agricultural Security Fund which has taken on commitments of roughly £20 mn.; or by dealing with the credit insurance companies set up by the agricultural credit banks. The latter, which have total insurances of about £10 mn., currently charge a premium of 0·8 per cent on the sum insured. In addition to its own mortgage loan activities the Eindhoven group also owns a mortgage bank, *NV Boeren-Hypotheekbank*, established about sixty years ago. Owing to the increase in demand for mortgage loans the Utrecht group has very recently set up a similar wholly-owned mortgage bank.

The term for loans varies, but is usually about twenty to thirty years. It can be as much as fifty-five years. Repayments of the loan are normally made at regular intervals but there is no penalty for early repayment of all or part of the loan. Interest rates are not fixed; they vary with prevailing rates. There is no government subsidy for agricultural credit in the Netherlands, nor are grants available for farm improvements except for experimental buildings. The time taken to obtain mortgage loans can be as little as two or three weeks from first application.

In comparison with the Netherlands the farm credit system in the Federal Republic of Germany is extremely complex. There are various categories of banks and individual credit institutions serving agriculture, some of which also lend to the non-agricultural sector. This variety arises partly from the different ways in which farm credit was organized in Germany before unification, and partly because of the changes that have occurred over forty or fifty years in the nature and extent of the need for farm credit. The most important institution, the *Landwirtschaftliche Rentenbank* in Frankfurt-am-Main, is the central credit organization for the whole of agriculture (including fisheries and forestry). This institution, founded in 1949, obtained its capital (as did also the *Deutsche Genossenschaftskasse*) through a special levy charged on most agricultural, forestry, and horticultural enterprises for ten years beginning in 1949. Its main task is to make use of its capital, reinforced by bond issues, to re-finance the lending of other institutions. Its business, particularly on long-term, has expanded very rapidly. Long-term credits outstanding are now about £300 mn. compared with about £100 mn. in 1960. Most of this business is secured by mortgages. The Bank is responsible for most of the subsidization of interest rates for agriculture, the cost of which to the Federal Republic is a little over £20 mn. a year.

Most villages of any size in Germany have an agricultural credit co-operative, often referred to as a savings and loan association (*Spar-und Darlehnkasse*), or *Raiffeisenkasse*, after the name of the founder of the movement. Local co-operative banks take deposits including short-term savings deposits and lend to farmers against a variety of types of security on short and medium-term. They are linked with a regional central bank (*ländliche Zentralkasse*) of which there are about a dozen in Germany. These regional co-operatives are in turn linked with the *Deutsche Genossenschaftskasse*, the central association for agricultural co-operative banks, which is also at Frankfurt-am-Main. One of the important tasks performed by the *Zentralkassen* and the *Genossenschaftskasse* is to even out the supply of savings throughout the movement in the Federal Republic. Farmers sometimes make use of the industrial credit co-operatives which are also organized regionally.

The savings banks are likewise organized in a pyramid form. Their activities are important to agriculture because they do a great deal of long-term lending as well as short and medium-term. Most of their regional banks, known as *Girozentralen*, act also as *Landesbanken* and as such are guaranteed by the *Land* in question. The apex of this pyramid is the *Deutsche Girozentrale-Deutsche Kommunalbank* in Düsseldorf. The *Landesbanken* are responsible for financing the very large number of agricultural improvement schemes, water undertakings, and the like which the *Land* governments undertake either on their own account or on behalf of the Federal Government under the provisions of the Green Plan.

E

In Belgium as in the Netherlands the agricultural co-operative banks play much the most important role in farm credit. At the head of the co-operative organization the *Caisse Centrale de Crédit Rurale du Boerenbond Belge* is, as its name implies, very closely linked with the *Boerenbond*, the most powerful of the Belgian farmers' unions. All the local co-operative banks are affiliated with the central bank which performs the same services for them as the two Dutch co-operative banks. For mortgage loans the *Caisse Centrale* takes a more active part than its opposite numbers in the Netherlands. Most of the long-term lending to farmers is done by the *Caisse Centrale* itself, the local co-operative acting as an intermediary.

The *Boerenbond* has about 80,000 members but only some 50,000 of these are full-time farmers. A little under half this number has taken long-term loans from the *Caisse Centrale* secured by mortgages. The normal term for mortgages is twenty years but this can be increased to twenty-five. Costs of taking up mortgage loans are very low. Valuations are usually free unless special buildings are involved or there is no local co-operative bank. Rates of interest are subsidized through the National Institute for Agricultural Credit in Brussels, a government organization responsible for the provision of cheap credit for certain specified agricultural objectives, and since February 1961 for the administration of the government's Agricultural Investment Fund. Rates vary according to the purpose and amount of the loan. The subsidized rate is available for a limited period, normally nine years. Rates can be as low as $1\frac{1}{2}$ per cent on loans to assist tenants to purchase their land, but are more often 3 per cent for a list of specified agricultural improvements, such as drainage, planting of fruit trees, and construction of poultry houses.

There are various sources of long-term credit for Italian agriculture. Some is contributed by the private banking system, especially the local savings banks, and some by private loans secured by mortgages arranged through lawyers. But far and away the biggest sources are the government itself and agencies largely dependent on government finance. The most important agency is the well-known *Cassa per il Mezzogiorno* established in 1950 to assist the development of southern Italy. Much of the *Cassa*'s vast expenditure has been directed towards helping agriculture but most of it has taken the form of direct expenditure rather than loans. An illustration is provided by the funds allocated at the review period after its first seven years. Of L.2,040 bn.[13] budgeted expenditure during the next period, L.1,138 bn. was allocated to agriculture, made up of L.638 bn. for various large-scale works including electrification, L.280 bn. for land reform, L.200 bn. for the cost of a wide range of land improvements, and only L.20 bn. for loans for agricultural improvements.

Two years after the *Cassa* started, the government introduced its Revolving Fund with an initial capital appropriation (subsequently increased) of L.125 bn. given over a period of five years. The Revolving Fund makes loans, often secured by mortgages, through special Agri-

[13] '000 million.

cultural Credit Institutes for three main purposes: purchasing agricultural machinery, irrigation works, and the construction of farm buildings. Preference is given to small and medium-sized farms. The rate of interest is usually 3 per cent. The Fund, which has been added to several times, has been largely responsible for the phenomenal growth in agricultural credit since 1952.

In a further effort to encourage development of agriculture Italy inaugurated its Green Plan in 1961, with an initial appropriation for the first five years of L.550 bn. Under the Green Plan public money can be spent on a wide range of farm investments including capital grants ranging from 10 per cent to 50 per cent of costs, and loans at very low rates. Interest charges vary from 1 per cent to 3 per cent, the latter being the same as under the Revolving Fund, depending on the type of investment and where it is to be made. Particularly favourable treatment is given to farmers in mountainous and other difficult areas.

While French private banks and insurance companies include farmers among their clients, the agricultural credit system in France essentially revolves round the *Crédit Agricole*. This organization dates from the nineties when a number of local co-operative agricultural banks were begun at the initiative of local farmers. A law of November 1894 gave them a legal constitution. Five years later regional co-operative banks (*caisses régionales*) were created in order to co-ordinate the activities of the local banks in their region. They were also given a co-operative form. Finally, in 1920 the organization was provided with a central bank in the form of the *Caisse nationale de crédit agricole* in Paris, which is state-owned. There are about 100 regional offices and over 3,000 local banks with a membership exceeding 15 million. The principal role of the *Caisse Nationale* is the provision of finance for the regional offices to which its medium and long-term loans total about £1,500 mn. Its own chief sources of funds are state-granted bonds and loans from FDES (*Fonds de développement économique et social*). The consolidated balance sheet of the regional offices amounts to £3,000 mn. Loans made by the *Crédit Agricole* have recently increased very rapidly and in the past ten years have risen threefold. Interest rates vary according to the purpose and term of the loan. Short-term loans are made at between $4\frac{1}{4}$ per cent and $5\frac{3}{4}$ per cent. Medium-term loans (up to fifteen years) are available at 5 per cent to $5\frac{1}{4}$ per cent, or for some special borrowers, including co-operative undertakings, at 3 per cent. Long-term loans, usually up to thirty years, are made at a basic rate of 3 per cent, but even cheaper terms are available under certain circumstances to war veterans (1 per cent) and to farmers from Algeria who are being resettled (2 per cent). Loans are secured by mortgages and other means. Limits are put on the amount that a borrower can take for any of these purposes. For instance young farmers (aged 21 to 35) equipping a farm for the first time can usually obtain a loan of about £1,000 at 2 per cent to help with initial improvements. Farmers who are being resettled can obtain a loan of up to £11,000 at 3 per cent on a term of thirty years in order to buy or improve a farm. Loans for improvements of buildings of up to about £2,000 are also available on a thirty year term at 3 per cent or on a five to fifteen year term at 5 per cent, reduced to 3 per cent in some circumstances.

The United Kingdom as a member of the EEC

The Community's intention is to harmonize interest rate policy for agriculture. The subsidization practised in varying ways by all member countries with the exception of the Netherlands represents a clear distortion of competition. So far harmonization has made little progress. The practice of giving special credit terms for agriculture in the majority of EEC countries is so long-established that it is likely to be allowed to continue, with the Dutch adjusting to their fellow members.

As a member the United Kingdom would have to make a similar adjustment. There would be little harm in this. Capital is already being attracted into agriculture in the United Kingdom through grants paid under the Farm Improvement Scheme. If the choice is between paying a grant of about one-third of the capital cost of a farm building or subsidizing the interest rate from, say, 9 per cent down to 6 per cent the former is not necessarily to be preferred.

Finally it is worth noting that Community institutions are providing some relief to national agricultural credit institutions. The European Investment Bank has made loans to large-scale agricultural undertakings including the irrigation and drainage schemes in the Bas-Rhône-Languedoc, which affects nearly half a million acres, the resettlement areas of the Landes and the Canal de Provence. The Guidance Section of FEOGA is also contributing capital for agriculture on an increasingly important scale.

(d) MACHINERY

Nowadays few farm tasks are performed without the assistance of a piece of machinery. Most successful farmers and well-paid farm workers have to exercise a wide range of mechanical skills. UK farmers' expenditure on repairs and depreciation of machinery comes to over £100 mn. a year.

Attempts are sometimes made to compare levels of agricultural mechanization in various countries. The usual way to do this is to show tractors available in the country per 100 hectares, which can be refined by expressing the comparison in terms of brake horse-power. Such comparisons are of very limited interest. It is obvious that a country with small farms and a predominantly intensive agriculture, such as Belgium, will be likely to have more tractors per 100 hectares than the United Kingdom where farms are larger and the type of activity more extensive. Of more interest are differences between the agricultural machinery industries of Britain and the EEC countries.

The British agricultural machinery industry is often pointed to as an example to other less dynamic, and in particular less export-minded, industries. About two-thirds of total output, amounting to about £180 mn.

a year, is exported. This is double the figure for 1957 and about seven times greater than in 1948. Far the most important item is tractors and tractor parts which together amount to nearly 90 per cent of exports. In 1966 the total number of tractors exported was 143,000. The next two most important exporters, Germany and the United States, sold only 40,000 and 35,000 units respectively. British exports of other farm machinery, totalling about £20 mn. a year, consist of combines, balers, rotary cultivators, and a wide range of miscellaneous products.

Farm machinery makes a useful contribution to British overseas trade. The industry's successes are due in part to good design, efficient management, and competent after-sales service. But a far more important factor is the structure and ownership of the industry. Companies producing tractors in the United Kingdom are mostly controlled from North America. They were established or very much expanded after the last war because the parent companies rightly regarded the United Kingdom as providing a more established and faster-growing home market than any EEC countries, convenient access to the Continent, an absence of language problems, and so on. The UK's predominance in the export market for tractors is largely due to this choice by the large North American tractor manufacturers of a base for overseas activity.

Appendix H gives details of trade in agricultural machinery between the EEC and the UK. The proportion of British exports going to the EEC, about 17 per cent, has not changed much over the past ten years. Imports from it have risen sharply. This again has been largely due to decisions over plant location by the North American companies. For instance, Ford finds it convenient to manufacture many of its tractor spare parts in Antwerp and ship them to the UK market. Massey-Ferguson is now making balers and International Harvester combines in France. Some important British companies like Rotary Hoes have plants in the EEC which they use to supply export markets.

The EEC common tariff, which applies from mid-1968, is generally speaking 9 per cent on agricultural machinery and 18 per cent on tractors. The UK tariffs are generally 12 per cent and 15 per cent respectively. The removal of these rather high rates of duty would undoubtedly be a stimulus to trade. On the other hand the Western European market for agricultural machinery has already become so specialized that tariffs on the present scale are not an important factor inhibiting trade. In a rather comparable position to Rotary Hoes from the point of view of specialization are companies like Clayson in Belgium, Vissers in the Netherlands and Welger in Germany.

Intra-community trade has been growing rapidly. About half the German exports of both tractors and agricultural implements (totalling about £77 mn. in 1966) went to EEC countries, as did roughly the same proportion of French exports, which amounted to about £35 mn. in 1966. The British agricultural machinery industry in welcoming UK membership of the EEC is making a reasonable assessment of its prospects, although some domestic sales will be lost owing to tariff-free competition from the Continent. The UK market is more or less saturated and its growth over the next ten years is likely to be less than that of the EEC.

(e) FERTILIZERS

Artificial fertilizers are not directly involved in the common agricultural policy but they constitute such an important farm input that a brief comment on the main differences between the EEC and UK as they affect fertilizers seems necessary.

Many of the characteristics of the artificial fertilizer industry in the EEC are common also to the UK. The industry is capital-intensive and concentrated, and frequently under suspicion of price-fixing through cartels. Expansion in recent years has been very rapid. Production of nitrogenous fertilizers in Western Europe, for instance, increased by about 40 per cent during the four years following 1961/62. Despite the closing down of many old-fashioned plants based on the coke-oven process, there is still over-capacity in nitrogen in Western Europe. Export prices are very considerably below domestic prices, UK nitrogen prices being higher than those in the EEC, where Belgian prices are the lowest. The future trend of prices is likely to be downwards. The situation is different for phosphates which are imported into Western Europe from North Africa, North America, and Eastern Europe, and for which prices are likely to remain firm. In potash Western Europe is about self-sufficient, but the market is affected by offers from surplus areas, especially from North America where there is a strongly established export association. Prices are highest in the UK and lowest in France and Germany, both of which are large producers.

Nearly three-quarters of all fertilizers in the UK are sold as compounds. This proportion is very much higher than in the EEC where only in France is more than half sold in compound form. In Italy, where consumption of fertilizers is anyway low, only about a quarter of all artificial fertilizers is compounded. The premium in the UK for compounding (about 12 per cent) is higher than elsewhere, being about double the premium in France. There is no premium at all in Germany. In both countries producers are trying to encourage farmers to use compounds in place of 'straights'.

Direct comparison between prices paid by farmers for fertilizers in the UK and EEC are complicated by differences in delivery terms, discounts, bagging and bulk prices, transportation subsidies, merchanting practices and so on. In the case of the EEC these differences have been carefully noted in Professor Albers' long report for the EEC Commission.[14] Published UK ex-works prices are higher than those in EEC. Allowance must be made for the fact that there is no retail price maintenance in the UK and merchants tend to give away a large proportion of their commission in order to obtain any sizeable order. But even after taking

[14] W. Albers, *Situation du marché, prix, et politique des prix des engrais dans les pays de la C.E.E.* (EEC Brussels, April 1963).

account of this difference, UK prices look high in relation to those in the EEC, something which is not wholly explained by the comparative advantage of EEC producers on raw materials.

The United Kingdom as a member of the EEC

The fertilizer industry would be influenced in two ways by UK membership of the EEC. First the tariff barriers between the UK and the EEC would be removed. Theoretically this might lead to increased competition in the UK market as the level of protection is about £4 per ton. The fertilizer industry does not seem to be particularly concerned about this and is even thinking of gaining more from this removal of the lower EEC tariff than it might lose from competition from duty-free EEC-produced fertilizers. In reality trade is unlikely to increase to any very great extent. Fertilizer producers have been careful in the past not to disturb the markets of their colleagues in near-by countries. It seems likely that in future the large-scale producers will appreciate the advantages of less than wholly cut-throat competition.

In the UK farmers enjoy a subsidy on fertilizers, high on nitrogen, modest on phosphates and nil on potash. In the EEC there are a few fairly unimportant transport subsidies affecting fertilizers but no price subsidization. The total cost of the subsidy in recent years has been about £30 mn. a year. Subsidies on fertilizers on one manufacturer's compounds in 1966/67 worked out as follows:

Type	Compound N P K	Price before subsidy	Subsidy per ton	Price after subsidy
High Nitrogen	25.10.10	£38. 2. 6	£10. 6.10	£27.15. 8
Low Nitrogen	0.14.28	£24.11. 6	£3. 7. 6	£21. 4. 0
Basic Slag	0.11. 0	£6.19. 6	£2. 0. 4	£4.18. 8
Muriate of Potash	0. 0.60	£19.16. 0	—	£19.16. 0

The survival of the fertilizer subsidy is one of the curiosities of UK agricultural policy. The reason usually advanced for subsidies of this kind is that they are educational, a convenient method of introducing farmers to the economic benefits that can accrue from a practice such as applying fertilizers. This argument can no longer be used in the UK where the benefits have been known for many years, and where the manufacturers are perfectly capable of putting right any ignorance that remains. In fact the fertilizer subsidy has become a form of income support. If the subsidy were removed the government would be under pressure to increase farm prices, particularly for grains. This might cause difficulties with overseas suppliers. The fertilizer subsidy has therefore remained.

Adoption of the CAP would, however, undoubtedly provide a useful opportunity of getting rid of it. What effect would this have? It is interesting to consider the experience of Germany which up to 1961 had a fertilizer subsidy costing about the same as the UK's and which was abolished over three years. The cost of the subsidy, which had averaged DM262 mn. between 1956 and 1961, fell to DM162 mn. in 1962, DM54 mn. in 1963 and became nil in 1964. Meanwhile fertilizer prices were increased. For instance, between 1962/63 and 1963/64 nitrogen fertilizer prices rose by 10 per cent, phosphate by 9 per cent and potash by $\frac{1}{2}$ per cent. This seems to have had very little effect on consumption. Over the three years that the subsidy was being removed expenditure on fertilizers increased by more than the previous cost of the subsidy.

The immediate effect of the CAP abolition of the subsidy would be to put up UK fertilizer prices. Judging from German experience, this will have little or no effect on consumption, especially as it will be accompanied by higher grain and beef prices. In the longer term UK farmers may enjoy lower net prices for fertilizers as manufacturers encounter somewhat greater competition from the EEC and are perhaps also able to buy some of their raw materials more cheaply.

(iv) PRICES, INCOMES, AND THE ANNUAL REVIEW

Article 39 of the Treaty of Rome, which forms the preamble to the section concerning agriculture, states:

The common agricultural policy shall have as its objectives:
(a) to increase agricultural productivity by developing technical progress and by ensuring the rational development of agricultural production and the optimum utilisation of the factors of production, particularly labour;
(b) to ensure thereby a fair standard of living for the agricultural population, particularly by increasing the individual earnings of persons engaged in agriculture;
(c) to stabilise markets;
(d) to guarantee regular supplies; and
(e) to ensure reasonable prices and supplies to consumers.

These objectives must be reckoned quite as acceptable to UK farmers, and consumers, as the aim of the preamble to the 1947 Agriculture Act to promote and maintain

a stable and efficient agricultural industry capable of producing such part of the nation's food and other agricultural products as in the national interest it is desirable to produce in the United Kingdom, and of producing it at minimum prices consistent with proper remuneration and living conditions for farmers and workers in agriculture and an adequate return on capital invested in the industry.

The inherent contradictions and lack of precision in this statement have already been discussed, as well as the historical setting of UK agriculture in international trade which it implies. Resemblance between the two sets of aims, proclaimed by the governments of the Six and of the UK, is all the same striking. Why, then, have British farmers' and growers' reactions, at least those expressed officially, to the prospect of entering the Community been mostly hostile or very reserved? There are two main aspects to these doubts and fears: first the direct result for farm incomes, and second the effect on the political influence of farmers and their Unions.

By accepting the EEC system the UK farmer would be sacrificing to a considerable extent the principle of price guarantees to which, over the past twenty or more years, he has become accustomed. Indeed he has become so accustomed to it that he sometimes tends to overlook the way in which the guaranteed prices determined each year with much publicity at the Annual Review are in fact watered down by the time they come to be applied to the products which he actually sells off his own farm. Many devices have been introduced in recent years to close the once open-ended deficiency payments and to adjust producers' returns to seasonal market trends: standard quantities for milk and cereals, flexible guarantees for pigs, indicator prices for eggs, abatements and supplements for fatstock, and the rest. The long-term assurances introduced in 1958, limiting annual reductions of the total value of the guarantees to $2\frac{1}{2}$ per cent, and to 4 per cent for any one commodity, operate at the lofty levels of gross agricultural income and gross returns from particular products, giving only limited security to the individual. Nevertheless it remains true that on entering the EEC the present guarantees, however qualified, for cereals, fatstock, and milk would be replaced by target or guide prices supported only by market intervention at certain minimum levels. The individual producer does not even obtain the intervention price,[15] let alone the target price. Nor is there the sort of long-term assurance which would limit reductions in target or intervention prices from year to year. For egg producers there is no intervention or target price. Not only would these changes in the support system result in a greater degree of uncertainty for farm incomes in general, but their level is likely to fluctuate more widely between one year and another than at present.

It is evident that adoption of EEC prices would involve sharp changes in both gross returns and in costs of production. Generally speaking costs will rise least for arable farmers, who would be mainly affected by the disappearance of the fertilizer subsidy. They will increase most for livestock producers in proportion that their products are dependent on converting cereals. The impact of these cost increases would fall in almost inverse proportion to the increases in gross returns, which would be highest for cereal growers, and, except in the case of beef, lowest for livestock producers. This is clearly brought out in a study by Mr. T. Kempinski, which shows that farm incomes on light arable land in Cambridgeshire and on Midland grazing farms would stand to gain substantially from adopting the CAP. Farms dependent for a greater proportion of their income on milk, poultry and eggs are seen to benefit relatively little or not at all.[16]

[15] Since all EEC prices are defined at the wholesale stage, the producer's minimum price is the local intervention price reduced by the amount of merchants' handling costs and profit margin.

[16] T. Kempinski, *Entry into the European Common Market and British Agricultural Income* (Department of Agricultural Economics, University of Manchester, November 1966).

Kempinski's estimates of farm income changes, like those made by T. K. Warley and Unilever in the studies already quoted, have to be adjusted in the light of the sterling devaluation of November 1967. Since its effect will have been, in terms of EEC prices, to increase potential returns to UK farmers considerably more than costs, the situation for British agriculture as a whole inside the EEC would be more favourable than before devaluation. Kempinski reached his conclusions by applying to 1965/66 UK production figures the EEC prices likely to be ruling at the moment of British entry. By this admittedly static method of approach, valid for not more than the first year after entry (and assuming some sort of interim running-in period, however brief, not valid for that), he estimated (pre-devaluation) that in the most favourable circumstances aggregate UK farm income would rise by just over 7 per cent, but that it could decline by as much as 22 per cent. So wide a range of probability was due to a number of alternative assumptions: first, about the possible levels of cereal prices; second, about the continuation or not of government grants and subsidies other than deficiency payments; and third, about the effect on horticultural incomes. The question of cereal prices is certainly of real significance and is discussed below. As far as grants and subsidies are concerned the alternative presented would not prove in fact to be as clear cut. It would not be a matter of all or none. Certain grants not clearly tied to a particular product would undoubtedly be allowed to continue. Horticultural income was assumed to remain either unchanged or to decline by 5 per cent. This is roughly in line with the other two studies.

The Unilever study, taking a more dynamic standpoint, considered the possible effects of price and policy changes over a ten-year period up to 1975, by which time it assumed that the UK would either be fully integrated into the EEC or still outside. Its authors did not, however, offer any estimate of changes in agricultural income as a whole, though they spelled out substantial rises in prices (ranging from 50 per cent to 5 per cent) and output of beef and veal, mutton and lamb, milk, and wheat and barley, all of which could involve relatively small increases in production costs. Even for pigs a price rise of 15 per cent is anticipated. No change is foreseen for broilers, and reductions only for sugar-beet, fruit and vegetables, and eggs. Unilever are particularly optimistic about the prospects for beef, output of which should, in their view, increase by 30 per cent considering the 35 per cent difference between the 1965/66 UK producer price of just under 180s. 0d. per live cwt. and an EEC target price of 242s. 0d. The difference might on balance have been somewhat narrower owing to a number of other factors, including the disappearance of the calf subsidy, not taken into account in these figures.[17] Given a 'devalued' target price of 288s. 0d., however, Unilever's optimism becomes justifiable.

Warley wished to avoid the additional assumptions and guesses about general price and consumption trends inseparable from looking as far forward as even the earliest date by which the UK might reasonably be

[17] For a discussion of these factors see pp. 138–9.

expected to have adopted the CAP in full. He therefore assessed the effects of entry by making his projections to 1970, the year by which the UK would undoubtedly have been fully involved in the CAP had its earlier application to join the EEC been successful. This had the considerable advantage of enabling him to make maximum use of verifiable data about supply, demand, prices, and policies. His calculations yielded a very reasonable picture of how, had farmers in 1967 been in the middle of changing over to the CAP, gross returns for each major type of production might have been affected by 1970. Thus it appeared that gross farm income could have risen about 5 per cent more inside the Community than out, but additional costs of production, particularly of feedgrains, would have more than outweighed this advantage, leaving a small overall margin of 3 per cent in favour of remaining out.

Devaluation will have altered this picture entirely. In the first place the price of feedgrains would, in terms of sterling, now be much higher, by at least £6 per ton, adding some £90 mn. to UK farmers' costs. Allowance must also be made for the revalued cost of imported store cattle. On the other hand, the effect of devaluation on farmers' returns would also be substantial. Retaining Warley's projections of what the volume of output might have been had the UK become a full member of the EEC by 1970, gross farm revenue could, at revalued prices,[18] amount to £2,100 mn. After deducting about £730 mn. for the cost of feedgrains, proteins, and net imports of cattle, this would leave a gross farm income of nearly £1,400 mn., or 12 per cent more than it would be, according to Warley's estimates, if the UK were to remain outside the Community. As a result of devaluation the net advantage of remaining outside has now disappeared. The comparative effects on gross returns for each of the main products of staying out or going in are illustrated in Table 8. It must be borne in mind that the main burden of the additional feedgrain costs would fall on producers of eggs, poultry-meat and pigmeat.

Cereals are the key to the CAP. Throughout all the negotiations which have taken place between the Six since 1961 there has never been any doubt that, whatever compromises might be reached about support measures for other commodities, a minimum price for soft wheat, barley, maize, and rye was to be ensured on all the major grain markets of the Community. For each of 840-odd markets an intervention price level is fixed at which the official agency is obliged to purchase all grain offered to it. This intervention price is, for much of the northern part of the Community, derived from the basic Community intervention price fixed at Duisburg in the Ruhr, deemed to be the zone of greatest deficit for grains. Derived intervention prices are lower by exactly the amount of the notional cost of transporting the grain from each intervention point to Duisburg. In the context of an agricultural economy traditionally dependent to a large extent on its income from

---

[18] Also taking into account absolute increases in intervention prices for feedgrains, beef, and veal, and of the introduction of support buying for pigmeat, authorized by the Council of Ministers since the publication of Warley's study.

TABLE 8. UK: FORECAST OF CHANGES IN GROSS
REVENUE AND GROSS FARM INCOME ATTRIBUT-
ABLE TO JOINING THE EEC

(£ mn.)

	'OUT'[a]	'IN'[b]
Wheat	91	200
Barley	186[c]	297
Oats	8	14
Dairy products	376	428
Beef and veal	250	298
Mutton and lamb	103	105
Pigmeat	182	153
Poultry and game	94	107
Horticultural products	111	105
Eggs	177	197
Sugar	34	38
Potatoes	78	80
Miscellaneous	82	91
Total revenue	1,772	2,113
Expenditure on		
Feedgrains	375	565
Protein feeds	143[d]	136[e]
Net cattle imports	17	28
Total	535	729
Gross farm income	1,237	1,384

a Warley, *op. cit.* Tables IX and XII.
b Warley, quantities in Table IX revalued.
c Includes allowance for revalued exports.
d Includes allowance for revalued imports.
e Allowance made for lower tariffs.

cash grain crops this so-called regionalization of the minimum guaranteed
prices has been unpopular in the remoter areas of the Community. For
markets in the southern part of the EEC, therefore, the level of intervention prices is calculated by reference to centres of other deficit zones
such as Marseilles and Rome. A decision would have to be reached about
the derivation of intervention prices in the UK. An obvious possibility
would be the establishment of a deficit zone in the Liverpool/Manchester
area, but the implications of such an arrangement need carefully assessing.
Derived from Duisburg intervention prices would be lower by anything
from 15s. 0d. to 65s. 0d. per ton at the main UK ports than they would be
if derived from Liverpool, taking into consideration handling charges at the
docks and freight to Duisburg. At possible inland intervention points in
surplus areas such as Lincoln or Bury St. Edmund's intervention prices
would be lower still, by the amount of the cost of road freight to the docks,
say 15s. 0d. to 20s. 0d. This would mean that corresponding to a basic
beginning of season intervention price at Duisburg for barley of £37 5s. 0d.
per ton, producer prices in East Anglia (assuming, as seems probable, they
were around intervention level) would be about £33 0s. 0d. per ton.

Owing to the high cost of road freight and relatively low sea and barge rates cereal growers in the eastern and southern parts of Great Britain would not be much affected by whether their local intervention prices were derived from Duisburg or from Liverpool: the notional cost of transporting their grain to either place would be about equal. But the impact of the choice of arrangement on the price of compound feeds, 62 per cent of which are still produced in the UK in the major ports, could be substantial, resulting in differences for some types of feed of up to as much as 26s. 0d. per ton between 'Duisburg' and 'Liverpool' prices. The implications for livestock producers of the level of cereal prices inside the EEC are considered in greater detail in Part II. We have attempted there to calculate for a number of products the additional costs of feed and fertilizers per unit of output. As these estimates are often based on known costings for particular enterprises we have not rounded our figures, which may therefore give an unjustifiable appearance of accuracy. Not only have the estimates involved a good many rather rough assumptions along the way (about freight rates for instance), but they present an essentially static picture. Applying new price to old practice, they assume that farmers do not adapt practice to price. But even on this unrealistic assumption we believe they may have some value in suggesting the order of magnitude of change in costs which adoption of the CAP could bring about.

Removal of the lime and fertilizer subsidies, worth about £35 mn. a year to UK farmers and unlikely to prove compatible with EEC rules, was not taken into account by Warley in the estimates of changes in gross farm income given above. Their disappearance would effectively reduce it by about 3 per cent. Our own estimates of feed cost increases per unit of output have, as already mentioned, assumed this additional cost to green forage production. It is, however, possible that the subsidies will in any case have been phased out by the time the UK joins the EEC. A beginning was made at the 1967 Annual Review with a 6 per cent reduction in the fertilizer subsidy, and, as in the case of the ploughing-up subsidy, now discontinued, it must be reckoned that their original educative impact is now spent.

Most of the grants of a generally 'structural' nature, estimated to cost some £30 mn. in 1967/68,[19] and not tied to any particular product, would appear to be unexceptionable to Community philosophy, and are, indeed, many of them the object of assistance under the Guidance Section of FEOGA. Far more serious would be the effect of the disappearance of the various aids to hill and upland farmers several of which, like the hill cow and hill sheep subsidies, are without doubt 'product orientated'. The impact of their removal is clearly shown by Kempinski,[20] who estimated

---

[19] Field drainage £3·6 mn.; water supply £0·5 mn.; livestock-rearing land and hill land £1·6 mn.; silos £0·2 mn.; farm improvements £13·2 mn.; farm structure £0·1 mn.; investment incentives £9·6 mn.; small farmers £2·2 mn.; farm business records £0·4 mn.; other £0·6 mn. *Annual Review and Determination of Guarantees*, 1967, Appendix V.

[20] *Op. cit.*, Table B.

that for predominantly livestock farms on poor land in Wales entry into the EEC would involve a 71 per cent reduction in income. He assumed all government grants, amounting to £180 for every 100 acres of these 450-acre farms, to have been cut off; certainly the major part of them would be likely to prove unacceptable in the Community. Such a sample of farms would be by no means exceptional in Wales, Scotland, and parts of northern and south-west England, in the considerable degree to which they rely on special assistance for their incomes. Kempinski's 'static' approach makes little difference in this case; there is very little room for hill farmers in the face of changes of this kind to make adjustments to their farming system, and the higher market prices for fatstock and store cattle and sheep obtainable in the EEC would be insufficient to compensate fully for the disappearance of the grants. Even allowing for the retention of some grants as well as for the favourable impact of devaluation on the beef guide price, loss of income, if not of the order of 70 per cent, is still not going to be at any level that could be considered tolerable.

Given that there are similar disadvantaged areas in the hills and uplands of France, Italy, and Germany, and that their problems are viewed sympathetically by the Commission, how can those of UK hill farmers be fitted into the framework of the CAP? The replacement of the present production grants by forms of assistance compatible with EEC philosophy would require a major re-thinking of government policy. This is evident from a glance at the sort of grants being made under FEOGA's Guidance Section. With all the calls being made on it the Fund would only provide a fraction of the expenditure on structural measures which might be considered adequate to yield increases in farm income on the scale of the former production grants. But there would of course be no limit to the amount of aid of this kind which the British government would be permitted to give. An example may be given from France, where even before the adoption of the CAP there was never any discriminatory price policy of the UK type in favour of hill farmers, but where the social and economic problem of upland farms in the Jura and Massif Central has been every bit as grave. As part of a plan for regional development in the Bas-Rhône-Languedoc large stretches of the south-western Massif Central have been subjected, commune (roughly equivalent to rural district) by commune, to structural analysis.[21] As a result holdings have been regrouped and divided between agriculture and forestry according to the suitability of the land, and part-time farmers given employment in forestry. Small hamlets have been allowed to disappear and the population gradually concentrated into a few of the larger villages. Roads and rural electrification have been extended, tourism attracted by the construction and equipment of camping sites and chalets, and rural industries encouraged.

---

[21] See, for instance *Etude d'un plan d'utilisation des terres et d'équilibre sylvo-agricole à l'échelon communal: commune de Colognac (Gard)* and *Etude d'aménagement socio-économique d'une commune en vue du reboisement: commune de Lunas (Hérault)*,—Compagnie Nationale d'Aménagement de la Région du Bas-Rhône et du Languedoc, Montpellier.

Action of this kind is likely to begin in the UK, independently of entry into the EEC, through the work of the Rural Development Boards set up under the 1967 Agricultural Act. If in making their plans the Boards make use, as they should, of the experience of EEC countries, an element of Community thinking may already have been introduced into government policy for hill farming by the end of a transition period. Such a period would logically include the gradual run-down of the special hill production grants. On the other hand one can envisage by that stage pressure from farmers' organizations inside the EEC in favour of the adoption in the CAP of some of the features of the UK system, including some form of direct aid to meat production in the hills. Pressure of this kind is unlikely by itself to lead to a radical departure from principle by the Commission. It is always possible, however, that once the agricultural population of the Community has declined to a manageable proportion of the whole, say under 10 per cent, and the cost of subsidizing it consequently become less, direct income support for disadvantaged minorities on the present UK model could one day find a place in official thinking.

The National Farmers' Unions will no doubt work hard to obtain the support of their fellow professionals in COPA over a number of issues where they may hope to persuade them that the interests of EEC farmers are also engaged. Production grants for hill farmers, market support for mutton and lamb, and for wool (to be treated as an agricultural and not an industrial product), and a wider seasonal price differential for milk should all be matters of mutual interest. Since these are points which will anyway be pressed at ministerial level during negotiations, COPA's handling of them will not provide for the NFU so serious a test of that organization's influence as a pressure group at the source of power as will some of the day-to-day issues later on in an enlarged Community. Fear of their loss of political influence has, apart from uncertainty about the effect on farm incomes, been a powerful motive of the NFU's attitude towards UK entry into the Community. As has been mentioned in Chapter 2 the union has since 1939, and especially since 1947, skilfully acquired for itself the right of officially representing the farmers' point of view at the discussions with the Ministry of Agriculture which precede the Annual Review. Even if its influence on government decisions about prices is not quite as decisive as it would wish, or at least wish its members to believe it to be, the union occupies a far more central role in the formulation of year-to-year agricultural policy in Whitehall than COPA ever does in Brussels. Once the UK entered the EEC the NFU's influence at home would count for much less, though it would continue to be able to press distinctively British points of view on agricultural policy through the UK permanent representation in Brussels participating in the Management Committees. As a member of COPA, on the other hand, the union would be bound by the tradition which has grown up over the past ten years within the various EEC pressure groups that national member unions should respect joint decisions freely arrived at by the standing committee of each professional association.[22] UK farmers would also be represented by COPA on the various Advisory Committees, one for each product covered by a common market regulation, which give producers some voice in the application, though not the drawing up, of each regulation. The work of these Committees is thus mainly of a technical nature, and, as has already been mentioned, they provide no kind of forum for discussions on policy.

Farmers' representatives are far less closely associated in Brussels than they are in Whitehall with the preliminaries to the review of farm prices which is conducted each year in both places. The EEC Commission intends nevertheless, as is evident from its first comprehensive price proposals (for 1968/69) submitted to the Council in June 1967,[23] to make a detailed annual examination of the issues involved. In a written submission to the House of Commons Select Committee on Agriculture on 21 June 1967 the NFU stated,[24]

We are aware of the steps taken by the Commission (e.g. a 'reservoir of information' [sic], a farm accounts scheme, etc.) to compile statistical data. There is no comparison, however, between a price-fixing system based on this sort of information and our annual review in which prices are fixed taking into account a wide range of criteria, e.g. changes in farmers' costs, the level and trend of farm income, the capital needs of the industry, the prospective course of demand, etc.

In fact each of these criteria, except that of capital needs, is dealt with, and for each member country in turn, in the Commission's report. It also makes a lengthy appreciation of the supply position both within the Community and on the world market for each of the products for which prices of one kind or another are to be fixed. The Commission offers an apology for the inadequacies of this report, due mainly to incomplete statistical information, increasingly to be made good in future years as its network of 10,000 farm accounts (*réseau d'information comptable agricole*) becomes established. First results are to be available by the 1968 review, which will contain price proposals for 1969/70. These have to be agreed by the Council before 1 August 1968. The Commission now recognizes its duty to support future annual price proposals with an economic analysis at least as comprehensive as that of the UK Annual Review. 'It is the Commission's intention in the future, which it wishes once again particularly to underline, to draw up a report each year on the agricultural situation and submit it to the Council at the same time as its price proposals.'[25] All the same it is evident that prior consultation with farmers' interests is to play little if any part in all this. Nor in present circumstances could any EEC review include a sentence even remotely analogous to the following

[22] H. von Verschuer, *Schriftenreihe für ländliche Sozialfragen*, Heft 44 (Schaper, Hanover, 1964).

[23] *Proposition de la Commission au Conseil concernant la fixation et la révision de prix pour certains produits agricoles*, Com (67) 290 final, Brussels, 14 June 1967.

[24] Select Committee on Agriculture, Session 1966–67, Minutes of Evidence, p. 310.

[25] *Proposition de la Commission au Conseil*, p. 9.

extract from the 1967 UK Annual Review: 'The Government have considered with the farmers' unions the economic condition of the industry; and it has been particularly useful to have available the additional economic and financial data prepared in agreement with the farmers' unions since the 1966 Annual Review.'

(v) THE FUTURE OF THE MARKETING BOARDS

It will be apparent from what has been said so far that there are broadly speaking two main impediments to reconciling UK domestic farm policy with the CAP. First, the tradition that food should be available to the general public at world market prices has led to the deficiency payment and the production grant as the main method of income support for British farmers. Second, also for a number of historical reasons, structural difficulties connected with both growing and selling their produce are far less serious for them than for EEC farmers. This means that the structural aspects of the CAP, on which so much stress is placed by the Commission, would seem to have relatively little to offer, translated into hard cash at any rate, to the individual British farmer. Particularly on the marketing side sound structure, in the shape of a concentration of farm supplies, is, for a number of major products, far better developed in the UK than in any country of the Six except the Netherlands. Since the original Agricultural Marketing Act of 1931 farmers have, with government assistance, gradually established, by means of statutory marketing boards, a considerable countervailing power to monopsonistic and oligopsonistic interests. These were previously able to take full advantage of farmers' ill-organized and unco-ordinated offers on the open market. Although official encouragement to co-operatives has to some extent taken the place of the UK type of marketing policy in a number of continental countries, notably in France, co-operatives could never expect to achieve the quasi-monopolistic position of some of the British Marketing Boards.

The general weakness of co-operative enterprise, taking the Community as a whole, in the field of marketing can be gauged from the efforts being made under the CAP to persuade farmers to concentrate their supply by forming producer groups. Officially recognized groups, which need not necessarily have the legal status of co-operatives, are to receive (from national but not from Community funds) cash grants to help them get going (*aides de démarrage*) during the first three years of operation, equivalent to not more than 3 per cent, 2 per cent and 1 per cent respectively of gross annual turnover, as well as investment grants over the first five years covering up to 40 per cent of the cost of new buildings and fixed equipment and up to 20 per cent of the cost of movable equipment. All members of a group, the purpose of which must be the collection, processing, and marketing of a single farm product, or group of products, are under the obligation to deliver their entire production to it, and may only

F

withdraw their membership after due notice given. Groups are exempt from the provisions of Article 85 of the Treaty of Rome forbidding price-fixing, market sharing, and other restrictive practices, but the throughput of any group may not normally (without a special ruling of the Council) exceed 5 per cent of total EEC production of the commodity concerned. Groups may also combine together into associations or *unions de groupements de producteurs*, on the volume of whose total production no upper limit appears to be placed.

Obviously a policy of this sort, essentially designed to help schemes starting from scratch, could only have rather limited application in the UK. There is still scope for new developments in fruit and vegetable marketing, and there are also interesting possibilities for marketing fatstock, a field in which producer interests have always been notably weak and divided. For most other major commodities, however—milk, eggs, potatoes, and wool—existing arrangements are far more comprehensive than any in the Six, and the exclusive powers enjoyed, in one form or another, by the Marketing Boards for these products exceed, generally speaking, the limits of exemption from the anti-monopoly clauses of the Treaty permitted to the producer groups. The exact nature of these limits has still to be defined, and will no doubt gradually emerge in the usual process of rulings by the Commission after consultation with the Management Committees on how the regulation is to be interpreted. A particular form of practice coming within this grey area is the French *extension des règles de discipline*, whereby, on the strength of a majority resolution, all producers, whether group members or not, in a given region are bound to market through a group and also become subject to a compulsory levy for financing group administration and any market support fund. There would appear to be some conflict here with the right of withdrawal written into the draft EEC regulation on producer groups. But, if only as the result of political pressures, the French system, already established for eggs and poultry meat before 1 July 1967, seems likely to prove acceptable to the Commission.

Particular issues connected with adapting each UK Marketing Board to EEC rules are discussed in the relevant chapters of Part II. Three general conclusions emerge. First, there would be no question of abolishing *in toto* the organizational set-up of any of the Boards. Second, the '5 per cent rule', if rigidly applied, would involve the breaking down of some of the Boards into smaller, regional, units. Third, under the CAP the Boards or their successors-in-title would have certain quasi-compulsory powers of levying contributions on producers in order to finance administration and, where appropriate, market intervention as well. Since this principle is conceded in the case of the first stage of intervention for fruit and vegetables,[26] there seems no reason why it should not be extended to other commodities as well.

[26] See pp. 201, *et seq.*

(vi) PROSPECTS FOR AGRICULTURAL CO-OPERATIVES AND ANCILLARY TRADES AND INDUSTRIES

(a) AGRICULTURAL CO-OPERATIVES

In any modifications to their organization which might prove necessary to bring the Marketing Boards into line with EEC principles, and even more where producer associations were to be built up *ab initio*, the agricultural co-operative movement would have an unparalleled opportunity of extending its activity and influence. Co-operation in agriculture has not on the whole greatly flourished in the UK. Historically this has been in large measure due to the relatively sound farm structure, and to the prevalence until quite recently of the landlord-tenant system which, for all its shortcomings at the level of the individual, was basically paternalistic. On the Continent hard necessity drove independent owner-occupiers of tiny holdings into forming co-operatives, mainly for the purpose of creating mutual sources of credit and working capital, but extending later into the field of marketing. In the UK, agricultural co-operatives, with some notable exceptions in marketing eggs and horticultural produce, have tended to develop as general organizations, supplying farmers' requirements and purchasing their produce, but making little if any claim upon their personal loyalty, and often indistinguishable, save in the payment of an annual trading rebate, from any other commercial enterprise. In the EEC, on the other hand, co-operatives related to particular products, notably cereals, milk, and wine, have built up, in most cases with government support, a strongly entrenched position backed with a considerable degree of producer solidarity. The official encouragement given to producer groups in so many of the EEC's agricultural regulations is not confined to those which have the narrowly defined legal status of co-operatives. Many different forms of association already exist within the Community such as the SICAs (*Sociétés d'Intérêt Collectif Agricole*) in France, the German *Erzeugergemeinschaften*, and Italian *federconsorzii*. In the UK machinery syndicates and buying and selling groups of various kinds have been formed here and there since the war, but it would probably need a major jolt such as the dismantling of the present system of price guarantees to make the movement in favour of co-operation, whether with a large or a small c, at all widespread.

(b) ANCILLARY TRADES AND INDUSTRIES

The organization of the domestic trade for products such as eggs and milk whose off-farm sales are at present strongly influenced by producer marketing boards, would be more closely affected by a transition to the CAP than it would be in the case of meat, for instance, or horticultural products in which official intervention hardly occurs at all in the UK. The outstanding exception to this generalization is, of course, the grain trade. Except for the stipulation that all off-farm sales of home-grown wheat must be made through a merchant in order to qualify for deficiency payment, there are no statutory limitations on the marketing of cereals by marketing boards or other means. Nevertheless introduction of the EEC cereals regulation would involve substantial shifts in both the pattern and volume of grain marketing. Home production of grains which may anyway have reached about 17 million tons a year by 1970 will be affected in a number of ways (described in Chapter 5) by EEC prices and regulations. The net effect might result in increased home production of some three to four million tons, thus drastically altering the balance between domestic and imported supplies. The location of so much of the grain-consuming industries in the ports would become even more uneconomic than now. Most affected would be the compounding industry which would be presented with an altogether different structure of price relationships between the ingredients it mostly uses at present and those it might use more extensively in the future. The composition of compound feeds is different in the EEC and it is difficult to predict exactly how UK compounders would react to EEC prices. With the present relationship between EEC grain prices maize would be likely to be used on at least the present scale. But as a member the UK would be likely to press for lower maize prices in order to encourage the domestic use of its very much increased supplies of barley and feed wheat. Home-grown beans would become a more important ingredient for the UK compounder, who would also have to pay more attention to a fairly wide range of by-products. These, at EEC prices, become attractive alternatives to other ingredients.

Flour millers may somewhat increase the amount of home-grown soft wheat that they take up. But the industry is geared to using a high proportion of North American hard wheat and its customers have developed a strong preference for bread dependent on these types of flour, close-textured, and with good keeping qualities, and, to the Continental taste, rather unpalatable. Consumption of bread per head is falling and this trend will continue. Adoption of the CAP will put up flour and bread prices, but as other food prices will rise too this is unlikely to have much effect on the consumption trend. The grain trade would, of course, welcome the larger quantity of cereals which it will have to move. A bigger volume of trade at considerably higher prices will present grain merchants, especially co-operatives with their present weak financial structure, with additional financing problems.

Changes for the dairying and milk manufacturing industries would arise mainly out of the need to amend the present UK milk marketing scheme in order to bring it into line with EEC rules. Whatever the name or constitution of the organizations which took over the Milk Marketing Boards' responsibility for collecting milk at farm-gate there seems little doubt that they would be under producer control. From that point onward in the distributive chain, however, dairies and manufacturers would compete to purchase raw milk from the producer organizations either for re-sale in liquid form or for processing. Manufacturers with an outlet for liquid sales would have a free choice as to its disposal. Under present arrangements the Boards allocate raw milk according to need, the demand for liquid milk taking absolute priority and that for manufacturing being merely residual. The implications of this loss of tight control of the market by the Boards for the maintenance of liquid milk supplies, especially in the winter months, are discussed in greater detail in Part II.[27] As far as the trade is concerned difficulties can be foreseen for dairies which do not have their own manufacturing outlets. They seem likely to have to contract for supplies of raw milk with individual producer organizations, with all the risks involved in forward buying of a perishable commodity for which demand may vary substantially from week to week, or even from day to day. This is a situation which has not arisen since before the war. Many manufacturers, particularly the larger ones, would welcome the disappearance of the dual market and the removal of the very close control which the Boards are able to exercise by means of a discriminatory pricing policy over the use to which supplies of manufacturing milk are put. The removal of the standard quantity restriction on production would be likely to give manufacturers access to additional quantities of milk sufficient to provide a more adequate and regular throughput for their plant than at present, though, whatever producer pricing system is adopted, there is always bound to be a winter 'trough'. The near doubling of the wholesale price of butter due to the high EEC threshold and intervention prices might, combined with any economies of scale arising from a larger throughput, make its manufacture marginally more profitable than at present. In any case home produced butter is likely to capture some of the UK demand lost to New Zealand imports which is not transferred to margarine. As part of this process of adjustment in the milk industry smaller firms would probably suffer most. The disappearance of the quotas of manufacturing milk at present allotted to them by the Milk Marketing Boards, combined with a very substantial increase in requirements of working capital due to higher raw material costs, would be likely to lead to further concentration.

Since important changes may in any case have been made to the UK egg marketing scheme by the time negotiations for entry into the EEC have been concluded, any consideration of the effects of entry on wholesalers and breakers must be exceptionally speculative. Much depends on the outcome of the Commission of Inquiry appointed in July 1967 to review the scheme. Whether the British Egg Marketing Board's powers are increased, as the Board has requested, or drastically reduced, as others would wish, two things are clear. In the first place, once inside the EEC there would have to be much more give and take, not to say collaboration of the French 'interprofessional' kind, between any producer marketing organization or organizations which succeeded the Board and the packing stations and processors. In this the producer co-operatives, which already

[27] See pp. 122, *et seq.*

have a large stake in the wholesaling of shell eggs, would have an important bridging role to play. Secondly, under EEC regulations, it would be obligatory for all eggs sold off farms (other than casual farm-gate sales of five dozen or less) to be graded at authorized packing stations, but Grade A eggs would be sold unstamped. Without these two rules any market intervention by producer organizations, financed by some form of levy on production, would be out of the question. But the co-operation of the trade would also be necessary. French plans for this type of action, in the absence from the CAP of any official market support for eggs, are described elsewhere.[28]

Finally, in the sugar sector the strongly centralized refining industry in the UK is likely to gain at least as much from a wider tariff-free market as it may lose from competition from French and other EEC refiners. Sugar refiners in Western Europe have already begun to make links across national frontiers and Tate & Lyle Ltd. have taken part in consortia concerned in concentrating and rationalizing the industry. Higher sugar prices might have some slight effect on consumption, but UK refiners will be more than compensated for this by greater export opportunities which they are well placed to take advantage of. Chapter 12 includes some comments on the possible effects of acceptance of the CAP on the monopolistic position of the British Sugar Corporation.

[28] See pp. 161-2.

4. Negotiating in Brussels

(i) 1961–1963

The full period of the first negotiations over the UK's entry into the EEC spanned nearly eighteen months, from the date of application to join, delivered on 9 August 1961, a week after Mr. Macmillan's statement in the House of Commons of the Government's intention, to 29 January 1963 when the negotiations were finally adjourned *sine die* in Brussels following General de Gaulle's famous press conference two weeks earlier. While the negotiations themselves were intermittent, during most of this period, the subject of membership of the Community filled the press and was a common topic for conversation even among the many who had little or no idea of what was involved.

For anyone who came into contact with the negotiations it was a time of some excitement. From the UK's point of view a sense of drama was produced by the difficulty and complexity of the issues, the number of interests that had to be reconciled, and the feeling that, in Mr. Heath's words,[1] 'a major turning-point in Britain's history' had arrived. Both in the preliminaries to the negotiations and in the negotiations themselves the government had to operate on a number of fronts. It had to educate the Conservative Party and preserve its solidarity, to pacify the EFTA countries, to reassure the Commonwealth, to preserve the Atlantic Alliance, and at the same time to convince the Community that a definite change of policy had occurred and that the UK was 'going European'. Understandably Conservative Ministers played down the difficulty of reconciling these and other interests affected by UK membership of the EEC. In the enthusiasm for obtaining membership some began to believe that no fundamental political choice had to be made.

The 1961–63 negotiations have been described in detail elsewhere.[2] Here we shall confine ourselves to their agricultural aspects. This obviously will present a distorted view of the events because the negotiations were concerned with numerous other problems, industrial, political, legal, and so on. Nevertheless, many of the worst difficulties encountered in the negotiations were concerned with agriculture.

The decision to apply for membership of the EEC represented a major change in the UK's European policy. Less than six years earlier, in

[1] Speech at Paris on 10 October 1961, issued as a White Paper, *The United Kingdom and the EEC*, Cmnd. 1565 (H.M.S.O., October 1961).
[2] Miriam Camps, *Britain and the European Community, 1955–1963* (O.U.P., 1964) and Nora Beloff, *The General says No* (Penguin Special, 1963).

November 1955, the UK had withdrawn from the Spaak Committee, set up after the Messina meetings, which effectively sowed the seeds of the Treaty of Rome. When withdrawing, the UK expressed a preference for continuing to work through OEEC rather than through new institutions, as well as a strong suspicion of any form of supranationalism, a point of view which was entirely different from that adopted in 1961. During the two years following the end of the Spaak Committee's work, while the Treaty of Rome was being drafted, signed (March 1957), and then ratified by the parliaments of the member countries, the UK's attitude remained negative to the possibility of joining the customs union that was being fashioned. For instance, in November 1956 Mr. Macmillan said in the House of Commons that he did not believe 'that this House would ever agree to our entering arrangements, which as a matter of principle, would prevent our treating the great range of imports from the Commonwealth at least as favourably as those from the European countries. So this objection, even if there were no other would be quite fatal to any proposal that the United Kingdom should seek to take part in a European Common Market by joining a Customs Union . . . so that is out.' At about this time the UK took a number of actions which, whatever their actual intentions, were interpreted on the Continent as being inimical to the creation of the EEC.[3] This hostility to the concept of a full customs union and the total refusal to contemplate the inclusion of agriculture in any agreements continued during the negotiations over the Free Trade Area proposals and for some two years after their breakdown at the end of 1958. Indeed it was commonly suspected in the Community, and with good reason, that the UK's enthusiasm for a Free Trade Area as a parallel development to the Common Market was really an attempt to weaken the cohesion of the EEC. When the UK finally decided to go ahead with the formation of EFTA as a second-best alternative to an arrangement with the EEC it seemed as though a final decision not to join the EEC had been made, as EFTA membership would obviously complicate any such attempt. But within two years of the Stockholm agreements which set up EFTA the UK was applying for membership of EEC. What happened to alter government policy so drastically?

In the first place the change in policy was not quite so abrupt as might appear since many people regarded EFTA from its very beginning as no more than a temporary grouping while new economic links with the EEC were worked out. It was felt that 'something had to be done' after the breakdown of the Free Trade Area discussions and an Association with six other approximately like-minded countries, mostly Scandinavian, seemed appropriate. By joining this Association the UK gained something through the tariff-cutting which followed, even though membership proved a limitation to subsequent negotiation with the EEC. From the UK's point of view the timing was perhaps unlucky. Within a short time from the creation of EFTA, the possibility of joining EEC as a full member was

[3] Described in Miriam Camps, *op. cit.*, Chapters 3, 4 and 5.

actively under consideration in the press and particularly in the *Financial Times*, the *Observer*, the *Economist* and the *Guardian*.[4] If EFTA had been delayed for a year it is most unlikely that the UK would have wished to join it. By July 1960 the Cabinet was reconsidering the problem of closer links with the EEC as is shown by the debate in the House of Commons of 25 July. It was thought that while the time was not ripe to start negotiations, membership of the EEC might ultimately be taken up in spite of the difficulties which were examined in greater detail during the second half of 1960 and the early months of 1961. Mr. Heath was made Lord Privy Seal with special responsibilities for European policy and the government was reconstructed so that some of the key ministries were filled with committed Europeans, Mr. Soames moving to the Ministry of Agriculture. Numerous inter-departmental Committees began to study problems associated with the UK's relations with EEC. By the early part of 1961 the political arguments in favour of trying for full membership began to be generally accepted.

Considering that it was well known that agriculture would be one of the biggest difficulties involved in UK membership of EEC, it received surprisingly little detailed consideration in public at this stage. There were several reasons for this. First, an attitude of mind prevailed, engendered by other negotiations with the EEC, which automatically tended to 'exclude agriculture', and this attitude took a long time to die. The reverse preference which would hit certain Commonwealth agricultural products such as butter and some fruits was almost too awful to be considered. Some special arrangement for agriculture was still hoped for. Further, the government was under some constraint in studying the agricultural problems of EEC membership as relations with the Farmers' Unions had deteriorated following the tough Annual Review of March 1960. During the second half of 1960 special talks took place between the Ministry of Agriculture and the unions, the results of which were published in a White Paper[5] at the end of the year. While this White Paper in effect said very little, its tone was affable, almost deferential, to the unions. The short section dealing with the EEC included this sentence: 'The Government and the Unions agree that the British system of agricultural support is the one best suited to the interests of this country'; a somewhat remarkable statement in the light of the Conservative Party's agricultural policy at the 1964 election which advocated a changeover to a levy-based system regardless of EEC membership.

A further reason advanced for the small amount of background work done on EEC agricultural policy was that the policy itself had not yet been formulated. As has already been shown in Chapter 1 the important decisions in this field, which enabled the Community to enter its second phase of development, were not taken until January 1962. It was also felt

[4] Miriam Camps quotes a number of examples of press and other comment on EEC in the first half of 1960, *op. cit.*, pp. 287–8.

[5] *Agriculture. Report on Talks between the Agricultural Departments and the Farmers' Unions, June–December 1960*. Cmnd. 1249 (H.M.S.O., December 1960).

(as it turned out, wrongly) that the UK would be able to influence the development of EEC agricultural policy as soon as an application for membership had been made. It remains odd that the new minister did not immediately form a much stronger EEC section to work on the fundamental agricultural problems in anticipation of the decision to apply for membership. Nor did the government make any special effort to encourage research in this field at universities or other non-governmental institutions. This lack of preparatory work was to prove a major handicap in 1962. Failure to do in good time the detailed preparatory work on agriculture is all the more surprising because in the summer of 1961 it was expected that the negotiations would be completed and the Treaty ratified during the following year so as to make it possible for the UK to take up formal membership of the EEC on 1 January 1963.

Another mistake was to underestimate the strength of Commonwealth objections to the UK joining the EEC. Before the Prime Minister's statement in the House of Commons on 31 July when the government's decision to apply was announced, senior ministers visited the principal Commonwealth countries to discuss the UK's policy objectives. These meetings achieved very little, the government appearing to be taken by surprise at the opposition from the old Dominions, all of which were major exporters of agricultural products. In the full-dress debate in the House on the EEC membership application on 2 August 1961 the Prime Minister reiterated that from the UK's point of view membership was conditional on satisfactory terms being obtained for the Commonwealth, for its partners in EFTA and for its farmers. These three conditions were endlessly repeated by politicians of all parties, usually without much elaboration, the third condition being frequently referred to as 'the vital interests of British farming'. Agricultural problems were also strongly involved in the other two conditions: with EFTA because it was obvious that Denmark, having strong trading links with the UK, would wish to join at about the same time and this would add to the Community an important new supplier of food; and with the Commonwealth because of the extent of the UK's agricultural trade, especially with the old Dominions.

The Council of Ministers accepted the UK's application to join under Article 237 of the Treaty at the end of September and on 10 October Mr. Heath, by then appointed the UK's chief negotiator, addressed a ministerial conference in Paris. In the course of this full and carefully constructed speech[6] he accepted the principle of the UK adopting the common agricultural policy, stressed the need for 'comparable outlets' for temperate-zone Commonwealth foodstuffs and suggested that UK agriculture would need at least as long a transition period as the existing member countries had had, indicating that a suitable period might be between twelve and fifteen years.

So far as agriculture was concerned there was then a lull in the negotia-

[6] Cmnd. 1565.

tions while the Six hammered out the basic principles of their common agricultural policy, the decisions being reached, after 'clock-stopping', on 14 January 1962 with retrospective effect to the beginning of the year. The UK took no part in these decisions, which largely followed the Commission's proposals. Regulations were agreed for grains, pigmeat, eggs, and poultry, based on the use of variable import levies and, in the case of grains, target prices. The basic form of agricultural support in the Community, levies on otherwise largely unrestricted imports in preference to quotas or deficiency payments, was firmly established.

The negotiations themselves can be divided into two periods, from early May, when serious discussions on topics including agriculture finally got under way, until 4 August, and from 8 October, when the negotiations resumed after the summer vacation and the Commonwealth Prime Ministers' conference, to their end in the following January. In the first part most attention was centred on problems of trade in agricultural products from the Commonwealth including the search for some worthwhile assurance for Commonwealth exporters in the light of the refusal of the Six to agree to anything which would give Commonwealth countries better treatment than other third countries after the end of a transition period. This complex problem was associated with the quest for international commodity agreements to take over before the end of the transition period, and also with the UK's hope of finding a formula to link the Community's agricultural price policy to a certain level of imports of agricultural products.[7] By the time that the negotiators broke off for the holidays on 5 August some progress had been made on the key question of imports of temperate-zone foodstuffs but without an agreement on a precise formula. Generally speaking the Six remained firm to their first stand, but were prepared to consider New Zealand as a special case, though even here France subsequently reserved its position following a fracas at the end of the meetings on the question of interpretation of a financial regulation. On domestic agriculture nothing was achieved except agreement in principle to the holding of Annual Reviews. This was a very modest concession, because the Community anyway intended to hold such a Review, as did some of its members already, but the form would be different from that in the UK, and in particular there was no likelihood of farming interests taking a direct part in the Review. When this phase of the negotiations ended on 5 August, just a year after the UK's application had been put in, the amount of positive results on agriculture was very small indeed.

The talks were resumed in October and serious negotiations on agriculture started at the end of the month. A major difficulty was immediately encountered over the transition period. The UK position was not only that the period should extend beyond 1970 (although this was resolutely and

---

[7] At the end of this phase of the negotiations a White Paper was published (*The United Kingdom and the European Economic Community*, Cmnd. 1805, H.M.S.O. August 1962) based on Mr. Heath's report to the House of Commons.

reasonably opposed by the Six) but also that during the transition guaranteed prices to farmers implemented by deficiency payments should continue to operate and be gradually phased out as variable levies were raised. This procedure was not acceptable to the Community which insisted that the change-over should be immediate (or at least by the end of the current parliament, which in effect meant about a year after entry), and that the UK should adopt the lowest wheat price in the Community, the French, which would have raised the UK market price by over 50 per cent. Subsidies could be used during the transition period to cushion the effect on consumer prices. The problem of the transition period for agriculture was discussed at length during November but without much progress being made. By the end of the year the atmosphere of the negotiations had deteriorated. On the UK side it was felt that the Six were being unnecessarily insensitive to the political difficulties (with the Commonwealth, with UK farmers, and with consumers over food prices). The Six began increasingly to regard the transition period as a test of the seriousness of the applicant's intentions and to harden their attitude accordingly. Among the French, both in Brussels and Paris, there was widespread suspicion that the UK would use flexibility in a transition period as a means of introducing modifications to the common agricultural policy which had been agreed among the Six with such difficulty.

The final stages of the negotiations can be briefly summarized. In an attempt to produce a package on agriculture a committee was set up under Dr. Mansholt. The report of this committee was presented on 15 January, the day following General de Gaulle's press conference. At this meeting Mr. Heath finally made the concession that all transitional arrangements for agriculture should terminate by the end of 1969. Under the influence of the French meetings remained indeterminate until the negotiations were finally broken off on 29 January 1963.

In the bitterness of the aftermath of the negotiations some attempt was made to analyse what had gone wrong. A popular, and for the UK a comforting view, was that the negotiations had always been doomed to failure because General de Gaulle would never have allowed them to succeed. According to this view the General's veto was the clearest indication that success was near at hand. However, it receives little support from a special report by the Commission[8] made immediately after the breakdown. This is a rather confusing document which shows signs of having been put together in a hurry, but it includes a number of very useful comments on the state of the negotiations and on the UK's attitude to them. The report shows that while a number of important issues were ready for a package solution, others of importance definitely were not. For instance, no outline agreement had been reached on horticulture. Lacking Community regulations little progress had been made on sugar, although a precise agreement on the status of the Commonwealth Sugar

[8] European Economic Community, Commission, *Report to the European Parliament on the state of the negotiations with the United Kingdom* (Brussels, 26 February 1963).

Agreement was clearly a 'must'. Arrangements for the other EFTA countries, one of the major pre-conditions of UK entry into the EEC, had not been defined. Most important of all a satisfactory agreement over the future of New Zealand's exports of agricultural produce was still a very long way off.

The NFU and the negotiations

Many received the news of the breakdown in Brussels with consternation. Among those who took a more relaxed view were the UK farmers' unions, whose attitude to the possibility of UK entry into EEC—never downright hostile while always negative and ultra-cautious—had had some effect on the course of the negotiations. Both the England and Wales Union's President, Mr. Woolley, and its chief economist, Mr. Winegarten, made a number of speeches on the subject. It is worth quoting from some of Mr. Woolley's speeches in order to illustrate the general attitude of the unions.

The vital interests of British agriculture are embodied in the Agriculture Act of 1947 and in the system of guarantees inherent in it. For horticulture . . . the Government's policy is to continue to support this important section of the industry with tariffs as the main instrument. Unless the Six are disposed to acknowledge these facts, negotiations could have no prospect of success.

July 1961

We do not accept . . . that this country should abandon something that is basically far in advance of any existing or proposed arrangements for European agriculture.

April 1962

Unless there is a marked change in the attitude of the Six, I see no prospect in the negotiations now taking place of coming to any satisfactory arrangements.

January 1963

The unions' three main preoccupations were over the institution of an Annual Review, the continuation of guaranteed prices, and special arrangements to safeguard horticulture beyond a transition period. The question of a Community Annual Review has already been commented on. The only reasonable explanation for the amount of emphasis laid on this point by the unions is that they felt that it would anyway be conceded (though not in the form the unions wanted). The impression might be created that the concession had been made as a result of pressure on their part. On the other two points nothing was obtained. So far as guaranteed prices were concerned nobody in the Six could understand why British farmers, acknowledged to be technically much further advanced and to enjoy a far better structure, should have firmer guarantees than their colleagues on the Continent. Much the same applied to the arguments over horticulture. It was pointed out by the Six that one of the principal reasons for the creation of a customs union was to foster production in areas which had the greatest economic advantage. If pears could be grown in Italy, a fellow member of the Community, and sold in the UK at prices which the local producer cannot meet, why should the latter receive special protection beyond a transition period? To the Community it seemed that to grant this protection was to run counter to the basic principles of the CAP.

How strong was the influence of UK farming interests on the negotiations? This is difficult to gauge, but one can certainly trace their influence on the UK delegation's efforts to obtain a transition period even longer than the existing member countries had had, and special residual guarantees for UK farmers. The emphasis on explaining and recommending the UK system of farm support must certainly have been done largely for home consumption, as must the stress on the peripheral issue of Annual Reviews. All of these crucially slowed down the negotiations which, as the government had realized from the outset, should have proceeded much more rapidly.

One of the main preoccupations of the UK farmers' unions is to preserve the cohesion of the agricultural industry and to prevent the creation of splinter groups representing special interest within the industry. The issue of joining EEC presented the unions with special difficulties. Following adoption of the CAP some producers, for instance cereal growers, would benefit, others like horticulturalists might suffer. Doubtless the unions felt that by taking up a very cautious attitude, by pointing out all the disadvantages and skimming over the advantages, they would at least run no risk of losing support.

To this extent an attitude to the EEC issue was forced upon the farmers' unions. But there was another reason. Since the war the farmers' unions had carefully built up a close relationship with Whitehall. 'Partnerships with the government' was often referred to with pride from both sides. In this the Annual Reviews played a particular role. Whatever the results of the Reviews—and they were often bitterly criticized by the unions—the decisions were, at least partly, reached in conjunction with the government. It seemed unlikely that a comparably close relationship could be established in Brussels. By the end of the fifties many leading farmers, noting the trend in farming income, were questioning the general system of support in the UK, and advocating a movement towards frontier control to avoid the baneful influence of the treasury on support costs. It was not a view which received support from the farmers' unions, which preferred the devil they knew, even though he seemed to keep farming income static.

Some conclusions to be drawn from the negotiations

Even if one accepts the most extreme view of the negotiations, that they were always doomed to failure, and that the General was waiting with his chopper from the outset, it is still possible in retrospect to draw some lessons from the way the negotiations went. In the first place the timing of the application proved troublesome. Not only were the Six heavily involved themselves in problems such as the formulation of the CAP regulations and talks on political union, but too little time was left before the next election in the UK. General de Gaulle could have chosen other methods of keeping the new applicant out. By early 1963 the British government had already to be thinking in terms of the next election. It might well have been possible for the General to keep things going without a conclusion during most of 1963, by which time the imminence of an election in the following year might well have forced the British government to withdraw.[9] Obviously it is a handicap to have to negotiate under political pressures of this kind.

Another mistake made in the 1961–63 negotiations has already been indicated. This is the lack of research and of competent staff on the agricultural side. The Select Committee which examined the Ministry of Agriculture in 1967, whose activities are commented on elsewhere, would certainly have found in 1960–61 that inadequate preparatory work had been done on problems of entry. Issues and choices had not been clarified. The result was that the UK delegation spent far too long over details before finding its way to the heart of the agricultural problems. Perhaps one of the reasons for this was over-optimism about the prospects of obtaining membership and an exaggeration of the Community's wish to have the UK in.

The negotiations contained a number of curiosities. In the early stages the UK spent a good deal of time defending parts of its existing agricultural policy, unrestricted entry of most foodstuffs, guaranteed prices and deficiency payments, and low retail food prices, which might well have been modified even without EEC membership. Nor did the negotiations always seem clear about the difference of interest between UK and Commonwealth farmers. A concession favourable to one was often adverse to the other. Again, it turned out to be important to define more clearly than did the negotiators the reasons why special privileges or concessions were being asked for. Why should Commonwealth countries have access arrangements to the enlarged EEC market for a longer period than was guaranteed to them by their existing agreements with the UK? Why do tomato growers in the UK require greater protection than those in the Netherlands?

The main lessons then to be drawn concern the need to define objectives after careful preparatory study, to work with despatch ignoring trivia, and to bring negotiations to a conclusion as soon as possible, very probably making use of the package-making skills of the Commission. In this connection the constant reporting-back to parliament, such as occurred in 1961–63 is no help to a UK negotiator, and might have been curtailed except for the Macmillan government's need to take the Conservative Party, including its landed interest, along with it. Finally it may be necessary to take a long view on certain matters, which, though troublesome in the short run, might be modified through UK influence after membership has been obtained.

[9] Miriam Camps quotes the *Daily Telegraph* Gallup poll of 12 December 1962 which showed that in two months the percentage of those in favour of joining had declined from 41 to 29 and the percentage against joining had risen from 28 to 37.

(ii) THE SECOND ATTEMPT

Not much more than five years separated the two UK applications for EEC membership. With such a short gap the basic problems have of course remained much the same. This applies to the agricultural as well as to the political and industrial issues. In general the negotiators in the second attempt will be trying to find answers to the same agricultural questions as last time: consumer food prices, contributions to the Fund, access for traditional food suppliers and so on. But there are a number of important differences which must be noted.

So far as EEC membership is concerned the Prime Minister's position is much more straightforward and secure than was Mr. Macmillan's. The amount of active domestic opposition to the principle of applying for membership is, perhaps surprisingly, close to negligible. He also has the advantage of having an Opposition which is rather more enthusiastic than his own party about getting the UK into the Community. To date, the question of what terms, particularly for agriculture, would be acceptable, has not become a political issue. The most one can say is that it seems unlikely that any terms which would commend themselves to the Prime Minister and a majority of the cabinet would not also be acceptable to the Parliamentary Labour Party and the two Opposition parties. On the terms, rather than the principle of entry, it is difficult at this stage to gauge public opinion or to know whether there is any grass roots opinion which might develop differently from the current views of informed members of the political parties. For instance, if the Australian government protest that the lack of special arrangements for their canned fruits will ruin their UK trade thus causing serious local unemployment, will a sympathetic ear be found in the British electorate? What sort of terms for New Zealand dairy produce would people in the UK regard as fair and reasonable? It is difficult to do more than guess at the answers to these questions before the public has been presented with them. Possibly the answers would be influenced by another change that has occurred since 1961. The first application was more or less sprung on the Commonwealth. Even at the Prime Ministers' conference of September 1962, about a year after the application, Commonwealth leaders still seemed to be genuinely shocked by the UK's decision. The position is different now. Nobody in their senses could have supposed that the French veto in 1963 was the end of the matter; indeed Mr. Heath made it very clear at the time that it was not. And after a brief intermission the possibility of a second application has been widely discussed ever since. Commonwealth and other exporters of agricultural products have therefore been under notice for more than five years that the odds were very strongly on the UK attempting once again to join the EEC.

Others who should have benefited from this notice include UK farmers. Over the past few years any sensible farmer making long-term plans for his farming business, including those affecting investment in fixed equipment, would have had to take account of the possibility of the UK adopting the CAP and EEC prices. The main effects of EEC membership on UK domestic agriculture have been known for some years. A well-informed farmer putting up a grain store would have to take account of the possibility that under the influence of EEC grain prices he would in future be likely to grow more grain and would therefore need more storage accommodation. Likewise a farmer considering the construction of a new poultry unit, or changing from beef to dairy production, would have to consider possible future price relationships as well as those current. This aspect is again touched on when we consider the length of transition period that would be desirable for UK agriculture.

There are other respects in which the UK is better placed to negotiate on the agricultural issues than in 1961–63. The government has profited from the lessons of the last negotiations by doing its preparatory homework in greater detail. After a rather slow start research on the possible effects of adopting the principles of the CAP was undertaken by the Ministry of Agriculture with much more care. As the details of the policy have been more closely defined this research has become increasingly meaningful. Here the activities of the Select Committee on Agriculture causing extra work at the Ministry as well as annoyance at the Foreign Office have had some beneficial effects. The need to produce clear-cut evidence before this Committee could only have sharpened the Ministry's inquiries. The Committee's general conclusion was that this work of preparation had been adequately performed and with this view we concur, although the burden of work thrown on the very small number of officials concerned in Whitehall and in the UK Delegation in Brussels was unnecessarily severe. It is apparently a characteristic of the machinery of government in the UK (unlike most other countries, and particularly the United States) to make do with the minimum staff for researches of this kind however important the issue which is being scrutinized. The preparation for the agricultural side of the second negotiations has proved no exception. Nevertheless the work has been done and the results clearly and validly displayed in White Papers and in particular in the evidence before the Select Committee on Agriculture. Many more advance consultations have taken place with various interest groups, for instance the UK farmers' unions and Commonwealth countries through their High Commissions in London and their Missions to the EEC in Brussels.

Finally, from the experiences of the 1961–63 negotiations the government should have developed a clearer idea of what is the most appropriate organizational framework for negotiating with the Community. The main requirement is that the team should be able to respond rapidly to proposals and suggestions from the other side. At the first attempt delays occurred and opportunities seemed to be missed due to the need to refer points back to Whitehall via the so-called 'Flying Knights', the senior civil servants who were constantly chasing between London and Brussels. The difficulty is to reconcile the need to have a team of skilled and experienced negotiators

G

with the likelihood that negotiations with EEC will be both protracted and intermittent. As any country negotiating with the EEC, for instance on terms for association, has found, there is a lot of other business going on in Brussels, and this is likely to make any negotiating programme rather lengthy. In 1961, and to a much greater extent in 1967, the British government was expecting the negotiations to be 'short and sharp'. But in fact all the evidence indicates that this would be most improbable. In these circumstances it would be difficult to have in Brussels a large team of senior officials who for much of the time would have very little to do. The best organization would consist of a closely-knit team under the leadership of one of the two or three men in the Foreign Office who have long experience of the EEC, the team being supplied beforehand with briefs from all the government departments concerned.

What is negotiable

The Foreign Secretary, Mr. George Brown, in a statement to the Council of Western European Union at The Hague on 4 July 1967,[10] listed the main agricultural questions which the UK government was convinced it was 'in our common interest to discuss together and resolve'. These consisted of an Annual Review, milk, support arrangements for pigmeat and eggs, the scale of financing for FEOGA, sugar, and New Zealand. He also mentioned hill farmers and noted the need for an adequate transition period.

The plea for an Annual Review seemed to be inserted largely for home consumption. Not only was the principle of a Review agreed to in the last negotiations but a system is being established in Brussels based on analysis of samples of farm incomes throughout the Community.[11] Mr. Brown in fact asked for a Review 'held in conjunction with the producer organizations'. According to the normal working pattern of the Commission, consultations with producer organizations in the Advisory Committees would be likely to be asked for while the report was being prepared and these might possibly include consultations on sampling procedures. Producer organizations would certainly be asked for their views after the Commission had finished the report, and no doubt these would include suggestions over future policy in the light of the report. But as things stand producer organizations would not work in conjunction with the Commission on its proposals to the Council of Ministers, nor be consulted direct by the Council while it is making its decisions. In short a comprehensive Community Annual Review of the agricultural industry will take place, but it will not be exactly similar to the present UK procedure.

On milk the plea was that 'Community arrangements should ensure that we have adequate supplies of liquid milk to meet demand for con-

[10] Issued as a White Paper *The United Kingdom and the European Communities*, Cmnd. 3345 (H.M.S.O., July 1967).
[11] See p. 66.

sumption throughout the year'. It is both obvious and widely recognized that the EEC milk regulations were introduced to meet an entirely different situation from that in the UK. These differences are described in Chapter 6. The entry of the UK into the EEC together with two important dairy producers and exporters, Ireland and Denmark, would necessarily involve reassessment of the regulations. Much publicity was given to the statement of a senior Ministry official before the Select Committee that the strict application to the UK of the existing EEC milk arrangements might give rise to serious shortages in the winter, and possibly even rationing. If this case can be established, however, it is inconceivable that suitable price adjustments would not be agreed to in order to avoid such a development, which could be in no one's interest. Provided that the UK agrees to accept that the general principles of the CAP extend to milk, that is to say that there is no question of sealing off the UK market from Continental competition, there should be no difficulty about including satisfactory arrangements to cover its special needs.

Pigmeat and eggs can be bracketed together because their situation and the effects on them of UK membership of EEC are much the same. Both industries are already going through a period of concentration and rationalization. Large-scale specialist producers have taken over a large part of the business previously done, often inefficiently, by small farmers. With the current EEC relationship between feed costs and product prices both would be squeezed further, accelerating the trend towards concentration. The EEC regulations for pigmeat and eggs do not provide ideal solutions to the problems of these sectors of the agricultural industry, nor are they likely to remain wholly unchanged in the future. But it is difficult to put forward any compelling argument why, with the UK in the EEC, producers in the enlarged community should require more favoured treatment than at present. Most of the largest and lowest cost producers in Europe are British. It would therefore be inappropriate for the UK to ask for special conditions for pigmeat and eggs as part of the negotiations for membership.

The effects on the UK's balance of payments to FEOGA, either through remitting the proceeds of levies or by direct supplemental payments have been discussed in Chapter 3. It is obviously an important issue for the UK. On the other hand in any immediate negotiations for membership of the EEC its importance was potentially much reduced by the fact that the Community anyway has to reassess the question of the Fund's finances and the scale of contributions by member countries before the end of 1969. On the assumption that 1969 was the earliest that the UK could expect to become a member, temporary arrangements for UK contributions made during the membership negotiations would have applied at the most to one year. The UK negotiators would merely have tried to ensure that the temporary arrangements were not regarded as precedents for the future. It now seems unlikely that the UK will have any influence over the future pattern of financing FEOGA. Any changes after 1969 would be of detail, to fix new contribution scales for the Guidance Section on the accession of new member countries for instance, rather than of substance. French interests are certainly better suited if the principle of contributions to the Guarantee Section is established before any new members are admitted.[12]

In the speech mentioned earlier the Foreign Secretary spoke of only two agricultural problems affecting third countries, the Commonwealth Sugar Agreement and the special case of New Zealand. This was a realistic approach. The UK negotiators will no doubt attempt to obtain as much as possible for other products and other countries, particularly Australia. In Australia's case the view held by the Commission that as none of its agricultural exports to the UK represent more than a small proportion of gross national product, or even of total exports, no special concession should be made, is likely to carry the day. The chapter on sugar in Part II arrives at the conclusion that there is no serious alternative to the UK being allowed to operate the Commonwealth Sugar Agreement for the remainder of its term, only the financial arrangement of the Agreement, including the disposition of the levies, being negotiable. This is the first of three *sine qua non* of the negotiations over UK membership. The second is concerned with New Zealand. We have shown earlier how uniquely dependent New Zealand is on exports of temperate agricultural products to the UK. EEC membership would not be taken up by the UK without agreement on special terms for New Zealand. As we have seen it is easier to say this than to work out what these terms realistically might be, but Chapter 3 outlines some of the alternative schemes that might be used to ensure that the New Zealand economy was not ruthlessly disrupted as a result of the UK joining the EEC.

Thirdly, there is the many-sided problem of the transition periods that the UK would require. The transition periods for a few individual countries or products, New Zealand, the signatories to the Commonwealth Sugar Agreement, and possibly some others, have already been mentioned. An administrative transition period would also be required. In the last negotiations the British negotiators maintained that it would take a long time to set up the necessary administrative machinery. They even argued, for instance, that it would take years to train grading inspectors to enforce a new set of quality standards in horticulture; whereupon the Dutch offered to do the job for them. This administrative transition period could be between six months and a year and would coincide with the time between final agreement on membership and the date on which membership is taken up.

Would farmers require a transition period longer than the one required to set up the administrative machinery? Given this minimum period of notice the agricultural industry would certainly be able to adapt to EEC prices and regulations without being thrown into hopeless confusion. Some farmers, including cereal-growers and producers of grass-fed beef, would

[12] See pp. 15–16.

be happy to be given no transition period at all. For others, including dairy farmers and producers of pigmeat and eggs, some transitional arrangements would be very beneficial. The UK negotiators could ask for a general transition period of five years during which time the threshold prices and levies would be gradually introduced and guaranteed prices and deficiency payments phased out. The advantage of this method is that it deals with all the problems of agricultural adjustment at the same time. Farmers are given an adjustment period to react to different prices and import costs; consumers are cushioned against a rapid rise in food prices; Commonwealth and other overseas suppliers get at least a few years when the disadvantages of the UK joining the EEC are gradually introduced; the ill-effects on the UK's balance of payments are phased in rather than being presented as a sudden jolt. It is therefore right to ask for a general transition period of this kind which might be shortened by one or two years. The problem remains that a request for a general transition period might not be agreed to by all the existing members of the EEC, even if the UK were prepared to accept detailed and binding conditions for it. Alternatively it might only be granted subject to terms on an industrial transition period which might not be acceptable to the UK. There might also be an attempt to link the UK's request for a general transition period with an offer from the EEC of a form of association leading to full membership at the end of the period. If a terminal date can be agreed this could prove a workable solution.

The British government has consistently exaggerated the length of transition period that would be required. In the first negotiations twelve to fifteen years was regarded as an acceptable length. Although this demand became reduced during 1962, the Minister of Agriculture's view in 1967 was that a transition period should be as long as possible. In fact the only categories of farmers who specially need a transition period are those who would be hard hit by higher feed prices, particularly producers of pigmeat and eggs, and hill farmers heavily dependent on special production grants which would come to an end if the UK adopted the CAP. The UK's future partners might reasonably agree that the UK could operate, over perhaps a three-year period, a subsidy scheme at national cost designed to ease the changeover to higher feed prices or, perhaps more appropriately, some direct income support, likewise over a limited period, on the analogy of the direct income support given to the German farmers. Some of the production grants might with advantage be phased out rather than ended abruptly. For instance the fertilizer and lime subsidies costing together about £40 mn. a year might be eliminated over two to three years and the various hill farming subsidies, which are so important to the livelihood of farmers in mid-Wales, the Pennines and many parts of Scotland, over perhaps seven years, during which time aid under Community schemes would take their place. Beyond this no special transition period is really required for UK farmers, nor for horticulturalists. They have been under notice for nearly a decade that they would be likely to suffer from

UK membership of the EEC and have over recent years been recipients of generous amounts of government aid.

A transition period for consumers' food prices could also be dealt with differently. If the present EEC members insisted on their wholesale prices being imposed on the new members from the outset, without any phasing-in, then the UK should be allowed over a limited period to use consumer subsidies. These would be applied at the wholesale level to foods such as butter, sugar, and flour which would otherwise rise steeply in price. The period for operating these consumer subsidies would be four to five years. The cost, which would be degressive, might amount to £200 mn. to £250 mn. for the first year, that is roughly half the total anticipated rise in wholesale food prices that would follow from adoption of the CAP.

Finally, there is the question of the transition period for overseas suppliers of foodstuffs to the UK which was discussed in the previous chapter. Terms arranged for New Zealand, the signatories of the Commonwealth Sugar Agreement, and any other traditional exporters to the UK will cover varying periods. These in turn should provide a transition period for the adverse effects of adoption of the CAP on the UK's balance of payments, for which the UK negotiators would certainly hope to obtain some relief through phasing-in.

The line taken by the UK negotiators on the question of the transition period for food and agriculture could be crucial to the future success of the UK's negotiations for EEC membership. In general this line should be that no special transition period is required beyond the minimum necessary for administrative purposes, that EEC prices and regulations will be adopted in full from the time when membership is taken up, but that some consumer and producer subsidies should be permitted over a limited period to ease the adjustment to different price levels, an adjustment as difficult as any undertaken previously by an existing member country in harmonizing national prices and policies to those of the Community.

PART II

Farm Production in the
United Kingdom and the
European Economic Community

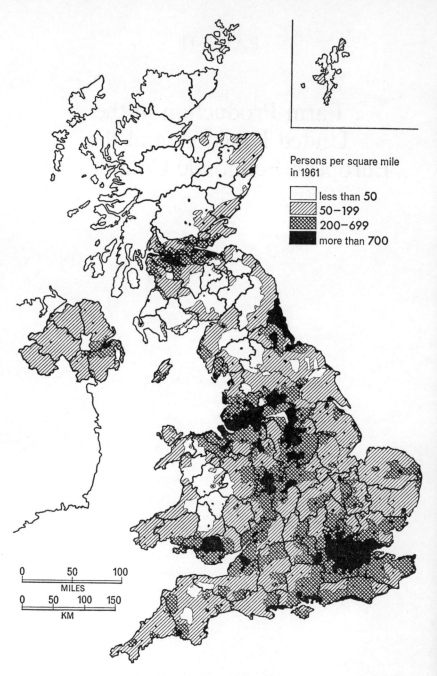

Persons per square mile
in 1961

less than **50**
50–199
200–699
more than **700**

0   50   100
MILES
0   50   100   150
KM

2. Population of the UK.

5. Grains

In any study of the principal EEC and UK agricultural products, priority must be given to grains. This is not primarily because of the importance of their production, which is less than some livestock products, including milk. There are several good reasons for putting particular emphasis on grains. In the first place the achievement of common grain prices in the EEC presented perhaps the biggest of all the difficulties involved in reaching a common agricultural policy. Before harmonization there were big differences in grain prices among the member countries, Germany having the highest and France the lowest. To many small farmers, especially in southern Germany, the wheat price had acquired an almost mystical significance. In farming areas in Western Europe which are not far from subsistence agriculture wheat is often the main cash crop, however uneconomic its production. For the many farm families who produce their own milk, butter, and cheese and often also their own eggs, potatoes, pork, and even wine and tobacco, wheat is the main means of getting shoes for the children. Agreement to cut the wheat and other grain prices in the interests of harmonization represented a very considerable political achievement.

Secondly, grains are an important input cost for many livestock products. Grain prices and livestock production costs are directly linked. Both the EEC and the UK take this into account in their support systems, particularly in the case of poultry and pigmeat where the proportion of total production costs represented by grain can be established accurately. Thirdly, the level of the harmonized EEC grain prices, far above world prices, shows the Community in its most absurdly protectionist light. And the big difference between these prices and those in the UK will present difficult problems for UK livestock producers if the CAP is adopted.

In addition, the basic regulations for grains in the EEC have been in existence since 1962 and the regulations for the period following harmonization (1 July 1967) are also established. Grains provide the best example of the Community system in practice. We shall therefore describe the mechanics of the regulations for grains in greater detail than those for other agricultural products. This will also provide an illustration of the complexity of the CAP. Likewise the UK situation will be covered in some detail.

TABLE 9. WHEAT AND BARLEY: PRODUCTION 1965/66

	Comparative acreage UK=100	Comparative production UK=100	Percentage of total production the Six	Percentage of total production the Ten	Average yield per hectare 100 kg.	Comparative yield UK=100	Degree of self-sufficiency per cent
Soft wheat (grain only)							
Germany (FR)	137·6	104·2	15·3	13·0	30·8	75·7	78·0
France	436·8	351·7	51·6	43·9	32·7	80·3	154·0
Italy	294·2	187·7	27·5	23·4	25·9	63·6	106·0
Netherlands	15·4	16·6	2·4	2·1	43·6	107·1	65·0[a]
Belgium	22·5	20·7	3·0	2·6	37·5	92·1	} 78·0
Luxemburg	1·8	1·1	0·2	0·1	25·5	62·7	
The Six	908·3	682·0	100·0	85·1		100·0	110·0[a]
United Kingdom	100·0	100·0		12·5	40·7	100·0	48·8[a]
Ireland	7·2	5·6		0·7	31·6	77·6	41·9[a]
Denmark	11·8	13·5		1·7	44·4	109·1	103·5[a]
Norway	0·4	0·3		(0·04)	27·8	68·3	3·0[a]
The Four				14·9			49·6[a]
The Ten				100·0			93·7[a]
Barley							
Germany (FR)	54·7	41·1	28·1	13·3	28·2	75·2	66·0
France	111·3	90·1	61·7	29·1	30·3	80·8	143·0
Italy	8·5	3·5	2·4	1·1	15·3	40·8	21·0
Netherlands	4·5	4·5	3·1	1·5	37·8	100·8	83·0
Belgium	6·7	6·3	4·4	2·0	35·3	94·1	} 74·0
Luxemburg	0·5	0·4	0·3	0·1	30·0	80·0	
The Six	186·2	145·9	100·0	47·1		100·0	94·0
United Kingdom	100·0	100·0		32·3	37·5	100·0	106·3
Ireland	8·6	7·5		2·4	32·8	87·5	93·3
Denmark	47·7	50·4		16·3	39·6	105·6	97·2
Norway	8·7	5·9		1·9	25·7	68·5	90·0
The Four				52·9			102·0
The Ten				100·0			95·6

[a] May include small quantities of hard wheat.

...al Statistics, 1967, No. 1. FAO: Monthly Bulletins of Agricultural Statistics. CEC: Grain Bulletins.

THE UNITED KINGDOM
Trends in production and imports

Post-war government policy towards grain production in the UK has been described in the first part of this book. It has varied from outright encouragement in the interests of import-saving to modest discouragement with an eye to the cost of deficiency payments and under pressures from traditional overseas suppliers. Currently, under the influence of self-sufficiency, or near self-sufficiency, in barley and soft wheat, policy lies about midway between these two extremes.

Livestock production can be rapidly expanded by importing larger quantities of feed. Grain production can only be increased by a larger acreage devoted to grain or by higher yields. Over the past twenty years UK grain production has roughly doubled. Production of wheat has risen from a little under two million tons a year at the end of the Second World War to an average over the past three years of about four million tons. Total coarse grains production has also doubled to reach the current figures of about ten million tons. As is well known there has been a big switch from oats to barley. Oat production, nearly three million tons in 1946/47, is now only slightly over one million tons. By contrast, barley production has risen from under two million tons to an average over the past three years of over eight million tons.

Much of this increase has been due to higher grain yields per acre. But in recent years rising yields per acre have not been the main cause of increased UK grain production. Comparing 1959 (admittedly a good harvest) with 1966, yields of wheat rose by about 8 per cent and of barley by 9 per cent, but over this period the barley acreage was doubled and the total acreage of cereals rose by nearly 30 per cent. The trend is illustrated by the following table.

TABLE 10. UK CEREAL ACREAGES AT 1 JUNE

('000 acres)

	1959	1960	1961	1962	1963	1964	1965	1966
Barley	3,059	3,372	3,828	2,987	4,713	5,032	5,395	6,130
Wheat	1,929	2,102	1,827	2,256	1,928	2,206	2,535	2,238
Oats	2,032	1,947	1,733	1,519	1,295	1,125	1,014	907
Other	236	222	166	143	120	101	91	83
Total, cereals	7,246	7,670	7,554	7,905	8,056	8,464	9,035	9,358

Source: Ministry of Agriculture, Fisheries, and Food.

In 1959 cereals constituted about 40 per cent of the total arable acreage including temporary grass. In 1966 they made up more than half. This remarkable change which has added over two million acres to cereal-growing (see Maps at the end of the chapter) has been brought about primarily by the increasing practice of continuous cereal-growing. As this practice will have such an important influence on cereal supplies in the future it is worth making some comments on it.

Only a few years ago any farmer growing more than three cereal crops in succession was regarded as pursuing a dangerous course. It was the sort of thing that was done by tenants, unless the landlord was on his toes, at the end of the farm tenancy. Indeed many tenancy agreements were drawn up specifically to prevent this practice. The pioneers of continuous cereal-growing, mostly on chalk land, were watched with mixed feelings by the bulk of traditional farmers. The extent of the change in cropping practices is illustrated by a recent survey of nearly 500 farms in Bedfordshire. This showed that 38·8 per cent of the farmers were currently taking *at least* four successive cereals crops whereas only 5·5 per cent had done so and given up the practice. These figures are all the more striking as soil conditions in Bedfordshire are not as generally suitable for continuous cereal-growing as in many parts of East Anglia or southern England. It shows how widespread the practice has become in spite of the well-known problems associated with it.

At present few farmers have been successful with continuous wheat. (An exceptional case is that provided by the Ministry's Boxworth Experimental Husbandry Farm where some of the fields have carried wheat for very many years and yields are still 1¾ tons to the acre.) The risks of disaster through disease are very much greater. This is, of course, the main reason for the upsurge in British barley production, a contributory cause being the unfavourable autumn weather conditions for drilling winter wheat in a number of recent years. Changes in the price relationships between wheat and barley (at present the difference is only about £1 per ton) would improve the odds for the gamble of continuous wheat growing and one can reasonably expect the odds to be further improved by technical improvement in disease control. But the most important factor for the future may well be developments in break-crop techniques. Traditional break-crops such as sugar beet, potatoes, or intensive grassland had disadvantages for farmers such as new machinery requirements, quota restrictions and more labour. Beans and oil-seed rape are examples of break-crops that can be fitted more easily into an existing farm system based on cereal-growing. At present, beans are grown on about 100,000 acres and oil-seed rape on only between 3,000 and 4,000 acres. Changes in production of these crops (stimulated in the case of beans by the new grant of £5 an acre, effective from 1968) will be worth observing carefully as much for their effect on cereal growing as on the market for the products themselves.

Changes in average yields of cereals have already been mentioned. The average covers a wide variation between best and worst. The same applies to averages of profitability. It might, however, be worth quoting one example from a survey of the 1964/65 financial results of some mainly arable farms of over 250 acres in the south-east of England.[1] Gross output averaged £41·4 per acre. Variable costs (seeds, fertilizers, etc.) were £11·5

[1] Wye College Department of Agricultural Economics, *Farm Business Statistics for South East England* (Supplement for 1966).

per acre and fixed costs (including regular labour, machinery depreciation and repairs, and rent) totalled £22·9 per acre, leaving an average profit for this type of farming of £7·0 per acre. Cereal yields averaged about 1½ tons to the acre. The effects on farm profitability of an increase in cereal prices of at least £7 a ton scarcely needs to be emphasized.

Compound feeds

Expenditure on feeding stuffs is the largest single item in UK farm expenditure. In 1966/67 it amounted to £463·5 million, equivalent to nearly one-third of all farm expenses. Nearly three-quarters of this expenditure was on products of the compound feed industry, whose Association (CAFMNA) estimates that 33 per cent of the industry's raw material requirements are drawn from domestic agriculture, mostly in the form of grains. This makes the industry the principal user of domestic grains, to the extent of about 3 mn. tons. Production of compound feeds in 1965 and 1966 is shown below.

TABLE 11. UK PRODUCTION OF COMPOUND FEEDS

	(thousand tons)		
	1965	1966	% change
Cattle and calf food	3,096·2	3,065·2	−1·0
Pig food	1,735·6	1,549·9	−10·6
Poultry food	3,694·5	3,577·3	−3·2
Sheep and lamb food	108·2	110·1	+4·8
Other compounds	59·8	62·7	+4·8
Total	8,694·3	8,365·2	−3·8

Source: Ministry of Agriculture, Fisheries, and Food.

The compound feed industry is also a large consumer of imported concentrated feed, particularly maize, mostly shipped from the United States, and oil cakes and meals. It also buys some by-products from the milling industry such as wheat offals, which could originate from either imported or domestic grain. The Ministry of Agriculture calculates the balance between imports and home production of concentrates by starting from farmers' purchases. The calculation is as follows (1966/67 estimate):[2]

	mn. tons
Concentrated feeds bought by farmers (including compounds)	12·6
Home grown concentrates retained on farms	3·7
Total consumption	16·3
Home feed production (including by-products)	10·0

[2] Annual Review and Determination of Guarantees, 1967.

Balance consisting of imported
concentrates, by-products from imported
grains, seeds, etc.   6·3

This balance, representing the quantity of all imported feeds required for UK livestock production, is made up approximately as follows:

	mn. tons
By-products from imported grains and seeds	1·7
Imports of coarse grains, mostly maize, including an estimation for feed wheat	3·5
Imports of oilcakes and meals	1·1
	6·3

There are nine companies in the UK selling compound feeds nationally, of which three are basically flour millers and four seed crushers. The other two are much smaller enterprises. These companies, which now account for about 70 per cent of total production, used to be based almost exclusively on the ports, utilizing mainly imported grains. The country compounders, of which there are several hundred, produce the remaining 30 per cent and, being located inland, have always tended to use more domestic grain.

The national compounders enjoy some fairly obvious advantages over the country compounders. There are definite economies of scale of compound feed production, at least up to about 70,000 to 100,000 tons a year. In addition they may possibly enjoy some economies in research and selling. Their location in ports gives them good access to imported raw materials and also to the by-products of the milling and seed-crushing industries which are similarly located. On the other hand the strong increase in self-sufficiency in grains (60 per cent now compared with 40 per cent before the war) has called in question whether these companies should be located in ports at all. At present, domestic grain, both feed wheat and barley, is being moved mostly by truck into the port districts, which are often extremely crowded, and then moved out again as compounds. Transportation costs, which are a crucial factor in the grain and compounding businesses, can be kept below £1 per ton if the journey is under 30 miles. Above this distance costs rise considerably, anything over 100 miles being usually in excess of £2 per ton.

The fact that country compounders are more than holding their own in competition with port compounders should not be taken as an indication that concentration in the industry is slowing down. Rather it is a question of the national companies becoming country compounders, either by purchasing existing mills or by building new ones inland. Concentration in compound feeds is still very much under way. The trend will continue as small firms find it even harder to compete with the technical service and high pressure selling of the larger companies. Even now, after taking account of the co-operatives, the amount that is being manufactured by small private compounders is certainly less than one million tons a year. The co-operatives play a very important part in the merchanting of compound feeds, accounting for nearly a quarter of total sales, but their manufacturing is on a comparatively small scale. Some of the bigger agricultural co-operatives, such as West Cumberland Farmers, do no compounding. This relatively small output is hardly surprising as the principal problem of all British agricultural co-operatives in the UK has been shortage of capital, and there is no agricultural co-operative bank. The money required to put up a modern compound feed plant is far beyond the resources of most of the agricultural co-operatives.

On-farm mixing of compounds, to which the structure of British agriculture is particularly well suited, is tending to increase. The larger farms often combine arable and livestock enterprises as well as possessing their own grain drying and storage facilities. Already about 45 per cent of total concentrated feeding stuffs is mixed on farms. The economies which can be obtained consist of two transportation costs (on the grain and on the compound) and the compounder's manufacturing and overhead (including selling) costs. Against these the main item which has to be offset is the capital costs of the milling, mixing, pelleting, etc., equipment. Case studies indicate that the break-even point is somewhere between 50 and 100 tons of compounds per year. Government grants are now available for on-farm mixing machinery and there are also considerable taxation incentives. Increased demand for additives and balancers has induced a somewhat ambiguous attitude in the compound feed industry towards on-farm mixing, as profit margins on the former tend to be higher than on compounds. The industry's public relations officer pointed out, very fairly, recently that 'where a large proportion of the cereal ingredients are available on the farm, and labour and capital are available, significant savings can be made particularly if the farmer still takes advantage of the skill and know-how of the compounder by using a manufactured protein/vitamin/mineral concentrate'. A further expansion of on-farm mixing of compounds must be expected in the future.

Millers, maltsters, and distillers, and exports

Apart from on-farm consumption and the compound feed industry the other major users of grain in the UK are the flour millers (about 5·0 mn. tons), the maltsters and distillers (about 1·5 mn. tons) and the export trade (about 1 mn. tons). Little needs to be said in this section about the flour-milling industry, which is concentrated in the hands of four large companies, based like the national compounders on the ports. The malting industry is also becoming concentrated, the largest company being responsible for about half UK malt output. Increases in production of malt in recent years have been largely due to growth in the distilling industry, whose consumption of malt has roughly doubled over the past ten years, whereas the demand for brewing rose by only 15 per cent. Production of high-grade malt used for the best pale ales has declined relatively to that of continental-type lagers, and this has reduced the incentive for farmers to produce a low-yielding high quality barley. The type of malting barley required for the home market and for export has become more similar, to the advantage of the export trade. The rise of UK barley exports for both malting and feed from a negligible quantity to over one million tons in about five years is something of a phenomenon. The trade, which goes through a large number of small ports, has developed without extensive silo or loading facilities. With the UK outside the EEC business should continue at about the million ton level. About half the total has been shipped to EEC countries with Germany the biggest buyer. Prospects for the trade if Britain joins the EEC are described later.

THE EEC

Roughly half the Community's grain production comes from France. Barley and soft wheat is grown throughout the country but particularly in the north and north-east where there are extensive areas in which large-scale, low-cost, mechanized cereal production is practised. As the Tables show, France has a large surplus in both these grains. Hard wheat is grown in small but increasing amounts in some of the southern departments, and rice in the Rhône estuary. Undoubtedly the most remarkable feature of French grain production since the war has been the development of maize growing. From being a crop for on-farm consumption, mainly on smallholdings in the Mediterranean and sub-Mediterranean climate of south-eastern and south-western France, maize has now become a major crop (nearly 4 mn. tons in 1966/67) grown in most departments. Not only has the introduction of US hybrids, and breeding of local variants, greatly increased average yields, but adoption of relatively drought-resistant and early-maturing strains in areas north of the Loire has enabled the traditional arable farmers of the Paris basin to apply their know-how and capital-intensive methods to maize production. Under the stimulus of relatively higher maize prices production is likely to increase still further. By 1970 production may be up by about 1·5 mn. tons and most of this increase will be exported.

The other principal grain producers in the EEC are Germany and Italy. Germany produces all the main cereals and is the principal grower of rye. Italy is an even larger producer of maize than France. Italian rice production, centred on the Po Valley, also greatly exceeds that of France. Both Belgium and the Netherlands have grain deficits, as will be seen from Table 9.

For each of the main grains basic target, intervention, and threshold prices are set which apply for the year following 1 August (for 1967/68 from 1 July). Durum wheat producers are given a guaranteed minimum price which is implemented by deficiency payments. Target prices are the prices at wholesale level which it is intended to maintain at Duisburg in the

Ruhr. This Rhine port has been selected as the centre of the area in the EEC where supplies of grains are in shortest supply, generally referred to as the area of greatest deficit. Prices are maintained at around this level in two ways. Threshold prices, equivalent to minimum import prices, are decided for each type of grain. These are implemented by variable levies which are designed to bring the price of imported grains at Rotterdam (and at other Community ports) up to the level of the threshold prices. Threshold prices are lower than the target prices by the cost of getting the grain to Duisburg. In other words, after the levy has been paid, imported grain should be sold at Duisburg at about the target price. The operation of the levies is described in greater detail below. The second method of maintaining the target prices is through intervention buying. A basic intervention price is decided in advance to apply to Duisburg, and so-called derived intervention prices are announced which operate at other grain marketing centres. Theoretically the difference between the basic intervention price at Duisburg and the derived version at, say, Rouen consists of the cost of transporting grain between the two. But there are some important exceptions. The 1967/68 prices for the principal grains are listed below, together with details of the agreed target prices for 1968/69 in units of account (US dollars) per ton.

TABLE 12. EEC GRAIN PRICES 1967/68

	Target price	Basic intervention	Threshold	Target price 1968/69
Soft wheat	106·25	98·75	104·38	106·25
Durum wheat[a]	125·00	117·50	123·13	125·00
Rye	93·75	87·50	91·88	97·50
Barley	91·25	85·00	89·00	94·44
Maize	90·63	b	88·38	94·94

a Minimum guaranteed price 145·00 implemented by a deficiency payment.
b Lowest derived (and uniform) intervention price 77·00 in 1967/68 with a proposal of 83·00 for 1968/69.

These prices apply to grain which meets certain quality standards. The specifications require grain that is sound, true to type, etc., and that fulfils a number of quantitative standards, for instance in respect of moisture content. Different threshold prices are established for the various qualities of imported grain. Complex regulations have been established for determining threshold prices and levies for products manufactured from grain, notably flour, and these are related to the grain prices. The prices shown in the Table above apply at the beginning of the season, and are increased by monthly increments up to a maximum of between 8 and 10 per cent in order to encourage orderly marketing through compensating producers for interest and storage costs incurred in retaining their grain.

Regulations affecting imports of grain

The threshold prices, common to all EEC ports, should not change

H

during the crop year except for the monthly increments, which commence from September. Levies are common to the whole Community, but they change to take account of changing offers of grain on the world market. If prices increase the levies are reduced and if prices fall the levies rise. By 2.15 p.m. each weekday the Commission's Price Information Office in Brussels receives up to 1,000 quotations for spot and future shipment from national agencies, and it can also check price developments direct with grain markets. This information is then processed, small or non-representative offers being ignored, and the lowest c.i.f. price for each of the main grains is then established by the Commission. National delegations give their approval to these by 6 p.m., thus giving legal validity to each levy, constituting the difference between the lowest c.i.f. price and the threshold price. The levy comes into force from midnight. In order to give some flexibility to the trade, levies are, however, not changed if market prices shift only slightly. In the case of maize, for instance, offers can rise or fall by 75 cents per ton (6s. 3d.) without the levy being changed. Further flexibility is given to the trade by its being able to fix levies in advance for future shipments. An importer generally fixes his levy when he applies to his national grain agency for permission to import a certain quantity of grain in a certain month. The licences, which are normally issued automatically, have the applicable rate of levy stamped on them. Levies can be fixed for shipment during the current month and the three following months, and are always the same for the current month and the next month. For the next two months levies may be different if the future market and the threshold price, allowing for the monthly increments, do not keep in step. If an importer wishes to fix the levy for these next two months he has to pay a fixation premium representing the difference between current and future levies, if this difference exceeds 12½ cents per ton. The premia are announced daily at the same time as are the levies for the current and the next months. Importers are penalized if they fail to make use of their import licence and if the shipment is not landed during the month indicated at the time of the licence application.

Despite the multitude of regulations and their admitted complexity, reasonable freedom and flexibility has been left to the EEC grain importing trade. In any regulated market system there is bound to be some conflict between the trade and the authorities, the former trying to find ways round the regulations as they are established, and the latter attempting to keep one jump ahead. A *modus vivendi* now seems to have been established. Expressions of serious discontent with the arrangements are very rare among the trade, the system in general being preferred to one based on quotas such as used to apply in Germany. There seems no reason why grain importers in the UK should not be able to adjust themselves to the system, though in this connection it is interesting to note that concentration in the trade seems to have been accelerated in EEC countries, the less go-ahead firms finding it difficult to cope with the new complexities.

Intervention and the domestic market

Grain marketing in EEC member countries is organized in much the same way as in the UK. Agricultural merchants buy grain from farmers for resale to compounders, maltsters, and other domestic users or move it for export either themselves or through specialist grain exporters. They sell back to farmers compound feeds, fertilizers and other farm requirements. There are two principal differences. The co-operative movement is much more strongly entrenched throughout the EEC. In France, for instance, the co-operatives handle about 80 per cent of the wheat and about 60 per cent of the barley and maize *collecte* and export roughly 2 mn. tons of grain a year. In the Netherlands the two co-operative groupings CEBECO and CIV are almost equally strongly placed and in addition produce nearly half the output of compound feeds. The second difference is in grain storage. Unlike the UK, where practically all grain is stored on farms, in EEC countries merchants, particularly co-operatives, own most of the silo capacity. This permits them to exercise a greater control over grain marketing.

Direct governmental intervention in agricultural markets is a common phenomenon, the UK being one of the few countries to avoid support buying to sustain farm prices. Market intervention is one of the key features of the EEC's common agricultural policy. It is worth describing how the system works in the case of grains. Details have already been given of the basic intervention prices for grains, which are set about 7 per cent below the target prices, and which apply in the first place at Duisburg. Actual market intervention is more likely to take place at the very numerous derived intervention points, of which there are now (1967/68) 124 in Germany, 279 in France, 4 in Benelux, and 431 in Italy. In Italy some of the intervention points are designated for only one grain whereas most of the French and German deal with more than one. This partly accounts for the very large number of intervention points in Italy, another reason being the predominance of local grain markets serving only very small areas of the country. Derived intervention prices, which can equal but not exceed the basic intervention price, are in principle set in accordance with national conditions of market price formation. For instance, in grain deficit areas partly supplied by non-EEC countries the intervention price would be related to that at which imported grain can be sold levy paid. In surplus areas which provide some of the grain for these deficit areas it would be related to the price in the deficit area less transport costs. Also the principle has been agreed that there should be no discrimination among farmers in the Community, which has ruled out specially high prices fixed for political or social causes in remote areas, such as Passau in Bavaria. It can reasonably be expected that the number of intervention points will be gradually reduced in the future.

Grain has to be offered to the intervention authority (a national agency acting on behalf of the Commission) in certain minimum quantities and at one of three points designated by the authority, transport costs to the centre being for the account of the seller. The minimum producer price is therefore below the intervention price, but as there are so many intervention points, the difference caused by transport costs is unlikely to be more than about 15s. 0d. per ton.

How do the intervention authorities dispose of their grain? Occasionally sales may be made on the domestic market, but obviously only if this can be done without disturbing the market. More normally grain is sold, by competitive tender to dealers throughout the EEC, for export from the Community. Clearly this is only possible under present conditions if exports are subsidized. Consequently general rules have been established for export restitutions (a euphemism for subsidies) under Regulation 139/67. These are calculated weekly, in much the same way as are levies, by taking account of market prices in non-EEC countries compared with Community prices in areas suitable for exports and also of transport and other marketing costs. The scale of restitutions tends, of course, to be very similar to that of levies, the two rising and falling together. Export restitutions can be varied according to the destination of the grain, and provision has been made for them to be increased at the end of the season to clear stocks which have accumulated high storage and interest costs.

THE UNITED KINGDOM AS A MEMBER OF THE EEC

Prices and production

What prices might UK producers expect to get for their grain under the CAP? Unfortunately this question cannot be answered precisely at this stage because it is impossible to do more than estimate what the intervention prices for grains in the UK would be. These could lie between the Duisburg basic intervention price and a price wholly derived from Duisburg, in other words after deducting the full cost of moving grain from the UK intervention point to Duisburg. The difference between the two is very considerable, over £4 per ton. On the latter assumption, after allowing for wholesale margins, and on the basis of the proposed 1968/69 intervention prices, producer prices in the UK might be about £38 per ton for wheat and £33 per ton for barley at the beginning of the season. These prices can be compared with the Ministry's calculations of average producers' returns for 1966/67 of about £25.7s.0d. for wheat and about £24. 10s. 0d. for barley. So that on the most pessimistic assumptions (from the producer's point of view), namely that the market is stuck at the intervention level and that intervention prices in the UK are set at the lowest possible level, grain producers would still receive at least £12. 10s. 0d. more for wheat and £8. 10s. 0d. for barley. Taking into account monthly increments, as well as the influence of marginal quantities of grain from third countries entering the market at threshold price levels, the actual increase in returns could be higher than this. After making allowance for the increased cost of fertilizers if the subsidy is removed, grain producers in the UK would still find their average profits per acre more than doubled.

This is admittedly a very rough estimate, but it is adequate to illustrate the effects that EEC grain prices will have on the UK.

How will producers respond to a price change of this magnitude and the considerable shift of the relative profitability of grain production compared with other farm activities? In trying to answer this question it is important to distinguish between the effects of this price increase and what is happening anyway. Over the past seven years about 2 mn. additional acres have been used for cereals, production of which in this period (assisted by higher yields) has risen by about 4 mn. tons. The National Plan calls for production by 1970 of about 17 mn. tons compared with the existing level of about 14 mn. tons. So a considerable increase in output is anyway expected. A change to EEC price levels will have four main effects. First there will be, of course, a strong inducement to plough up more grassland. Second, the odds on the gamble of continuous corn growing will be much improved. Third, the economies of fertilizer application to cereals will be altered. This may not be a major factor. Many farmers are already applying quantities technically near to optimum. Fourth, the price relationship between wheat and barley will be altered to the advantage of wheat growing. Here again it is extremely difficult to assess what the effects on output of the two grains will be, not least because weather conditions in the autumn have a significant influence on the ratio between planting of wheat and barley. Most of the extra wheat will anyway have to be used for feed.

One guess—and it cannot be very much more than that—is that EEC grain prices might boost UK production by about 3 to 4 mn. tons within two or three years of their introduction. A brief transition period of perhaps three to five years would not appreciably slow down the switch to grain production. On this basis the UK might therefore be producing at least 20 mn. tons of grain in the mid-seventies. Some of this increased production would be exported. But it seems likely that most would be used domestically, thus reducing the amount of grains imported. The position would be particularly severe for non-EEC grain exporters who would be likely to lose business to EEC countries in the UK market. Worst hit would be non-EEC maize exports as French maize could be conveniently and cheaply substituted for US and Argentine.

Effect on compound feed prices

There are a number of complications involved in calculating the effect of higher grain prices on the prices for compound feeds. One has already been mentioned: the difficulty of estimating what will be the UK intervention prices for areas close to the centres of the compounding industry and how much above these prices market prices will be. The most sensible way of coping with this difficulty is to take the two extremes for intervention prices, the highest representing the Duisburg price applied to a deficit area like Liverpool/Manchester or London, and the lowest a price derived from the Duisburg price by the full extent of transport, handling and other merchanting costs. The other problem is to forecast how com-pounders would respond to changes in price relationships between the various ingredients. We are grateful to some of the principal national compounders for carrying out formulation exercises for us. These have indicated how the changed price relationship between the main cereals used in compound feeds, wheat, barley, and maize, would involve re-adjustments in the cereal element of present formulae in order to maintain the necessary nutritional standards on a least-cost basis. The following typical results have been computed for production in the Liverpool area:

TABLE 13. COMPOUND FEEDS: POSSIBLE PRICE INCREASES ATTRIBUTABLE TO EEC CEREAL PRICES
(1968/69)
(shillings per ton)

	at 'low' intervention prices for cereals	at 'high' intervention prices for cereals
High quality cattle food	138s. 7d.	151s. 9d.
Good quality poultry food	156s. 10d.	163s. 6d.
Top quality poultry food	192s. 8d.	195s. 0d.
Standard food for growing pigs	137s. 1d.	163s. 0d.
Broiler finishing food	196s. 6d.	224s. 5d.

Thus, on the basis of cereal prices alone prices of compound feeds as traditionally formulated in the UK could go up by between about £7 and £11 a ton, with an average rise of about £8 per ton. The impact of such possible increases on livestock production costs are dis-cussed in the course of the following chapters. In order to modify this impact and enable UK producers within the EEC to remain competitive with the most efficient producers on the Continent, compounders would have to reconsider their traditional formulae based on the availability of grains at world market prices. They would have to take advantage of the lower prices of imported vegetable proteins. Duties on oil-cakes, and on soya-bean and other meals under the common external tariff are mainly nil or at any rate lower than those under the non-preferential UK tariff. The new price situation would be a challenge to the resourcefulness of UK compounders. They would have increasingly to turn their attention to ingredients such as maize gluten feed, copra expellers, hominy chop, rapeseed extracts and beans, at present regarded as of second quality in the UK or inconvenient, but commonly used, evidently to the satis-faction of efficient producers, in the Netherlands and elsewhere.

Structural changes already occurring in the compound feed industry have been mentioned earlier. The increase in home production of grains which would follow from UK membership of the EEC would, of course, further reduce the case for being located in a port. On-farm mixing of feed would be likely to increase as farmers became even more cost-conscious on feed, and because more livestock farmers would be likely to be growing some of their own grain. The attractions of livestock rearing mainly based on grass would be enhanced at the expense of feeds containing a very high proportion of grains. All of these points suggest that, at least in the short run, the compound feed industry in the UK does not stand to benefit from adoption of the CAP.

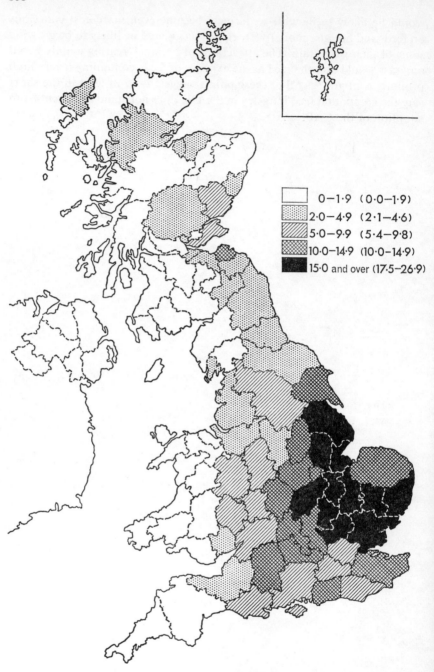

	0–1·9 (0·0–1·9)
	2·0–4·9 (2·1–4·6)
	5·0–9·9 (5·4–9·8)
	10·0–14·9 (10·0–14·9)
	15·0 and over (17·5–26·9)

3. Wheat in the UK (excluding Isle of Man).

Acreage as percentage of total crops and grass, Ø 1964/65–1966/67. For 1964/65
Middlesex figures have been used for Greater London. Figures for Northern Ireland
are for that area as a whole.

(Source: UK Agricultural Statistics)

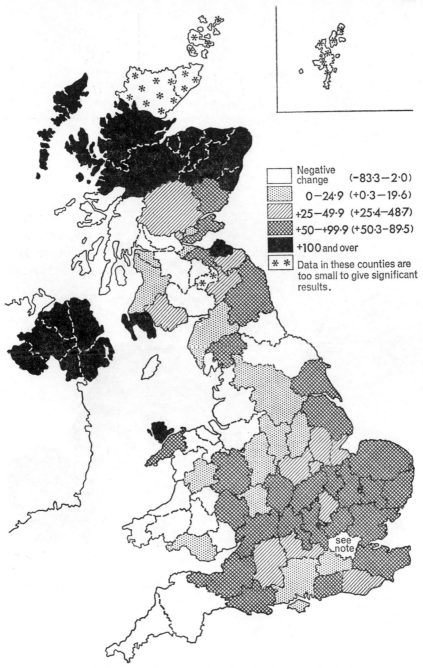

Negative change (−83·3 − 2·0)

0 − 24·9 (+0·3 − 19·6)

+25 − 49·9 (+25·4 − 48·7)

+50 − +99·9 (+50·3 − 89·5)

+100 and over

* * Data in these counties are too small to give significant results.

see note

4. Percentage change in wheat production in the UK (excluding Isle of Man)

Ø 1951/52–1953/54 to Ø 1963/64–1965/66 (Scotland Ø 1951/52–1953/54 to Ø 1962/63–1964/65) Figures for Northern Ireland relate to that area as a whole. Owing to boundary changes comparable data are not available for Middlesex and Greater London and these areas have been omitted.

(Source: UK Agricultural Statistics)

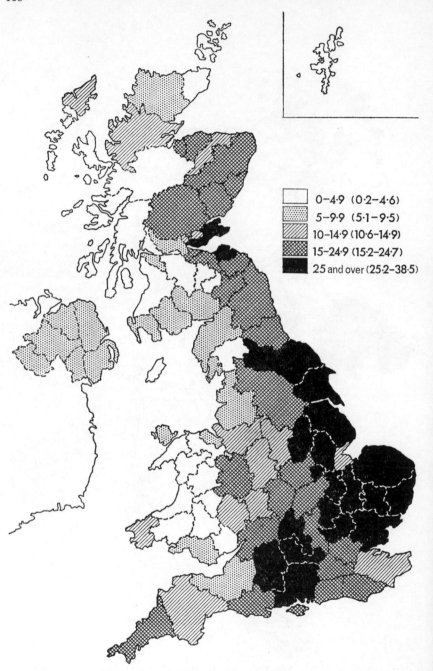

5. Barley in the UK (excluding Isle of Man)

Acreage as percentage of total crops and grass, Ø 1964/65–1966/67. For 1964/65 Middlesex figures have been used for Greater London. Figures for Northern Ireland are for that area as a whole.

(Source: UK Agricultural Statistics)

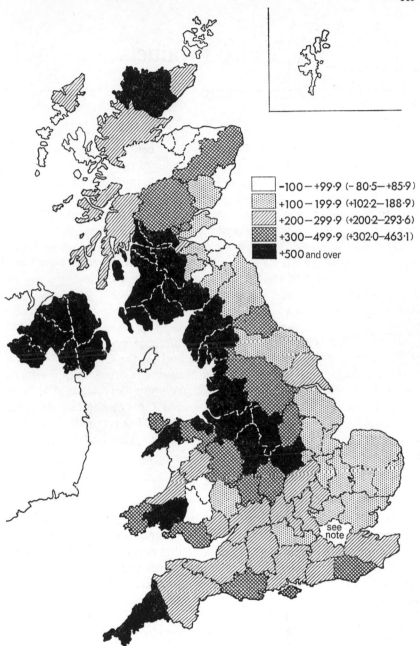

-100 – +99·9 (– 80·5 – +85·9)
+100 – 199·9 (+102·2 – 188·9)
+200 – 299·9 (+200·2 – 293·6)
+300 – 499·9 (+302·0 – 463·1)
+500 and over

see
note

6. Percentage change in barley production in the UK (excluding Isle of
Man)

Ø 1951/52–1953/54 to Ø 1963/64–1965/66 (Scotland Ø 1951/52–1953/54 to Ø 1962/63–
1964/65). Figures for Northern Ireland relate to that area as a whole. Owing to
boundary changes comparable data are not available for Middlesex and Greater London
and these areas have been omitted.

(Source: UK Agricultural Statistics)

6. Dairy Products

In the UK, where it accounts for about 23 per cent of total farm sales, as well as in the Community and in the economies of the other applicants for membership, where the proportion is on average much the same (ranging from 11 per cent in Italy to 35 per cent in Luxemburg), dairying is of outstanding importance to farmers. The dairy cow, through her daily supply of milk, her annual progeny and her eventual carcass, gives farmers in almost all countries their largest single, and most regular, source of income, and provides the basic livelihood of several million small and medium-sized holdings. The level of milk and milk product prices is thus of major political importance everywhere. It is paradoxical that such a vital common denominator of farm income should of all commodities involve one of the more awkward adjustments of the UK support system to that of the EEC. This is due to a fundamental difference, evident from Table 14, in the pattern of milk consumption here and on the Continent, where a relatively small proportion of the milk produced is drunk in liquid form. There the problem of maintaining adequate supplies of liquid milk in winter hardly exists, and those responsible for drawing up the EEC regulations have had to give it little attention. Their thinking has been dominated by the constant threat of excessive spring and summer milk supplies transformed into surplus butter.

THE UNITED KINGDOM

Recent government policy has been to restrict the expansion of milk production by limiting any increases in the guaranteed price to a standard quantity of milk roughly corresponding to that needed for liquid consumption. The threat of diminishing average returns per gallon on increased output which this implies is a main factor accelerating changes in the structure of production. Many farmers with small herds have given up milk, those staying in being obliged to enlarge their herds to maintain their incomes and take advantage of economies of scale. There were 119,000 registered producers in 1966, 20 per cent fewer than in 1960, but owning only 3 per cent fewer cows and heifers and selling about 6 per cent more milk. Although the average size of dairy herd in the UK is still only 25 cows (Scottish herds are nearly twice this size and those in Northern Ireland less than half), 31 per cent of all cows in England and Wales were, by 1965, in herds of 50 cows and over, compared with 20 per cent in 1960. Despite these changes milk production is still predominantly the occupation of the smaller farmer; 61 per cent of producers were occupying holdings of 99 acres or less in 1964.

Milk distribution is controlled by the Milk Marketing Boards[1] which purchase all milk produced within their respective regions, other than that consumed on farm or sold direct by licensed producer retailers (most of whom sell wholesale to the Boards as well). In 1967 there were 9,801 producer retailers (32 per cent fewer than in 1960), well under a tenth of all producers. The Board for England and Wales, often known loosely as 'the Milk Marketing Board', exercises, as far the largest board, a co-ordinating role in the Federation of Milk Marketing Boards, but only as *primus inter pares*. The Boards' expenditure on administration, research and development, and on their extensive advertising of liquid milk, represents just over 0·6d. per gallon of total sales. They also operate AI and milk recording services, and a milk costing scheme.

Since 1962 there has been no exchequer liability for milk, but producer prices are supported in a number of indirect ways. The government fixes a maximum (effectively also a minimum) retail price for liquid milk sold to the public. The Boards use their statutory monopoly to obtain this relatively high price for as much milk as can be sold in the liquid market. They dispose of the balance for manufacturing at whatever price is obtainable on a market influenced by world prices for butter and other products. Imports of butter are limited by quotas allotted to individual exporting countries. Imports of liquid milk, being entirely at the discretion of the Boards, are effectively nil, although nominally permissible subject to certain health regulations. The English Board has never made any imports from the Continent and wholesalers are only permitted to purchase raw milk produced 'within the scheme'.

Government price support to milk producers takes the form of a guaranteed price for liquid milk limited to a standard quantity of milk. This quantity, shared out between the Board regions, is adjusted upwards or downwards each year to reflect increases or decreases in sales of liquid milk during the previous year, and also allows for a reserve of up to 20 per cent of total supplies. Any increase in the guaranteed price, or in the agreed margins received by distributors and retailers, is passed on to the consumer and is not borne by the exchequer. In deciding whether to award a higher milk price at the Annual Review, therefore, the government is motivated by the direct effect on the cost of living rather than, as in the case of all other review products, by mainly budgetary considerations. Milk produced over and above the standard quantity for which the Boards cannot find an outlet on the liquid market is sold at the much lower manufacturing price (currently about 46 per cent of the Boards' net realization price for liquid milk). Payment to producers by the Boards thus takes the form of a pool price, varied seasonally to encourage winter supplies, which averages out the Board's combined income from sales on

[1] The MMB of England and Wales, the Scottish MMB, the Aberdeen and District MMB, the north of Scotland MMB, and the MMB for Northern Ireland.

TABLE 14. MILK AND DAIRY PRODUCTS: PRODUCTION AND CONSUMPTION, 1965

	Cow numbers (Dairy herd) UK=100	Comparative production UK=100	Percentage of total production: the Six	Percentage of total production: the Ten	Average yield per cow, lb.	Comparative yield UK=100	Degree of self-sufficiency (1964/5) per cent	Total Consumption per head per year kg.
Raw milk								
Germany (FR)	117·8b	164·3	32·0	23·8	8,029	99·3	99·8c	77·5c
France	218·5a	184·0	35·8	26·6	6,076	75·1	100·3c	103·8c
Italy	96·7a	74·7	14·6	10·8	6,173	76·3	99·9c	63·7c
Netherlands	34·7b	56·6	11·0	8·2	9,275	114·7	101·0c	116·9c
Belgium	20·3b	32·1	6·3	4·6	8,516	105·3	} 100·2c	103·8c
Luxemburg	1·1b	1·6	0·3	0·2	7,474	92·4		
The Six	489·1	513·3	100·0	74·2				
United Kingdom	100·0a	100·0		14·4	8,089	100·0	100·0	148·0
Ireland	31·0b	24·8		3·6	5,183	64·1	100·0	216·4
Denmark	27·2a	41·4		6·0	8,706	107·6	100·6	132·2
Norway	10·4b	12·6		1·8	7,139	88·3	100·0c	181·5c
The Four				25·8				
The Ten				100·0				
Butter								
Germany (FR)		1,237·0	40·7	32·9			100·8	8·7
France		1,167·9	38·4	31·0			102·9	8·5
Italy		160·5	5·3	4·3			64·9	2·0
Netherlands		253·3	8·3	6·7			151·6	4·6
Belgium		204·7	6·8	5·4			} 113·4	8·9
Luxemburg		14·8	0·5	0·4				
The Six		3,038·3	100·0	80·7			102·3	6·4
United Kingdom		100·0		2·7			8·3	8·8
Ireland		166·7		4·4			142·1	16·0
Denmark		409·6		10·9			311·8	10·3
Norway		48·6		1·3			125·5	4·2
The Four				19·3			48·5	
The Ten				100·0			84·3	

Cheese					
Germany (FR)	160·0[a]	12·6[d]	10·5[d]	64·9	8·0
France	534·0[d]	42·0	35·0	106·0	11·3
Italy	352·3	27·7	23·1	90·8	8·2
Netherlands	193·1	15·2	12·7	202·8	7·9
Belgium	30·5	2·4	2·0	} 58·3	6·2
Luxemburg	1·0	0·1	0·1		
The Six	1,271·2	100·0	83·4	98·7	9·0
United Kingdom	100·0		6·5	43·2	4·8
Ireland	14·2		0·9	250·8	1·5
Denmark	100·3		6·6	281·8	8·9
Norway	39·0		2·6	129·7	8·6
The Four			16·6	83·7	
The Ten			100·0	95·9	
Powdered milk					
Germany, (FR)	232·3	30·0	24·2	91	1·4
France	321·9	41·5	33·5	131	1·4
Italy	10·4	1·3	1·1	30	0·6
Netherlands	130·2	16·8	13·6	68	1·3
Belgium	} 80·2	10·4	8·4	133	5·9
Luxemburg					
The Six	775·0	100·0	80·9	98	2·3
United Kingdom	100·0		10·4	75	2·0
Ireland	24·0		2·5	267	0·6[e]
Denmark	52·1		5·4	167	nil
Norway	7·3		0·8	100	0·4
The Four			19·1	101	
The Ten			100·0	99	

[a] Cows and heifers 2 yrs of age and over.
[b] Cows, including heifers in calf, kept primarily for milk.
[c] Including goat and sheep milk.
[d] Factory production only.
[e] 1963.

Sources: FAO/ECE Review of Agricultural Situation in Europe, 1966. FAO Monthly Bulletin of Agricultural Economics, December 1966. World Agricultural Production and Trade, June 1966. CEC Dairy Produce, 1965. EEC Agricultural Statistics, 1967, No. 2. Food Consumption in OECD countries 1962/63–1964/65.

TABLE 15. EEC/UK: MILK PRODUCTION AND UTILIZATION, 1965

	Germany (FR)	France	Italy	Netherlands	Belgium	Luxemburg	EEC	UK[a]
Production								
'000 metric tons	21,268	27,733	10,158	7,181	3,930	188	70,458[b]	12,821
kg per head[c]	361	544	189	588	416[d]		379	236
Utilization—per cent								
Direct								
liquid[e]	20·4	17·3	32·5	19·9	24·1	21·3	21·0	63·4
fresh cream	5·5	1·1	*	3·1	1·5	7·4	2·5	4·3
other fresh products	0·3	*	*	0·2	0·3	0·5	0·2	0·8
Total direct	26·2	18·4	32·5	23·2	25·9	29·2	23·7	68·5
Manufacture								
butter	52·4	41·9	14·9	31·2	53·7	63·8	40·8	7·7
cheese	6·4	15·9	32·9	22·1	6·0	1·1	15·5	9·3
condensed milk	4·9	1·5	0·1	13·1	1·6	–	3·5	5·1
dried milk	1·0	1·1	0·1	4·7	5·1	–	1·5	1·7
Total manufacture	64·7	60·4	48·0	71·1	67·4	64·9	61·3	23·8
Stockfeed	8·8	20·3	19·5	3·8	8·4	5·9	14·4	6·8
Other	0·3	0·9	–	1·9	0·7	–	0·6	0·9
Total	100·0	100·0	100·0	100·0	100·0	100·0	100·0	100·0

a 1965/66   b Incl. sheep and goats milk 1,710 (Germany, 85; France, 953; Italy, 672).   c 1964/65.   d BLEU.

e Incl. human consumption on farm.   * = not available.   – = Nil.

Source: EEC Agricultural Statistics, 1967, Vol. 2, Federation of UK Milk Marketing Boards, Dairy Facts and Figures, 1967.

the liquid and manufacturing markets. Prices paid by the Boards to producers also involve a pooling of the costs of collection from farm gate to first point of sale, and to a considerable extent of the wholesale distribution of milk for the liquid market as well.

Some indirect support to milk production is also afforded by the government subsidies providing free milk in schools and subsidized milk to nursing mothers and young children, costing £66 mn. in 1966/67. Over the past thirty years the school milk scheme has encouraged lifelong habits of milk drinking from which producers have greatly benefited.

For two main reasons the lion's share of British farmers' income from milk is derived from liquid sales: first, the relatively low elasticity of demand for milk in face of a fixed price administered, even if not actually decided, by a producer monopoly, and, second, the availability to the British consumer of butter and cheese at relatively low prices on a world market mainly influenced by his own demand and the kindliness of the New Zealand climate. The 24 per cent of home produced milk going for manufacturing satisfies under 10 per cent of demand for butter and just over 40 per cent of that for cheese. Since the policy of the government and of the Milk Marketing Boards is directed towards maintaining a price relationship as favourable as possible to producers and discouraging large surpluses for manufacturing, processing firms although obtaining their raw milk from the Boards at a low price are inevitably restricted as to quantity. With the Unigate group controlling about a third of national throughput, the rest of this limited market is shared by the Co-operative Wholesale Society, the Boards themselves and four large firms. Eighty per cent of manufactured milk is processed by the 5 per cent of organizations which have a throughput of 4,600 tons and more a year.

In the distribution of liquid milk, on the other hand, it is the consumer co-operatives which control about a third of the market. Unigate and Express Dairy have about a quarter and 12 to 15 per cent respectively, and six medium-sized firms share a further 5 to 10 per cent between them. The remaining 20 to 25 per cent is divided among a large number of small local enterprises.

THE EEC

Although herd size in the EEC has been slowly increasing in recent years, milk production, as the main source of income of farmers in every member country except Italy, remains essentially a small-holding activity. Some idea of the scale of production may be gained from the fact that even in the Netherlands, the Community's main exporter of butter and cheese and the country with outstandingly the highest milk yields, a quarter of all herds still had fewer than 5 cows in 1966. The average herd only had 12, and there were fewer than 150 herds in the whole country with over 50 cows. In Germany the average herd was 6 in 1965. Only 9 per cent of the cow population was in herds of over 20 cows.

As might be expected from this small scale of production, processing and distribution of milk in the Community is to a considerable extent in the hands of producer co-operatives. In the Netherlands about three-quarters of the 480-odd creameries, and in Belgium about half the total of 260, are run co-operatively. In Germany, which has 2,750 creameries, the proportion is over three-quarters, and in France, with 4,300, nearly 60 per cent are co-operatives.

The French manufacturing industry is dominated by half a dozen private firms (including two subsidiaries of Swiss companies), and co-operatives generally operate on a smaller scale than the private sector. A recent study[2] has examined the current trend towards concentration. Although total national throughput of milk increased by nearly 40 per cent between 1958 and 1965, the number of private and co-operative creameries fell by 30 per cent, or over 200 a year. Parallel with this technical concentration small private firms are being absorbed by the larger groups. These operate oligopolistically in the traditional markets for cheese, butter and skim, sharing them out by regions, but compete monopolistically across the whole country in the rapidly expanding market for fresh products like cream cheese and yoghurt. About 45 per cent of yoghurt sales are now made by Danone, with one or two other firms and a co-operative, Sodima-Yoplait, taking a major share of the rest of the market. Generally speaking the big firms have derived profits from economies of scale in the manufacturing processes, concentrating on the high marginal returns obtainable there rather than attempting to cut raw material costs. The economies at present to be achieved by extending their monopoly power into the field of milk collection, for instance, would be very small by comparison. To a great extent government support of the butter market has precluded any need for close attention to raw milk costs, but exposed to international competition in the unified EEC market French manufacturers will in future have to watch all production costs much more closely. They will certainly be in no mood to concede to farmers higher prices than intervention levels dictate. The bargaining position of farmers will not in any case be improved by rising production due to increased yields. Even if milk prices do not rise many small and medium-sized firms will be in a difficult position and further concentration seems inevitable. In this connection it is interesting to note that a number of the very large firms have already received substantial investment aids (one a loan of 5 mn. fr.) from the French government as part of the policy under the Fifth Plan of supporting enterprises capable of competing in the international field. Concentration in the dairy and dairy products industry has also occurred, though more slowly, during the sixties in Belgium and Germany.[3]

The basic regulation for the common market in dairy products, instituted in 1964, provided for the gradual alignment of national policies and prices which took place during the four years preceding the introduction of

[2] D. Hairy et al. Croissance et concentration dans l'industrie laitière (INRA, Paris, 1967).

[3] See L. Ackerman and A. Verkinderen, Structure de l'industrie laitière en Belgique (Cahiers de l'IEA, Brussels, September 1966). H. Stamer, Distributionswege von Milch und Milcherzeugnissen in der BRD (Kiel, 1966).

a unified market on 1 April 1968. Almost two years before the passing of the new regulation governing the unified market, the Council of Ministers published, in July 1966, a decision on the pricing policy to be adopted in the Community from 1 April 1968 onwards. Constitutionally a formal 'decision' of this kind by the Council is binding on member governments, which must adapt their national regulations to conform to it. The unified price structure for 1968, laid down in 1966, reflects the predominant importance of dairy products, as opposed to liquid milk, in the EEC. A common producer target price for milk is closely related to the wholesale price for butter. A maximum producer price is set for milk destined for the liquid market, member governments also being required to control its retail price. Pooling of returns to producers from sales of liquid and manufacturing milk, on a national basis, is forbidden, and all production subsidies are to cease. A draft regulation for liquid milk, submitted by the Commission to the Council in January 1968, establishes certain principles of health and hygiene for production and marketing (testing of herds for brucellosis and tuberculosis, equipment of milk-sheds and dairies, compositional criteria for milk, etc.). It provides that no milk, other than raw milk sold at farm-gate, may be marketed by dairies which has a fat content of between 0·1 and 1·5 per cent or of between 1·8 and 3·5 per cent. It also elaborates the basis for fixing maximum retail prices for liquid milk, which may be differentiated by regions. Member governments must take into account

(a) the average price for manufacturing milk prevailing in the region,
(b) the special costs incurred by producers, dairies, and retailers in taking the measures necessary to prepare liquid milk for human consumption, and
(c) an additional amount sufficient to encourage them to undertake such measures.

The 1966 decision fixed a common target price for milk of $10.30 per 100 kg. at 3·7 per cent fat content (48·23d. per gallon) delivered at dairy. This is an average annual price aimed at for producers throughout the Community which it is hoped to achieve by tariff protection and various methods of internal market management. It is not a guaranteed or minimum price. The main measures designed to bring about this general level of free market prices concern butter, and to a lesser extent cheese and other products. They are:

(a) *Tariffs.* Variable levies will be applied to butter, cheese, processed milk, and lactose. Threshold prices from which the levies will be derived are based, as with other processed commodities, on the internal target price of the base product and on average manufacturing costs, plus an element of protection for the home processing industry.

The threshold price for butter is $191.25 per 100 kg. (809s. 9d. per cwt.). All other products, except Cheddar and Tilsit cheese, are divided into twelve groups, each designated by a pilot product, to which a number of other products are assimilated, and each with a different threshold price (see Appendix J).

(b) *Intervention*. The internal market for butter will be supported by an intervention price of $176.25 per 100 kg. (746s. 3d. per cwt.), a level estimated to give a return to producers of $0·3125 per 100 kg. (about 1·5d. per gallon) below the target price of $10.30 (48·23d.).

In Italy, where butter consumption is customarily low, a similar milk price will be aimed at through support buying of Parmesan type cheese.

There is a general provision for official storage of other types of cheese at times of seasonal surplus.

(c) *Subsidies*. Sales of skim milk and manufacture of skim powder for stockfeed will be subsidized to the amount of $1·375 per 100 kg (6·3d. per gallon) and $15.00 per 100 kg. (63s. 6d. per cwt.) respectively, in order to make them competitive with other protein feeds.

Subsidies, equivalent to about 241s. 6d. per cwt., will be paid on Cheddar, Emmenthal, and Sbrinz cheese to compensate for the amount by which the lower duties bound in GATT on these products differ from the Community threshold prices. A similar arrangement is necessary for skim milk processed into casein.

Consumer subsidies are to be permitted until the end of 1969 on butter in the Netherlands and on butter and Gouda cheese in Germany, where the sharp price increase in these commodities as a result of the unified market could lead to a marked fall in consumption, and thus prove a threat to the Community target price. Direct subsidies, also on a degressive basis, are authorized to producers in Luxemburg until 1974. These exceptional aids are to be met out of national budgets.

(d) *Export restitutions*. These will be granted on all products exported to third countries.

In forbidding direct subsidies to producers or on milk products and bringing to an end all regulations aimed at pooling returns from liquid milk and manufacturing milk on a national basis, the Council and the Commission have had two main objectives: first to prevent any unfair competition between producers and manufacturers in different member countries, and second to discourage the emergence of unmanageable surpluses. To this end also member states are required to fix their retail prices of liquid milk in such a way that the return from liquid milk does not exceed that of manufacturing milk by more than $0.50 per 100 kg. (2·3d. per gallon). It seems questionable whether this can be reconciled with the requirement that governments should in fixing prices, take into account an incentive to producers. If pooling at a national level were allowed within member countries national governments might be encouraged to subsidize their manufacturing industry, and to some extent insulate it against competition from that of other member countries, by raising the retail price of liquid milk for which demand is fairly inelastic and in which there is virtually no international trade. Pooling would then enable the processing industry to pay a lower price for manufacturing milk at no net loss to producers.

The total annual cost to FEOGA of the support measures will in 1968/69 according to the Commission's latest estimates,[4] amount to $800 mn., consisting of export restitutions $260 mn. (about 4 mn. tons at $65), skim milk subsidy $223 mn., cheese subsidy $37 mn., and intervention on the butter market $280 mn. Total expenditure out of national budgets in subsidies to the milk sector in 1963, the last year before the introduction of the CAP for milk, was over $502 mn.

In fixing a target price of $10.30 per 100 kg (48·23d. per gallon) free at dairy the Council over-ruled the Commission's proposal for a farm-gate target price of $9.50. Since average collection costs for the EEC as a whole are reckoned to be $0.55 per 100 kg. the Council appeared to be offering producers an extra $0.25, or two and a half per cent more than was in the Commission's view the safety limit. Although the Council's decision was undoubtedly a political one its benefit to a large number of producers will be more apparent than real: in Belgium, Germany, and the Netherlands where collection costs from farm to dairy are below average (as low as $0.28 in the Netherlands) the change will be advantageous, but in Italy and France where they are well over $0·70 the Council's bonus works out at less than $0.10 per 100 kg.

In proposing the lower figure the Commission were concerned to preserve into the period of a unified market the somewhat precarious balance between supply and demand for milk and milk products achieved since the early sixties, when the Community as a whole had been about 102 per cent self-sufficient. Serious surpluses by 1970 could only be avoided given a combination of static dairy-cow numbers, rising consumption of milk products per head of population, and no increase in the rate of use of milk substitutes for calf rearing, or in the earlier weaning of calves from whole milk on to compound feeds and other concentrates. In the event, though cow numbers have remained steady, average yields have continued to rise, and are now 13 per cent higher than in 1960. With increased prices, butter consumption has reached a virtual standstill, and is further threatened by removal of intra-Community tariffs and certain national restrictions on margarine. Use of substitutes for calf-rearing has risen eightfold since 1960, and deliveries of milk to dairies are over a third higher. In 1967/68 excess of butter supplies over demand was 50,000 tons, and is expected to go up by 40,000 tons a year over the next four years. Disposal of these surpluses, as well as of the 150,000 tons already in cold storage on 1 April 1968, presents formidable problems. Apart from subsidized exports to third countries, various expedients are proposed: sale to the public out of cold store at reduced prices, subsidized sales to institutions, de-naturing for cooking and industrial purposes, and raising the fat content of powdered milk for calf-rearing.[5] The draft regulation on liquid milk authorizes national subsidies for school milk, but there is nowhere any mention in the Commission's latest report of measures to encourage greater consumption of liquid milk.

[4] *Rapport de la Commission au Conseil, sur la situation économique du secteur laitier,* Brussels, 20 January, 1968, p. 18.
[5] Ibid., pp. 14–16.

THE UNITED KINGDOM AS A MEMBER OF THE EEC

Producer prices and costs

At the 1967 Price Review the guaranteed price for the standard quantities of liquid milk was raised by 1·25d. per gallon for 1967/68. The pool price to be received by producers at farm-gate in England and Wales over the year ending 31 March 1968 should therefore average nearly 40d. per gallon, the pool price for 1966/67 having worked out at 38·75d. Barring any changes in the guaranteed price made at the 1968 Price Review producers in England and Wales can expect to receive about the same return during 1968/69. For those in the Scottish Board's region it will as usual be higher, and in the Aberdeen and District Board's region lower, by a fraction of a penny. Producers in the north of Scotland will receive between 2d. and 3d. more, and those in Northern Ireland between 3d. and 4d. less per gallon, than English producers. In all cases the actual pool price realized will depend on the amounts by which production exceeds the standard quantities and on current levels of milk product prices on the free market.

The EEC target price of 48·23d. per gallon at dairy represents about 47·0d. at farm-gate in England and Wales, the region with the lowest collection costs, which were 1·25d. per gallon in 1966/67.[6] The Community target price is geared to a situation where only 22 per cent of milk produced is assumed to go for liquid consumption, at a maximum premium of 2·3d. per gallon above the target price, and 37 per cent for butter, the intervention price for which is calculated to return not less than 1·5d. per gallon below the target price. Given the opposite pattern of consumption in the UK this weighting ought to enable producers with ready access to a liquid market to obtain on average something above the target level, though at the expense of those in remoter areas whose milk would mostly go for manufacture. With surpluses in other parts of the Community wholesale prices for butter, even in a deficit area such as the UK, are unlikely to rise much above intervention level. There is also some risk that a premium of only 2·3d. per gallon might prove insufficient to elicit adequate supplies of liquid milk to meet the present level of demand in the UK in the late autumn and winter. The further implications of this for consumers are discussed below. As far as producers are concerned a switch to summer milk could only result in an increase in the amount having to go for manufacturing. The opportunities for them to achieve, or improve on, the target price by sales in the liquid market are therefore a good deal more limited than at first appears. Generally speaking, however, milk producers' gross returns would, at current price levels, be higher in the EEC than they are under the present UK system. This state of affairs is largely due to devaluation, and should dispel some of the apprehension felt about the future for dairy farmers inside the Community.

Costs will also rise, but not proportionately. Some idea of changes in

[6] This low figure, compared with average costs in the Community, is, however, only achieved by pooling arrangements and allowances which would almost certainly not be permitted under the EEC system.

these may be obtained by applying to the costings published annually by the Milk Marketing Board for England and Wales[7] the likely higher prices of compound feeds and of barley, as well as making an allowance for the effect of increased fertilizer prices on the cost of forage crops.[8] On this basis costs per gallon for the 434 herds covered by the 1965/66 inquiry might rise by 2·6d. a gallon or 2·8d. a gallon according to whether cereal prices are assumed to be derived from Duisburg or Liverpool.[9] Exercises of this kind are inevitably subject to the unrealistic assumption that farmers do not adapt their feeding plan to changing prices of inputs. For this reason any close approximation to actual changes in feed costs or individual herd size groups is particularly difficult to arrive at. A literal application of the new prices, for instance, raises costs (by over 3d. a gallon) for most herds of the 70·0–99·9 cow class, which make greater use of home-grown cereals to achieve their relatively higher yields than smaller herds. The increased profitability of barley growing under EEC conditions, combined with the disappearance of the acreage-based deficiency payment, would in fact be likely to result in a shift to more intensive use of grassland by owners of large herds in order to keep to a minimum the extra cost of production per gallon directly attributable to joining the EEC.

The same considerations apply if one tries to estimate the different amounts by which increases in feed costs per gallon would vary from region to region. Not only do the Board's costings of the sample according to geographical distribution omit the proportion of compounds to straights of purchased concentrates, but estimates about the relative intervention prices for cereals in each region involve a large number of assumptions about transport costs from Duisburg or Liverpool. Such tentative calculations as we have made, however, lead to the rather obvious conclusion that costs per gallon would be likely to rise less in the south-west and in the Midlands-and-north-west (with their greater reliance on fodder crops) than in East Anglia and Wales. This is to a large extent confirmed by the report on the MMB's scheme for low cost milk production.[10] Of 673 Friesian herds recorded in 1966, and averaging 883 gallons (4,134 kg.) per cow, those in the Midlands-and-south and South-west regions consumed below average (for the sample) amounts of concentrates per gallon both in winter and summer. In the West-and-Wales region, where the lowest cost per gallon of any region was recorded in the summer, winter concentrate costs were higher than in any region except the North. Differences between summer and winter costs of production would be likely to be accentuated by EEC conditions. Three samples, grouping 103, 141 and 156 summer milk and winter milk herds costed in 1965 and 1966, indicate a consumption of 2·3 lbs of concentrates per gallon in summer and 3·0 lbs in

---

[7] *Costs of Milk Production in England and Wales, April 1965 to March 1966*, compiled on behalf of the Milk Costs Committee of the Conference of Provincial Agricultural Economists (MMB, Thames Ditton). See especially Tables 6, 8 and 9.

[8] 6·0d., 4·0d., and 2·0d. respectively per cwt. of hay, silage, and roots/kale.

[9] See pp. 103–4.

[10] *Low Cost Production, an assessment of the past four years* (MMB, Thames Ditton, 1967).

winter. The additional concentrate cost per gallon due to price increases could be 2·0d. in summer and 2·6d. in winter at 'Duisburg' prices, or 2·3d. and 2·9d. at 'Liverpool' prices.

Taking into consideration that these are essentially results achieved by low cost producers, and allowing for the fertilizer element in the cost of forage, the assumption of an overall rise in feed costs for milk producers of 2·6d. or 2·8d. per gallon, according to the system of cereal price derivation agreed upon, would not therefore seem to be unreasonable. Against the unfavourable difference caused by changes in costs, and in some regions in returns as well, for milk producers must, however, be set the increased sale value of calves not required as replacements, and of barren cows for which there is a stronger demand on the continent than in the UK. Given a guide price for veal in the Community of 387s. 4d. per live cwt. and one for fat cattle some 15 per cent higher than the existing UK guaranteed price (including an allowance for the calf and beef-cow subsidies), producers might hope to obtain an extra £5 per calf and £25 per cow, giving an average of about £10 per lactation. Allowing for the extra costs of herd replacements this might represent about a 1·5d. per gallon advantage on a 800-gallon cow to compensate for all or part of the rise in feed costs.

Ensuring liquid supplies

The most notable effects of adopting the EEC milk regulations without any modification might be felt not by the dairy farmer but by the consumer. In the course of the past thirty-five years a system of milk marketing has been evolved one of whose main objectives has been to provide sufficient liquid milk to meet demand throughout the year. In achieving this, and other aims more directly beneficial to producers, the Boards, as producer monopolies, have had their share of criticism from all sides. Manufacturers, especially the larger firms, have been impatient of the Boards' powers to allocate supplies of milk for manufacturing from particular farms to particular factories and, through its influence on prices, to particular products. This is said for instance to have inhibited the development of new lines of milk products. Many producers close to large centres of liquid consumption have felt that the Boards' pooling system deprives them of the full economic benefit of their location, to the unfair advantage of geographically remote producers. Although the government after the war retained and did not restore to the Boards their original powers of fixing retail prices and distributive margins there has also been a feeling that the artificial division of the liquid and manufacturing markets has operated to the disadvantage of the consumer. He has been made to pay a higher price for liquid milk than was warranted by the valuation of milk on the international market for milk products. None of these arguments is without substance. The system, while admittedly keeping producers' interests well to the fore, has at least enabled the consumer to buy as much liquid milk as he could afford all the year round. He has paid a price which, however much lower it might in theory have been on an entirely free market, at least has not been so high as to reduce per head consumption.

It is this fairly delicate balance of interests which a rigid application of the EEC regulation to the peculiar British situation threatens to upset. Assuming a willingness on the part of the Six to adapt the regulation, any exception must be based on the Community principle that no major distortion of competition should be involved either for producers or for manufacturers in the other member countries. Complete freedom of movement of liquid milk and cream and of milk products is an evident first step. An efficient and regular roll-on roll-off service (or eventually a Channel tunnel) might so reduce the cost of delivering liquid supplies from the Continent as to make them competitive in the south-east of England with those from more remote areas of England and Wales. It may be observed that French dairies at present export about 25 mn. gallons a year to Italy by road and rail, some of it from as far afield as Auxerre and Le Mans. Only the prospect of regular all-the-year-round contracts in England, giving the advantage of higher winter prices but also providing some outlet for local spring and summer surpluses, would, however, seem to justify the capital cost of new dairy installations along the northern European seaboard (present ones being mainly geared to manufacturing) and be likely to attract sufficiently low freight rates. But even if such a trade never developed free movement would at any rate have to be theoretically possible. For this to be so the Milk Marketing Boards' present system of pooling collection and distribution costs virtually over the whole UK, bringing collection costs down to almost half the present average in the Six, would undoubtedly be deemed to distort competition.

To what extent might other forms of pooling be forbidden? The Council of Ministers has ruled that 'arrangements made by individual member states to fix a balance between fresh milk and milk for processing' is among the national measures incompatible with the application of common prices. The aim of this, as has been explained, is to forestall a blanket protection of national manufacturing industries. It does not in any way exclude local pooling arrangements, and clearly could not do so since in the case of any given dairy or factory, whether private or co-operative, it would be inequitable, even if it were physically possible, to allocate individual producers' milk supplies to particular purposes at differentiated prices. Not only is this form of price pooling commonly practised, but collection costs are shared, and seasonal price differentials and quality premia are normally paid, by co-operatives covering a fairly wide area (two or three French departments for instance). There would appear to be nothing to prevent practices of this kind being adopted by recognized producer groups, the only limitation on whose size, it will be remembered, is at present that their throughput shall not exceed 5 per cent of that of the Community. In the case of a Community of Ten this would have represented in 1964 something of the order of 4·5 mn. tons, or about 960 mn. gallons. The three Scottish Milk Marketing Boards' and the Northern Ireland Board's throughputs would each come well within this limit. Since the Board for England and Wales has a throughput of just over twice the amount it might have to be sub-divided into a number of groupings of its present regions, say one for Wales and two or three for England, which could thus constitute ready-made producer groups. Acceptance by the Commission of the principle of '*extension des règles de discipline*' provided for in the French Agriculture Act of 1962 would mean that legislation extending to such regional groupings the Boards' present exclusive rights of purchase of all home-produced milk would be considered compatible with EEC rules. It is in any case unlikely that after over thirty years of selling to the Board more than a small minority of producers would even wish to exercise a right to opt out of such an arrangement and negotiate contracts direct with dairies. The somewhat more regionalized price structure which might emerge, while disadvantaging producers in Wales and the south-west, for instance, would bring to those in the east and south-east the full benefits of closer access to the liquid market of which they have felt themselves to some extent deprived. The average annual price difference between the south-east and the remotest regions of England is never more than 1·25d. per gallon at present.

On the organizational level, then, the difficulties of adopting the EEC regulations are by no means insuperable. Much of the Boards' present activity would continue undisturbed, including, of course, the AI, milk recording, and other services. There remains the thorny problem of ensuring all-the-year-round liquid milk supplies, to the maintenance of which the Boards would claim that their present policy and powers were primarily dedicated. The 2·3d. per gallon maximum above the target price permitted for liquid sales would not be adequate to provide the large differential between winter and summer prices which experience has shown to be necessary in existing circumstances to cover the November to February gap. In England and Wales for the six winter months of 1966/67 prices payable to producers ranged between 42·1d. and 45·6d. according to region and month. During the summer the spread was 29·7d. to 39·7d.[11] This maximum all-the-year-round variation of over 20 per cent of mean may be compared with about 6 per cent current in Germany or with the 3·5 per cent offered to members of a typical dairy co-operative south-east of Paris. In the Netherlands the variation is between 6·0 and 9·0 per cent according to the region. Since retail prices for liquid milk in the UK seldom change by more than 5 per cent between summer and winter and distributive margins are also fixed, both the high winter prices and the low summer prices paid to producers are artificially contrived through the Boards' pooling arrangements.

What would happen if the UK joined the EEC? If the present seasonal differential for liquid milk were retained while prices for manufacturing milk rose to the level set by an intervention price for butter of 746s. per

---

[11] The average price (net of collection and administrative charges) was 40·5d., the Board pooling a return of 48·1d. on its liquid sales with one of 22·6d. on those of manufacturing milk.

cwt. (designed, it will be remembered, to ensure a return of 46·77d. per gallon of milk to the producer), average producer returns would exceed the 48·23 target level by a substantial amount. Any producer groups sub-stituted for the Boards, assuming they were not debarred by EEC regula-tions from operating a pooling system on a regional basis, would be faced with a complicated pricing problem. In selecting a winter price they must avoid fixing it so low as to be insufficient to elicit adequate supplies. Nor must they fix it so high that the summer price required to average out the return on sales to the liquid market at the maximum permitted level would have to be so low as to be unremunerative even to the efficient producer. But whatever the levels chosen they must ultimately reflect the price at retail. It is well known that seasonal alterations in the retail price of liquid milk tend to discourage total consumption over a period, which is more elastic to upward price changes than to downward ones. It is therefore in producers' interests that there should be little or no differentiation between summer and winter retail prices, and seasonal differentials, if any, applied to producer prices only.

The alternative is to have little or no seasonal differential. This works well enough in the Community where mainly very small herds are pro-ducing for a limited liquid milk market. At present, at any rate, there seem to be enough farmers practising, whether from deliberate choice or force of habit, all-the-year-round calving, which conveniently spreads family farm income and labour load in the milk-shed evenly over time, without over-much regard to higher winter feed costs. To what extent would both economic and psychological motives encourage UK producers to shift from winter milk if the present price incentives were removed, or much reduced? For the owners of larger herds, usually the most cost-conscious, the attraction of much higher summer prices than at present would be con-siderable. In the first place there would be an overall saving in the feeding of concentrates, whose price inside the EEC would be £7 or more a ton higher. Secondly, reduction of working hours during the short winter days would be a psychological advantage for hired labour. Thirdly, grass could be more cheaply and efficiently converted into milk during spring and summer, hay and silage being utilized mainly for winter maintenance rations. A trend towards cutting out winter milk is already apparent. In anticipation of a lowering of the pooled price even in winter, due to increas-ing supplies over and above the standard quantity and to the virtual saturation of the liquid market, a growing number of large herds are being calved down in the spring and dried off in November. Use of an outdoor milking bail in these cases also eliminates the need for new capital expendi-ture on winter housing. The effect on milk production from smaller herds of having little or no seasonal price differential would probably be less pronounced. As on the Continent the smaller producer will tend to respond to a level all-year-round price by spreading out calvings. This would of course involve some shift in supplies from winter to summer. On the other hand, although the EEC target price, now equivalent to 48·23d. per gallon at dairy, would mean a substantial increase over present UK summer prices, winter prices would still remain much the same as now, and could even be a little higher in some areas.

Under the present price structure about 46 per cent of milk in England and Wales is produced between October and March. In 1965 probably something over half of this, say 490 mn. gallons, came from herds of under 40 cows on farms of under 200 acres. If winter production from all the larger herds were reduced by, say, half, to 235 mn. gallons, just over 500 mn. gallons would still be needed from the smaller herds to satisfy the present level of demand for liquid milk during the winter months, about 740 mn. gallons. This leaves no room at all for any switch by smaller producers to summer milk, surely an unrealistic assumption. It is possible that higher prices will somewhat reduce total demand; but even if the switch by larger producers were less than 50 per cent, the prospect of satisfying demand in the winter seems doubtful unless some form of fairly strong price incentive is retained. It might take the form of a special price agreed between the Boards (or their successors) and individual producers contracting with them to supply minimum quantities of winter milk. This would probably involve modifying, for the UK only, the Community's present '2d. a gallon' rule.

On balance there seems a case for this, and not only to help protect the British consumer from possible winter milk shortages—even if the UK producer were thereby to receive a higher average return than other dairy farmers in the Community, and competition were to that extent distorted. Otherwise summer surpluses for manufacturing would be stimulated. This, while benefiting the UK balance of payments, would be to the disadvantage of milk producers elsewhere in the Community who will be looking to the UK as a large importer of their own surpluses. The continuing encouragement of winter milk production for the liquid market in this country would therefore be in their interest.

The maximum likely increase in off-farm sales of milk might, given an unrestricted market, be about 850 mn. gallons over the next ten years, an increase of just over a third, and the equivalent of 170,000 tons of butter.[12] Whether the removal of the present restraints on the volume of production resulted in the whole of this increase or not, a substantial proportion of it would go towards filling the gap left by the reduction in butter imports which, whatever the agreement reached about New Zealand, would be bound to occur.

The manufacturing market

On the manufacturing side adoption of the EEC system is likely to benefit mainly the major groups and firms, which will be free to buy milk when and where they want, taking advantage of the greater economies of scale and lower overheads per unit of output made possible by a relatively large and regular throughput of manufacturing milk. Under

[12] See Imperial Chemical Industries Ltd. *The Dairy Industries in the UK and EEC and the Common Market policy for milk and milk products*, May 1967.

present circumstances this is not always obtainable. Smaller firms on the other hand enjoy some protection from the allocation of quotas by the Boards. The powers exercised by the Boards over disposal of the milk which they purchase from producers make it possible for them to make sure that the supply of liquid milk has first priority. The manufacturing market is residual. In this situation producers' and consumers' interests coincide, but not with those of manufacturers. Firms whose potential supplies may be switched at the Boards' expense to satisfy liquid demand elsewhere have to take second place. With the disappearance of the dual market, arrangements of this kind could not be maintained. Producer groups would make the best contracts they could for specific quantities of milk at a uniform price, with minor seasonal variations. They would then have to adjust payment to their members in such a way as to elicit the volume of winter milk which they had contracted to supply. Although the highest bids would be likely to come from firms obtaining a substantial proportion of their returns from the higher priced liquid market, there could be no attempt by producer groups to control the ultimate disposal of the milk which they sold.

Processers who also have an interest in the liquid milk market would find themselves at some advantage compared with the distributors of liquid milk with no manufacturing capacity to fall back on. These would be faced with the unfamiliar problem, common enough before the war, of having to make forward contracts and budget ahead for a highly perishable commodity the day-to-day demand for which is inclined to be very variable. In fact the liquid milk distributors would have to start remembering how to buy milk. For nearly thirty years now the Boards have virtually guaranteed them whatever they required, switching supplies from manufacturers in times of shortage and relieving them of their surpluses when demand was slack. Some of the smaller firms would undoubtedly find the adjustment difficult to make.

Since it is fairly unlikely that seasonal surpluses of home-produced butter would occur on the UK market, support for storage will hardly be necessary. Subsidies from FEOGA for cheese manufacture will, however, be required to enable imports of Cheddar from third countries to enter at the price bound in GATT, not much higher than at present, and at the same time maintain the target price of milk to producers. Internal prices for Cheddar may in any case tend to rise above present levels; with the entry of the UK into the Community it would become a cheese in its own right instead of, as at present, merely a raw material for German processed cheese. Consumption of cheese in Britain might not be much affected by this price rise, as it would be substituted to some extent for meat, and might even increase.

A subsidy of 63s. 6d. per cwt. will also be payable on home-produced skim powder for stockfeed, reducing it from a threshold price of 229s. 9d. per cwt. Even at the subsidized price it will be some 50s. 0d. per cwt. above current UK import prices. Milk for fresh cream being priced in the

EEC on the same basis as all other liquid milk, cream prices would increase substantially, leading to a decline in consumption. In the UK it is at present sold by the Board at a manufacturing price of 28·0d. per gallon; in the EEC by 1968 manufacturers will be paying around 50·0d. though they will obtain a price for skim equivalent to about 15·0d. per gallon of wholemilk higher than present UK levels.[13]

It seems clear, in conclusion, that adoption in the UK of the EEC milk regulations would present the British milk manufacturing industry with considerable opportunities for expanding its output and concentrating its structure.

[13] E. Strauss, 'Common Market Challenge to Britain's Dairy Industry', *Dairy Industries*, January 1967.

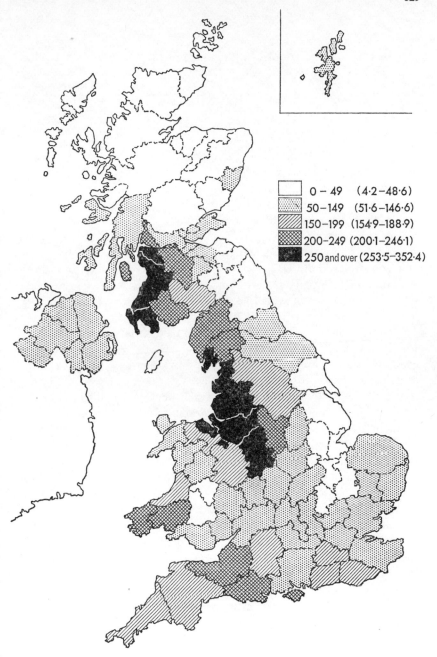

7. Dairy cattle in the UK (excluding Isle of Man)

Per 1,000 acres of crops and grass, 1965. Figures for Northern Ireland are for that area
as a whole.

(Source: UK Agricultural Statistics)

7. Beef and Veal

Whatever the efforts of travel agents and other professional promoters of the British image to project the beef-eater as a national symbol, cold statistics show that considerably more beef is eaten per head of the population in France and Belgium than in England. Even the traditional liking for veal in some parts of the Community, memorable by the monotonous appearance on menus of various forms of *Kalbsbraten* and *vitello*, has been giving way to a growing desire for red meat, demand for which now constitutes about 80 per cent of the total. Average consumption per head of the Community of beef and veal taken together, including parts of southern Italy where it is still less than 10 kg. a year, is now greater than in the UK. If the UK enters the EEC the disparity seems likely to increase. The British housewife and her family will have little stomach for steak at 17s. 6d. a pound, and even the price of the cheaper cuts will be enough to encourage her a good deal of the time to buy other less expensive forms of protein. On the Continent, however, where beef at well above UK prices is already an established fact of domestic life, it seems likely to continue to be, as P. G. Wodehouse once remarked about jute in the days before synthetic fibres, something the populace is pretty keen on.

The fact that not enough beef is produced inside the Community to satisfy this craving presents to the EEC farmer, and should continue to present to the farmer in an enlarged Community, a unique situation in which his product is, taking one year with another, actually in keen demand. Unfortunately structural factors such as an inefficient distributive system or shortage of working capital may result in the consumer's message not being clearly transmitted to the producer's pocket. He will prefer to stick to the short-term security of the monthly milk cheque, rather than face the cyclical hazards and rewards of beef production. Official incentives have therefore had to be progressively jacked up on both sides of the Channel. On balance they are at present surer in the UK but higher in the Community.

THE UNITED KINGDOM

Beef and veal production has, despite some fairly sharp year-to-year fluctuations, been maintained during the sixties at an average of about 850,000 tons, or 13 per cent above the level of 1960/61, satisfying between 70 and 75 per cent of total demand. This has been achieved partly by an enlargement, by nearly one-third, of the pure-bred beef herd. For every

TABLE 16. BEEF AND VEAL:
PRODUCTION AND CONSUMPTION, 1965

	Total cattle numbers UK=100		Compara-tive produc-tion[a]: UK=100	Percent-age of total produc-tion[a]: the Six	Percent-age of total produc-tion[a]: the Ten	Degree of self-sufficiency per cent	Consump-tion per head per year[b] kg.
Germany (FR)	116·2	(June)	108·7	27·3	19·4	87·1	21·3
France	172·8	(Oct)	185·7	46·7	33·2	100·4	31·9
Italy	76·9	(Jan)	53·0	13·3	9·5	64·9	15·4
Netherlands	31·4	(May)	27·8	7·0	5·0	123·6	18·6
Belgium	21·1	(Jan)	21·3	5·4	3·8	}92·9	23·7
Luxemburg	1·4	(May)	1·3	0·3	0·2	}	
The Six	419·8		397·8	100·0	71·1	90·8	
United Kingdom	100·0	(June)	100·0c		17·9c	75·6	21·0
Ireland	44·9	(June)	29·6		5·3	126·7	17·0d
Denmark	28·0	(July)	25·9		4·6	138·6	16·0
Norway	8·9	(June)	6·4		1·1	100·0	15·2
The Four					28·9	89·6	
The Ten					100·0	89·4	

a Production from indigenous animals only, including where applicable, the meat equivalent of exported live animals and excluding meat equivalent of imported live animals.
b 1964/65.
c Including meat equivalent of imported store cattle.   d 1963/64.
Sources: FAO: *Monthly Bulletin of Agricultural Statistics*, Feb. 1967. FAO/ECE *Review of the Agricultural Situation in Europe, 1966. Irish Statistical Bulletin*, December 1966. *Food Consumption in OECD Countries, 1962/63 to 1964/65.*

three dairy cows there is now nearly one of beef breed. The increase is also due to more frequent crossing of dairy cows with beef bulls. The dairy herd provides about two-thirds of home produced beef. In 1965/66 35 per cent of artificial inseminations carried out for the Milk Marketing Board in England and Wales were by bulls of pure beef breed (nearly two-thirds of them Hereford), compared with 30 per cent in 1960/61. It is also notable that the proportion of Friesian inseminations, still nominally a dairy breed but effectively dual purpose, was 52 per cent (an increase of 3 per cent since 1960/61).

Since beef production necessarily takes up a relatively small proportion of space on cereal farms (in some cases occupying no farmland at all), and is comparatively rare on small and medium-sized dairy farms, the map at the end of the chapter, rather than emphasizing the density of the livestock population, illustrates the relative importance of beef to the economy of the upland regions of the UK. Except for two or three Mid-land counties where cattle are traditionally finished on permanent pastures, the heavily hatched areas mostly have a preponderance of moorland, hill, and mountain.

Price support for beef is by deficiency payment and production grant. In the case of fatstock, however, there is not, as for eggs and milk, any Marketing Board to act as statutory buyer of first instance. Producers are

K

free to sell where they will, at public auction markets or by private treaty direct to butchers or dealers. The Fatstock Marketing Corporation, a public company in which farmers, through the National Farmers' Union, retain a majority shareholding, has since its foundation in 1954 provided the only means whereby beasts can be sold on a carcass grade and dead-weight basis. Payment of the subsidy is made by the Ministry of Agriculture direct to producers on the basis of a certificate issued, subject to certain standards of weight and quality, by a representative of the Ministry at the point of sale. The guaranteed price, announced annually after the Price Review, represents an average of 52 standard weekly prices fixed to reflect seasonal variations in supply and demand. A number of additional refinements have been introduced in recent years in line with government policy of adjusting guarantee payments to correspond as closely as possible to market fluctuations.

There are no deficiency payments for veal, production of which is relatively small and confined mainly to specialized units. The calf subsidy is a further element of government support for beef. A fixed lump sum (£11. 5s. for steers and £9 for heifers), it is payable at eight months on calves of beef beef-cross or dual-purpose breed. An annual subsidy of £7. 10s. per head payable on cows of beef breed, other than hill cows, was introduced in 1966. Farmers in recognized hill areas were already receiving a subsidy of £14. 5s. per breeding cow, plus £5 towards winter keep.

The cost of deficiency payments inevitably fluctuates from one year to another according to the general level of prices on the home market (see Appendix G), which are greatly influenced by imported supplies of chilled beef and of forward Irish store cattle. The level of Argentine shipments, whose marginal effect on prices is particularly strong, has been subject over the years to a good deal of climatic and political variation. Attempts to reach an agreement with the Argentine government on greater regularity of exports and a more even seasonal spread have not been successful. UK market prices are also sensitive to the availability of export outlets for live cattle from Great Britain (mainly fat barren cows, which do not qualify for any deficiency payment), as well as for Irish stores, in the EEC. The imposition of levies by the Commission in the middle of 1966 shut off this trade and the consequent general fall in UK market prices for all types of fat cattle is reflected in a return to earlier levels of exchequer liability. The cost of deficiency payments, which averaged little over £7 mn. during 1964/65 and 1965/66, was treble that amount in 1966/67 and a further large bill must be expected for 1967/68.

New developments in rearing techniques during the sixties have brought about a considerable acceleration in the process of fattening beef cattle. The number of heavy two-year-old beasts has declined by about a quarter since 1960, in response to a growing demand for the leaner 12- to 18-month-old animal going out at between $7\frac{1}{2}$ and $8\frac{1}{2}$ cwt. (380 and 430 kg.) live-weight. Production of this type of beast, of which only a proportion is achieved by intensive indoor methods, makes considerable use of grass silage and arable by-products. Those not bred by the finisher are usually bought in either as week-old cross-bred calves for early weaning or as weaned single-suckled calves off cows of beef breed. Many fewer beef cattle change hands as stores than in the past, the most important trade being in Irish imports, which qualify for deficiency payment on slaughter in the normal way on condition they have been in the country for a minimum period of time (usually about two months, depending on the date of importation). As a result of these trends store markets, a feature of the beef trade peculiar to the UK and of relatively small importance in the EEC except in the Netherlands, are tending to decline.

THE EEC

In the EEC a much larger proportion of beef and veal is produced from dual-purpose cattle than in the UK. As herds of extreme dairy breed are fairly rare in any member country, crossing with beef bulls is little practised. The pure beef breeds, Charollaise and Limousine in France, Romagnola, Marcheggiana, and Chianina in Italy, account for little more than 20 per cent of total cattle population in either country. Most beef production thus takes place jointly with milk on smallholdings, although large feed lots are to be found here and there. Bought-in beef stores are fattened on the big arable farms of the Paris basin, for instance, and in the Po valley, and a few produced co-operatively in the former land reform areas of Italy. Only in the Netherlands is there virtually no joint production of milk and beef, calves unwanted as dairy replacements being either reared to veal weights on their farms of origin or sold as young beef stores in the predominantly arable areas. Some of these are finished out of winter yards, some off summer grass by specialist graziers.

Subject to the usual determining factors of end price, cereal and forage costs and availability of land, labour and capital, particularly working capital, the EEC producer has five broad choices of finished product. First there is in general a much stronger demand than in the UK for vealers, either between 2 cwt. and 3 cwt. (liveweight) intensively reared on whole or skim milk plus concentrates, or larger calves of 4 to $4\frac{1}{2}$ cwt. reared to six months with small quantities of roughage in their later ration. These are mainly produced on small family dairy farms, though the steady growth in volume of deliveries of milk to creameries over recent years suggests that the use of milk substitutes is increasingly widespread. The French *veaux de Lyon* or *veaux de St. Etienne* (named after the markets to which producers in the Charollais traditionally had access) and the *vitelloni* of the lower Po valley, young fat cattle reaching 7 cwt. or 8 cwt. in 12 to 14 months, are a traditional form of so-called 'calf' production. Usually single-suckled and finished indoors, on fodder and concentrates, this type of beast may even, in the case of heavy-boned breeds like the Chianina, reach weights of up to 10 cwt. at that age.

The baby-beef intensively reared on cereals which it to some extent resembles is a third product increasingly favoured by larger-scale farmers in the EEC, particularly by French and Italian maize growers, as well as being popular with politicians looking for the means of creating the large supplies of income-elastic beef which they have conjured up in their Plans. Buyers and eaters of meat in the Community, particularly the French housewife, have so far treated these transatlantic production methods with a certain reserve, though it seems likely that with the spread of self-service retailing, economic considerations will, as elsewhere, in the end prevail over gastronomic ones. A fourth option for the EEC farmer, more suited than baby-beef to his small scale of operations, though calling for greater resources of working capital than veal production, is the rearing of 18- to 20-month beasts of up to 10 cwt. liveweight. These require substantial quantities of non-concentrate feed, which may include silage and sugar-beet tops, and are usually finished off the grass. This type of rearing is widely practised in combination with (and, as far as resources are concerned, in competition with) milk production in all member countries except the Netherlands, and especially in Germany, the bulls mainly reared there being particularly apt for quick-grown lean meat with low proportion of bone to flesh.[1]

Finally, there is a class of very heavy beast, much less commonly produced than in the past, slaughtered at anything from two to four years old and going out at between 10 and 14 cwt. Mainly confined to non-dairy farms this labour-extensive form of production involves a prolonged store period at grass, the stock being only brought into yards for final winter fattening. A sixth and important type of production hardly qualifying as a choice for producers, since it is ineluctable, is cow-beef from barreners. The meat of the *vache de réforme* is more highly valued by continental butchers than British ones, as dairy farmers in the south of England will remember who experienced the halcyon days before the EEC levies were applied.

The very close link involved in the production methods most widely employed in the EEC between milk, veal, and beef has made the market for beef, despite a background of rising demand, even more vulnerable than elsewhere to cyclical movements in supply. The way in which a lengthy chain reaction of this sort can be set off by some exogenous factor like the weather is well illustrated by the course of events during the past five years. Between 1955/56 and 1963 per head consumption of beef and veal in the Community rose by 65 per cent, to 24·3 kg. In 1966 it had reached nearly 26 kg., and by 1970, when it is expected to be over 27 kg., people all over the EEC will be eating on average almost double the amount they were eating 15 years before. Though a growing taste for red meat can be without difficulty linked to a general rise in real incomes, the process has been far from straightforward for the producer. Fluctuations which have occurred in home supplies illustrate vividly the uncertainties encountered by

---

[1] UK entry into the EEC would seem to offer an opportunity to the Ministry of Agriculture to amend its licensing regulations to permit the production of bull beef.

farmers, especially those with slender reserves of working capital, even when producing a commodity for which there is known to be a steadily upward trend in demand. Two consecutive dry summers in 1962 and 1963 led to large numbers of beef animals being sold in an unfinished state or prematurely as veal, and at prices depressed by an over-supplied market. High beef and veal prices induced by scarcity in the following year checked the upward trend in consumption, causing a switch to cheaper pig and poultry meat, but encouraged cattle farmers to rebuild their depleted stocks. Continued high prices during most of 1965 resulted in a further expansion of beef production, the appearance of whose finished output on the market during the latter part of 1966 and during 1967, accompanied by economic recession in Germany and the Netherlands, led to a renewed collapse of prices.

Regulation 14 of 1964 for beef and veal, which came into force at the end of that year, can evidently not be blamed for failing to prevent a situation whose origins dated from 1962, and it could be argued that, by excluding imports and providing a common framework for support buying by national intervention agencies, the CAP at least mitigated its worst possible consequences. The final stage of the CAP, beginning 1 April 1968, involves the abolition of all intra-Community levies and the substitution of a price *fourchette* by a single unified guide price for medium grade cattle for the whole Community. The purpose of fixing a guide price is twofold: to set a level of external protection and provide a trip for internal market intervention. A basic level of protection against imports of live cattle is provided by a common external tariff of 20 per cent *ad valorem*. When weighted average prices for medium grade fat cattle on selected internal markets of the Community fall to 105 per cent of the guide price, a levy is also applied, at a reduced rate of 50 per cent of the full levy. Once internal prices fall to the actual guide price level, however, imports become liable to the full rate of levy. The levy consists of the difference between the guide price and the duty-paid import price. For the purposes of calculating the amount of the levy the import price is deemed to be the prevailing weighted average price for equivalent medium grade cattle on a number of representative third country markets in Europe. Since the imposition of a levy by the EEC authorities automatically depresses prices on these markets its effect tends to be cumulative, lower prices begetting a still higher levy. Denmark, whose markets count for about 50 per cent in the weighting of the officially declared import price was especially hard hit by this arrangement, but was accorded preferential rates of levy, particularly favourable between 1 February and 15 August, in the Kennedy Round. East European state-trading countries, where the market mechanisms are, to say the least, muffled, have on the other hand tended to benefit.

The Regulation also covers all carcass meat, offals, and derived beef and veal products, levies on which are calculated according to a large variety of co-efficients relating them to fresh meat and live cattle. There is a 26 per cent tariff bound in GATT for corned beef and one of 20 per cent on frozen meat for an annual levy-free quota of 22,000 tons. Any supplementary quotas of frozen and chilled meat (treated indifferently for this purpose) fixed by the Council on a proposal by the Commission are subject not only to the common tariff but to any levy which may be applicable.

Support of the internal market through intervention buying may occur at the discretion of national agencies (though its cost is chargeable to FEOGA) when prices on national markets have fallen to between 96 and 93 per cent of the guide price.

It must be one of the main objectives of the CAP for beef and veal to forestall cyclical movements by announcing each year's guide price as far as possible in advance so as to encourage farmers to take long-term production decisions. With this in view a guide price for 1969/70 was proposed at the time of the general price review for 1968/69, a year earlier than technically it need have been. A second objective must take into account the dual nature of most herds and the comparative ease with which farmers operating on a small scale can switch between milk, beef, and veal. A price relationship must be maintained between milk and beef sufficient not to encourage over-production of one at the expense of the other. This ratio has been observed over a number of years to be not less than 1 : 7,[2] and its maintenance has become something of an article of faith with the Commission. Between 1964 and 1966 milk production, which during the early sixties seemed to have been rising less rapidly than had been feared (two years of drought having to some extent masked the effect of increasing yields), went up by 7 per cent. More alarmingly, deliveries to creameries rose by over 12 per cent, and, despite much increased exports, stocks of butter had mounted to 122,000 tons by the end of 1966. In making its recommendations for 1968/69 the Commission had in the previous March been careful to balance the target and guide prices for milk and beef in a 1 : 7 ratio ($9.50 : $66.50 per 100 Kg.). By raising the target price of milk the Council reduced the ratio to about 1 : 6·8. Understandably the Commission took the opportunity a year later to redress the balance, the additional $1.0 per 100 kg. on beef restoring it exactly to 1 : 7. The $70.00 per 100 kg. guide price proposed for 1969/70 is designed to be an even more ample incentive, though the Commission must fear that irresistible political pressure on the Council to raise the price of milk to $10.00 may in the end prevent the ratio rising above 1 : 7. But at least by then some of the extra beef should be safely in the pipeline.[3]

The third objective of the CAP for beef, bridging the other two, must be to keep the producer price of veal high enough in relation to milk to

[2] See L. Malassis and H. J. Mittendorf, *L'augmentation de la production bovine dans les pays de la CEE; étude sur les possibilités techniques et les conditions économiques,* Agricultural Series Study No. 5 (Brussels, 1961), pp. 40–43.

[3] It is interesting to note that in the UK the ratio between the guaranteed prices for milk and for beef (including the calf and beef-cow subsidies) declined from 1 : 7·1 in 1962/63 to 1 : 6·7 for the three years 1965/66 to 1967/68.

encourage rearing of calves, and yet low enough in relation to the price of beef to discourage their premature slaughter as vealers in such large numbers as to endanger beef supplies. The proper ratio of beef to veal prices is reckoned by the Commission to be not more than 1 : 1·35. Fixed in July 1966 at $89.50 per 100 Kg. the guide price for veal was therefore increased to $91.15 (387s. 4d.) when that for beef was raised to $68.00 (288s. 0d.) per cwt. For 1969/70 a price of $94.50 (400s. 0d.) has been proposed.

High prices for beef in relation to milk, even announced well in advance, are unlikely to eliminate the risk either of beef cycles or of milk surpluses; import demand for beef and export supplies of butter will continue to fluctuate in the foreseeable future. Net imports into the EEC of beef and veal, including live cattle, rose from 607,000 tons in 1963 to 781,000 tons in 1964, and remained at 771,000 tons in the following year. By 1966 the Community is reckoned to have supplied 88 per cent of an increased demand, compared with 85 per cent in 1965, and net imports seem to have fallen again. Continuing restrictions on imports, including a supplementary levy to Germany, suggest that in 1967 the Community's degree of self-sufficiency will have been further increased. Since imports regularly include between 200,000 and 250,000 tons of frozen and chilled meat, supplies of fresh meat and live cattle from European third countries tend to be rather highly marginal to those of the Community, which produces around 4 mn. tons a year. This is a phenomenon of which producers in Denmark, Ireland, and the UK have become painfully aware.

THE UNITED KINGDOM AS A MEMBER OF THE EEC

There being no marketing board for meat, transition from the UK to the EEC support system presents no major organizational problem. The nature of the intervention agencies in the Community at present varies somewhat from country to country. In Germany the Import and Storage Agency (EVSt) and in Belgium the *Office Commercial du Ravitaillement* are official institutions originating from the days of food rationing. The French SIBEV (*Société Interprofessionnelle du Bétail et de la Viande*) more directly represents, as its name implies, producers' and distributors' interests. In no case does intervention fall to a ministry of agriculture. Entry into the EEC would seem to offer the possibility of a practical role for the recently constituted British Meat and Livestock Commission.

Support buying of meat in the unified market is intended to be optional, though a ruling has to be given by the Council before 1 April 1968 on the degree of autonomy to be enjoyed by national agencies in exercising their discretion to intervene. In general the Council has laid down that support measures shall not impede intra-Community trade; that they must aim to stabilize both producer and consumer prices; that they must be 'selective and regionalized'; and that they must conform with supply trends for different types of cattle and meat in the most important areas of the Community. Intervention may in the end be by two stages: optional at, say,

98 per cent of guide price, and only mandatory if market prices fall to around the present intervention level.

Given the importance of encouraging beef production it seems unlikely that any British government would put pressure on its intervention agency not to enter the market if market prices remained obstinately within the intervention range. At the present authorized level of 96 per cent to 93 per cent of the guide price (276s. 3d. to 267s. 9d. per live cwt. for 1968/69, 284s. 6d. to 275s. 6d. proposed for 1969/70, for average grade cattle), intervention could thus by 1970 in theory ensure a return from the market not less than 91s. 6d. per cwt. above the average price received for all certified cattle by UK producers in 1966/67[4] or, the guarantee having been raised by 5s. 0d. a cwt. at the 1967 Price Review, not less than 86s. 6d. above the probable 1967/68 realization price. This statement requires qualifying in four ways. First, on the debit side of the account as far as the comparison is concerned for the UK producer, the price of 184s. 0d. does not take into account the additional value of the beef-cow and the calf subsidies. These must be reckoned at something between 20s. 0d. and 29s. 0d. a cwt. depending on the liveweight of the beast, its sex, and the fact that only about one in four beef cattle are out of cows eligible for the subsidy. Second, comparing 1967/68 UK prices with 1968/69 or 1969/70 EEC prices leaves out of account further increases in the guarantee which may occur at the 1968 and 1969 price reviews and thus narrow down the advantage for the beef producer of going into the EEC. Third, on the credit side, 184s. 0d. represents an average market price in which cows, not being eligible for deficiency payment, receive no weighting. The EEC guide price is an average weighted to include cows of all grades as well as a higher proportion of medium and lower grade beasts than would normally be found among certificated cattle in the UK. The average price received for all cattle is estimated by the Ministry of Agriculture to have been 163s. 0d. per cwt in 1966/67. Finally, also in the UK producer's favour, the 184s. 0d. is an all-the-year-round average price. It would certainly not be reasonable to assume that in an enlarged Community, which will not in the foreseeable future be self-sufficient in beef, prices per cwt. would average no more than intervention level over the whole year. Although they are bound to become depressed during the late summer and early autumn this should induce an increasing proportion of farmers to spread their marketings and, despite the high marginal cost of doing so, profit by finishing cattle at other times of the year.[5]

Taking these conflicting considerations into account a fair assessment of the additional return to the beef producer from going into the EEC in

[4] 184s. 0d., including a deficiency payment of 23s. 10½d., as estimated in the *Annual Review and Determination of Guarantees 1967*, Cmnd. 3229, Table B, p. 42.

[5] It should, however, be noted that seasonal fluctuations have tended to be smaller on continental markets than those built into the UK price guarantees. Whereas the highest level of guarantee for any month in 1966/67 was 114 per cent of the lowest, in no country of the EEC were average market prices for any month of the same year more than 112 per cent of the lowest. That was in Belgium. In France and Italy there was only a difference of 6·5 per cent, with Germany (10·5 per cent), and the Netherlands (9·5 per cent) in between.

1970 might be in the region of 87s. 0d. per cwt. on the sale of his end product.[6] What are likely to be the marginal costs to be set against this? Obviously they will vary according to the method of rearing and finishing employed. Reckoning up the additional cost of cereals,[7] fertilizers and skim milk, the estimates given below, based on costings actually carried out[8] suggest the order of magnitude of the effects for UK rearers of EEC levels of prices for these inputs. The first three rearing methods examined cover nine separate batches, containing between 10 and 104 cattle each, on nine different arable farms in East Anglia. The marginal cost figure per live cwt. given is in each case a weighted average. Method (d) refers to a single batch of 26 cattle.

(a) Early weaning of purchased calves, and finishing at 18 months at 9 cwt.:   25s. 9d. per cwt. liveweight

(b) In-wintered, autumn calving, single-suckled herd, with progeny finished at 18 months at 8 to 9 cwt.:   26s. 0d. per cwt. liveweight

(c) Spring calving, single-suckled herd, with progeny finished at either 12 months or 15 months: 26s. 6d. per cwt. liveweight

(d) Friesian steers purchased as calves and reared intensively to be finished at 11 to 12 months at 7 to 8 cwt.:   18s. 0d. per cwt. liveweight

Rearing and management methods were of varying efficiency. Gross margins per beast and per acre at these prices differed considerably both between farms and between methods. Since extensive use was made of arable by-products such as pea-haulm silage, sugar-beet tops and barley straw, marginal costs of adopting EEC prices, which are mainly those of cereals, would be correspondingly lower than on farms where by-products were not available.

The estimates given above suggest that for the majority of rearers a switch to EEC costs and prices would prove on balance advantageous, to the tune of £22 and upwards for a first quality beast. It would, however, be unwise to assume that taking one year with another beef production inside the Community would, despite the continuing rise in demand on the Continent, necessarily ensure the UK producer the same regularity of net return which he at present derives from the market plus subsidies and deficiency payments. Those who have worked out an efficient and

[6] 98 per cent of EEC guide price (290s. 6d.) *minus* average UK price for 1966/67 (184s. 0d.) *minus* increased guarantees to 1970 (15s. 0d.) *plus* adjustment for comparability to include non-certificated cattle (20s. 0d.) *minus* allowance for calf and beef-cow subsidies (24s. 6d.) *equals* 87s. 0d.

[7] Assuming intervention levels derived from Duisburg.

[8] P. G. James and R. J. Gayton, *Beef on the arable farm* (Farm Economics Branch, Cambridge University, October 1961), Report No. 56. This was chosen from a fairly wide selection of beef cost studies, some of more recent date, since it recorded quantities of feed and not only costs. Fertilizer usage has been estimated from silage and hay consumption. EEC price assumptions are based on the reasoning put forward on other pages.

profitable production method mainly based on green forage would be encouraged to continue, and even expand, but whether a substantial number of new entrants would be drawn into the beef business seems doubtful. The hill farmer, who may now draw in subsidies the equivalent of an additional 47s. 0d. per cwt. (on an 8 cwt. beast), would find himself only a little better off than at present.

There can be no doubt that demand for beef in the EEC will continue to rise, owing partly to population increase but mainly to rising incomes. Even if, as happened in the early sixties, short-term cyclical factors continue to disturb this general trend, production is unlikely to exceed demand, except seasonally, for the foreseeable future. A recent report by OECD,[9] basing its calculations on the individual estimates of member governments, assesses the Community's deficit at 600,000 tons of beef and veal by 1970. According to the Commission's forecasts,[10] however, average import requirements for the three years 1969/70, 1970/71 and 1971/72 could be anything between 125,000 and 430,000 tons. The difference between these two alternatives, corresponding to 97·5 per cent and 92 per cent of self-sufficiency, springs mainly from assumptions about the proportion of live calves being carried on to beef weights. At present it is about 65 per cent. The smaller import need would imply an increase to 85 per cent, giving a maximum yield of beef and veal for the whole Community of over 5 mn. tons. This is hardly a realistic assumption. Though the switch in demand from veal to beef which has become evident, especially in Italy, is likely to continue, it will not of itself be enough to account for a major reduction in the number of calves slaughtered as vealers. The change will come about rather as a result of more widespread use of intensive methods of beef production, giving a quicker turnover of a larger number of lightweight beasts. In the meantime the 35 per cent rate of calf slaughter, resulting in an import requirement of over 430,000 tons, seems likely to persist until the early seventies.

To this probable deficit of the Six would have to be added, in an enlarged Community, the UK's import demand forecast by the National Plan at nearly 600,000 tons by 1970.[11] Export surpluses available from Denmark (145,000 tons) and the Republic of Ireland (325,000) would reduce the larger Community's theoretical deficit to about 560,000 tons. Allowance must, however, be made for the net fall in UK demands for beef and veal due to higher retail prices. Warley[12] estimates that UK consumption inside the EEC would be about 150,000 tons below its present level. This would bring back the Community of Ten's deficit to 410,000 tons, not far short of the current deficit of the Community of Six. Experience suggests that to close this gap at least another 10 per cent of calves in the Six

[9] *The market for beef and veal* (OECD, Paris, 1967).

[10] *Informations Internes sur l'agriculture* No. 7 (EEC, Brussels, June 1966).

[11] The figure is not specified in the Plan, but a net import requirement of 585,000 tons of carcass meat, including canned meat equivalent, has been deduced in the OECD report, *op. cit.*, Table S, p. 55.

[12] Warley, *Agriculture: the Cost of Joining the Common Market*, Table IX.

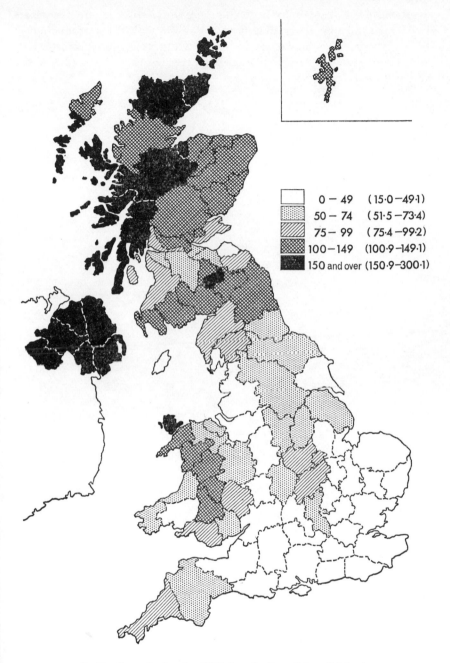

	0 – 49	(15·0 –49·1)
	50 – 74	(51·5 –73·4)
	75 – 99	(75·4 –99·2)
	100 –149	(100·9 –149·1)
	150 and over	(150·9 –300·1)

8. Beef cattle in the UK (excluding Isle of Man)

Per 1,000 acres of crops and grass, 1965. Figures for Northern Ireland are for that area as a whole.

(Source: UK Agricultural Statistics)

would have to be kept on for beef, and there would still be current increases in demand to be met over and above this. Even with rising production in the new member countries as well, the prospect of 100 per cent self-sufficiency for an enlarged Community recedes to the far end of the seventies.

8. Mutton, Lamb, and Wool

Sheep have traditionally played an important part in the husbandry of the British Isles, both in the hills and the lowlands. A multiplicity of local breeds and crosses is evidence of a native passion for genetical experiment and of nearly two centuries of trying to reconcile conflicting requirements of fleece and carcass meat. The British have as a result acquired a taste for the meat not generally shared by their continental neighbours, so that they normally eat at least half as much mutton and lamb as they do beef and veal. Among the members of the EEC only the French like lamb in any significant quantity, but even they eat not much more than a quarter the amount that the British or Irish do. Elsewhere in the Community sheep are rarely seen on the farms, or, as will be apparent from Table 17, on the menu either.

THE UNITED KINGDOM

Over the past ten years the UK sheep flock has increased by about 20 per cent, although the rate of expansion has slowed down since 1960. Home production, 244,000 tons in 1966/67, supplies about 40 per cent of demand, imports, mainly from New Zealand and the Irish Republic, having averaged about 350,000 tons over the past five years. Mutton and lamb constitute a fifth of total meat supplies, including poultry, and just over 10 per cent of home supplies. Although sheep only provide about 5 per cent of gross agricultural income (mutton and lamb 4·3 per cent and wool 0·8 per cent in 1966/67), a large proportion of it is earned, as can be seen from Map 9, on farms in the upland areas of Wales and Scotland.

Government support consists of deficiency payments on fat sheep and lambs and on wool. The guarantees announced each year after the Price Review are average prices subject to seasonal variations. The 1966/67 guaranteed price was 3s. 3·75d. per lb. (estimated dressed carcass weight) ($0.87 per kg.). Of the price actually received by producers, 3s. 2·75d., the deficiency payment amounted to 5·25d. or 13·5 per cent. The guaranteed price for wool, 4s. 5·25d. per lb. ($1.17 per kg.), involved a deficiency estimated at 1s. 5d. or nearly one-third. The deficiency payment for 1967/68 is likely to be about 2s. 0d. per lb. On the other hand, when world wool prices are high and the average realization price exceeds the guaranteed price, the exchequer receives a refund. In addition to the guaranteed prices farmers in upland areas also receive a hill subsidy of 21s. 0d. per ewe in the case of self-maintained flocks and of 10s. 6d. a head for flocks whose replacements are bought in.

TABLE 17. MUTTON, LAMB, AND WOOL:
PRODUCTION AND CONSUMPTION, 1965

	Total sheep numbers: UK=100	Comparative meat production: UK=100	Percentage of total meat production: the Six	Percentage of total meat production: the Ten	Degree of self-sufficiency per cent	Consumption per head per year[b] kg.	Comparative wool production: UK=100
Germany (FR)	3·4 (June)	5·7	7·2	2·8	82·4	0·2	6·4
France	30·3 (Oct)	54·9	68·7	26·4	90·5	2·9	46·3
Italy	26·4 (Jan)	12·7	15·9	6·1	83·8	0·8	20·6
Netherlands	1·6 (May)	4·5	5·6	2·2	—[a]	0·2	2·1
Belgium	0·53 (May)	2·1	2·6	1·0	} 62·5	0·4	1·2
Luxemburg	0·01 (May)	0·0	0·0	0·0			
The Six	62·3	79·9	100·0	38·5	92·0		76·6
United Kingdom	100·0 (June)	100·0		48·1	41·2	10·3	100·0
Ireland	15·6 (June)	20·9		10·0	137·8	10·7	20·6
Denmark	0·3 (July)	0·4		0·2	100·0	0·2	—
Norway	6·5 (June)	6·6		3·2	94·1	4·3	9·0
The Four				61·5	48·2		
The Ten				100·0	59·0		

[a] The Netherlands are a net exporter of mutton and lamb, but owing to the small volume of production and trade involved the self-sufficiency figure (550·0) is without significance.   [b] 1964/65.
Sources: FAO *Monthly Bulletin of Statistics*, February 1967. FAO, ECE, *Review of the Agricultural Situation in Europe*, 1966. *Food Consumption in the OECD Countries 1962/63–1964/65*. *Irish Statistical Bulletin*, December 1966. United Kingdom Statistics. CEC Intelligence *Bulletin*, September 1966. International Wool Secretariat.

As in the case of beef and cereals deficiency payments on fat sheep and lambs are made direct to producers by the Ministry of Agriculture and not through any marketing board. The subsidy for wool, however, is administered by the Wool Marketing Board, the sole purchaser of all home-produced wool. The wool is then sold by the Board to the merchant taking delivery of the wool with whom the producer has chosen to register. The Board deducts its marketing costs (about 6·25d. per lb.) from the guarantee payments.

THE EEC

In 1965 there were 18 mn. sheep in the whole EEC compared with 30 mn. in the UK. Numbers have been falling steadily, at a rate of about 200,000 a year, over the past fifteen years. In Germany there are only half as many as in 1950, and the Italian flock has been reduced by about 20 per cent during the same period. Since 1960, however, numbers have remained steady in France and increased slightly in the Netherlands. Almost the whole of the output from the Dutch saltmarshes is exported to France, which also accounts for 80 per cent of all EEC imports from third countries, totalling 16,000 tons in 1964/65.

In Germany and Italy, where the exodus from agriculture to industry, especially from upland areas, has been most marked, the reduction can be largely attributed to shortage of suitable labour for milking ewes, which are mainly used for cheese production. In France, not only is there a bigger demand for meat, whose production requires a less labour-intensive form of shepherding, but there is a somewhat wider market for French cheeses, such as Roquefort, made from sheep's milk.

There is a 20 per cent common external tariff on mutton and lamb bound in GATT, and in addition to this the French impose minimum import prices. But given the small scale of both production and consumption in the EEC it is not surprising that no steps have yet been taken to bring sheep meat under the CAP. National farmers' organizations have at times suggested that it should be. The question is as much a social as an agricultural one in backward mountainous areas of the Community like the Massif Central and the Apennines. The Commission seem to have considered three possible solutions, to be adopted either singly or in combination: import quotas, import levies based on a minimum internal reference price, and deficiency payments to producers to bridge the gap between market realizations and a guaranteed minimum price. However, with a large number of regulations for more important commodities having to meet deadlines by 1968, proposals for mutton and lamb are not likely to be given very high priority for the time being.

Wool, treated as an industrial product, bears no duty at the common frontier, and does not come under the Directorate-General for Agriculture.

THE UNITED KINGDOM AS A MEMBER OF THE EEC

If the present arrangements for sheep were extended to an enlarged Community the 20 per cent external tariff would, at recent price levels, represent an average of 6d. per lb. on imports on New Zealand lamb, raising its price to about 3s. 0d. Unless the New Zealanders were to absorb some of the tariff the UK producer should not therefore have much difficulty in obtaining from the market the 1967/68 guaranteed price of 3s. 3·75d., especially in view of the substantial rise in retail prices of beef resulting from adoption of the CAP. Without even a tariff to help him, however, he could hardly hope to get the same return as at present for wool. Over the past four years the deficiency payment has averaged about a fifth of gross returns. Further, Community practice hitherto suggests that the hill sheep subsidy, being 'product orientated', would be inadmissible. So that even though his costs, being largely grazing, would rise less than those of most other types of farmer, the sheep farmer in the UK, and particularly the hill sheep farmer (who besides getting the special subsidy receives a relatively larger return from wool than the lowlander), could suffer some loss of income.

Of the possible support systems which might be adopted by the EEC for fat sheep and lambs deficiency payments would seem to be the most desirable. A levy system would place a wholly inequitable burden on the UK. Precedents for durum wheat, olive oil, and oilseeds suggest that in cases involving a minority of producers or a commodity in which the Community has a very low degree of self-sufficiency, deficiency payments are deemed to be not incompatible with the Rome Treaty. The same reasoning could presumably be applied to wool, though it would first have to be reclassified as an agricultural product. The compatibility of the hill sheep subsidy is certainly more questionable. It properly falls into the range of problems, discussed elsewhere, concerned with special measures for disadvantaged regions. There would certainly seem to be a case for tempering the wind to the shorn hill lamb.

The Wool Marketing Board if converted into a union of producer groups would be handling more than half the output of an enlarged Community. The 5 per cent of turnover rule for groups is not, however, absolute and may be varied at the discretion of the Commission. It seems unlikely that a continuation of the Board's activities could constitute unfair competition for wool producers in other member countries (though it might be considered so for wool merchants). In Germany the *Wollverein*, a producer organization, has existed for a number of years, and attempts are being made by French producers to co-ordinate their marketing. The Board has since its inception provided producers with a measure of countervailing power in a market where merchant interests were notably dominant. Merchants might be glad to find an excuse to have its powers clipped.

There remains the problem of New Zealand imports, also referred to elsewhere. If concessions are to be made by the Community on the even more vital question of dairy products it seems likely that it would insist on

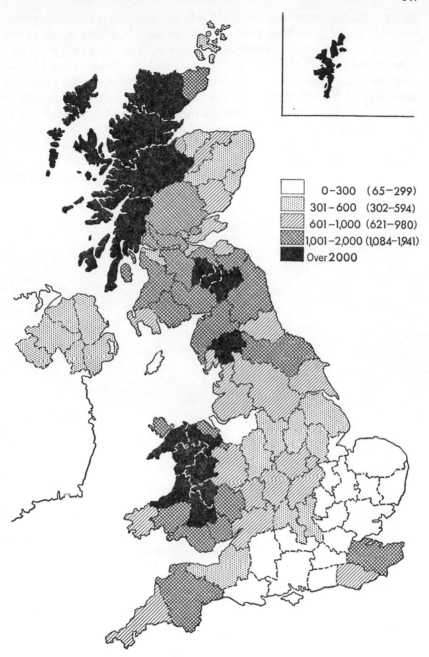

9. Sheep in the UK (excluding Isle of Man)

Per 1,000 acres of crops and grass, 1966 (Scotland 1965). Figures for Northern Ireland
are for that area as a whole.

(Source: UK Agricultural Statistics)

L

maintaining the 20 per cent tariff on lamb. It is impossible to estimate what the price elasticity of New Zealand lamb in the UK might be, given the unprecedented changes in the price of other meat which would be taking place at the same time, but inevitably there will be a substitution of Irish supplies from within an enlarged Community and home suppliers will take advantage of the higher price of imports to obtain a larger proportion of the UK market. Traditional disinclination on the part of the French housewife to purchase chilled or frozen meat limits the possibility for expanding New Zealand exports in other parts of the Community. Development of a rather specialized export market across the Channel by UK producers would, on the other hand, no longer be inhibited, as it has hitherto been, by levies.

9. Pigmeat

Few probably share the extreme devotion to the pig which Lord Emsworth gave to his 'Empress of Blandings', whose large and contented form gave him such comfort in the vicissitudes of aristocratic life. But it is hard to avoid being impressed by some of the peculiar qualities of the pig, its fecundity, its remarkable appetite, and its efficiency in making use of feed to put on weight. In the UK the pig's public image is further improved by association with the traditional breakfast of eggs and bacon.

The word pigmeat is American and is rarely heard on this side of the Atlantic where pork, bacon, and ham are preferred to the more general term. EEC statistics generally do not distinguish between the various forms which the pig can take after it has been slaughtered. For this reason we have used the word pigmeat both in the text and in the statistical summary, although it is an oddity in the English language.

TABLE 18. PIGMEAT: PRODUCTION AND CONSUMPTION, 1965

	Total pig numbers UK=100	Comparative production[a] UK=100	Percentage of total production:[a] the Six	Percentage of total production:[a] the Ten	Degree of self-sufficiency per cent	Consumption per head per year[b] kg.
Germany (FR)	214·9	208·2	44·2	30·7	98·1	39·8
France	115·8	142·1	30·2	21·6	94·6	29·4
Italy	67·8	40·2	8·5	5·9	96·2	9·7
Netherlands	47·0	48·5	10·3	7·1	129·0	25·6
Belgium	23·1	30·6	6·5	4·5	} 96·5	27·7
Luxemburg	1·3	1·4	0·3	0·2		
The Six	470·0	470·9	100·0	69·4	99·1	
United Kingdom	100·0	100·0		14·7	68·3	23·6
Ireland	15·9	15·3		2·3	150·8	29·0
Denmark	106·0	85·2		12·6	211·0	34·9
Norway	7·1	6·5		1·0	98·3	15·2
The Four				30·6	101·7	
The Ten				100·0	101·7	

a From indigenous animals. Wherever possible includes meat equivalent of exported live animals and excludes lard and offals.   b 1964/65 for EEC.

Sources: FAO/ECE, *Review of the agricultural situation in Europe, 1966*. FAO, *Monthly Bulletin of Agricultural Statistics*, February 1967. CEC *Intelligence Bulletin*, September 1966. EEC *Agricultural Statistics*, 1967 No. 8.

THE UNITED KINGDOM

The UK is more or less self-sufficient in pork. Supplies of bacon are limited by percentage quotas which are awarded annually, the biggest two quotas being given to Denmark and to domestic producers. Supplies from the latter source are largely determined by complicated pricing arrangements, made no easier for the layman to understand by prices being expressed per score (20 lb.) of deadweight (sheep prices are, perversely, expressed per lb. of estimated dressed carcass weight, and cattle per live hundredweight). The guaranteed price announced at the Annual Review is an average price subject to seasonal adjustment. It is also related to a stated compound feed price, representing a selection of compound feeds. The guaranteed price is automatically changed to take account of alterations during the year in this feed price. A further complication is provided by the flexible guarantee scale. The basic guaranteed price (46s. 0d. per score deadweight for 1966/67) applies to a forecast level of pigs marketed, in 1966/67 12·8 mn. to 13·6 mn. If numbers fall below this the price is automatically increased, for example, by 1·6 per cent if the level is between 12·5 mn. and 12·8 mn. or by 3 per cent if the level is between 12·2 mn. and 12·5 mn. Similarly, as numbers increase the guaranteed price is lowered. The effect of this can be quite severe. In May 1965 when there was a substantial increase in production the effective guaranteed price was reduced by a total of 5 per cent. While the pig market will always remain a difficult one to manage, the Ministry of Agriculture has through this complicated pricing system achieved some success in dealing with the pig cycle. It is now assisted by the activities of the Meat and Livestock Commission, previously carried out by the Pig Industry Development Authority, which is responsible, among other things (e.g. maintaining quality standards), for market information. The cost of implementing the guarantee has been as high as £51 mn. in 1962/63, and as low as £7 mn. in 1966/67. The average in recent years has been about £20 mn., equivalent to about 10 per cent of producers' returns.

Modern pigmeat production is a standardized factory-type operation, with feed constituting about two-thirds of costs, and conversion rates normally the key to profitability. Production techniques are so standardized that international comparisons of efficiency can be particularly revealing. The most relevant countries with which to compare the UK on costs of production are the Netherlands, acknowledged to be the leaders in pigmeat production in the EEC, and Denmark, the principal non-EEC pigmeat producer with a long-established trade in bacon with the UK amounting to more than half of the total market. A recent study[1] made use of statistics obtained from the Cambridge Pig Management Scheme which has been in operation for more than thirty years and of comparable material drawn from surveys carried out in the Netherlands and Denmark.

[1] F. G. Sturrock and R. F. Ridgeon, *A comparison of pig production in England, Denmark and Holland* (Farm Economics Branch, School of Agriculture, Cambridge University, December 1966).

Differences exist between the structure of the industry in the three countries, herds tending to be largest in the UK and smallest in the Netherlands. The Cambridge report found that differences in labour and overhead costs, which are likely to be associated with structural character-istics, are less important than feed costs, feed conversion rates, feed consumed by breeding stock, and number of weaners produced per sow per year. For all these costs, however, there had been a significant narrow-ing in national differences, compared with the situation ten years earlier when costs of production in the UK were about 60 per cent above the Danish level. As a result of improvements in all aspects of management, costs in the UK had fallen to only about 12 per cent above the Danish and less than 3 per cent above the Dutch. It seems likely that a further narrow-ing of the gap has occurred in the past two or three years with the result that UK, Danish and Dutch pig producers would now compete on nearly equal terms if it were not for artificial trade barriers and special government assistance.

THE EEC

In formulating a common agricultural policy for pigmeat the Com-munity has had to contend with the usual difficulties presented by differ-ences in price levels, production methods, and consumption patterns between member countries. Additionally, it has had to cope with some special problems, of which the notorious pig cycle is perhaps the most severe. Even before the full removal of intra-Community trade barriers this cycle, which had existed independently in all member countries, had become gradually synchronized in the Community. It is worth giving an example to show how severe the effects of this cycle can be. In early January 1964 prices exceeded the average for 1959–61 (the reference price) by 53 per cent in Belgium/Luxemburg, by 21 per cent in Germany, by 23 per cent in Italy, and by 41 per cent in the Netherlands. But by the end of that year prices had fallen back again by between 15 and 20 per cent.

As in the case of most other EEC agricultural commodities, domestic prices can be influenced by control at the common frontier. For pigmeat this is less effective partly because of the relatively high degree of Com-munity self-sufficiency and partly because the Community's cycle may correspond with that of other countries. For instance, reductions in the levies in the latter part of 1963 which should have affected prices in the period mentioned above were of limited value because non-member countries were also short of pigmeat.

The third special difficulty associated with pigmeat is its importance for the incomes of many small-scale farmers. In spite of the changes, already noted, that have occurred in the structure and efficiency of the industry, there are still many small producers whose incomes are severely affected by slumps in pigmeat prices. Consequently the Community has been com-pelled to introduce intervention buying and special assistance for storage.

The Community regulations governing pigmeat are contained in

Regulation 121/67 of June 1967, introduced just before the single market stage began on 1 July 1967. Protection against imports from third countries is provided by sluice-gate prices and levies. The latter comprise two components, one consisting of the difference between feed grain prices in the EEC and world market prices, and the other an element to give special protection to EEC producers. The latter now consists of a 7 per cent tariff based on the average sluice-gate price in the previous year. Sluice-gate prices, which are effectively minimum import prices, are determined by the Council of Ministers, on recommendations from the Commission, for three months in advance. Additional protection is given to EEC producers by the fixing of a basic price and by intervention on representative Community markets if prices fall below a certain percentage of this.

The basic price for 1967/68 was fixed at the equivalent of 55s. 7d. per score deadweight. Intervention may be made by the national intervention agencies, when authorized by the Management Committee in Brussels, provided that the price at which the intervention is made lies between 85 and 82 per cent of the basic price. These are equivalent to 47s. 10d. and 45s. 7d. per score deadweight. To encourage stock-piling in times of surpluses and low prices aids will be given to assist private storage of pigmeat.

THE UNITED KINGDOM AS A MEMBER OF THE EEC

As a result of higher cereal prices feed costs would rise very considerably. A fair estimate is that their effect would be to put up fattening costs by about 6s. 6d. per score deadweight for porkers, 10s. 0d. a score for baconers and 11s. 0d. a score for heavy hogs.[2] So far as returns are concerned widely differing results are obtained depending on what stage of the pig cycle is taken. In evidence before the 1967 Select Committee on Agriculture, the Ministry of Agriculture took 1965 for comparison's sake, when the average return to Community producers was 50s. and to UK producers 42s., both per score deadweight (calculated before devaluation). With a difference of food costs of 10s. the two appeared to be about equally placed at the time. The Pig Industry Development Authority's estimates, also quoted to the Select Committee, being based on Community prices in the latter half of 1966, which were considerably higher, make the prospects of EEC membership look rather more attractive to the UK pig producer. Under both systems the potential floor price is quite low, and the lowest point in the EEC intervention system, equivalent to 45s. 7d. per score, is just below the 1967/68 UK guaranteed price.

The main immediate worry of UK pigmeat producers is concerned with the simultaneous entry of Denmark, their traditional rival in the bacon market. Quota arrangements between Denmark and the UK would not, as fellow members of the EEC, be permitted. While Denmark would

---

[2] Based on typical costings for south-eastern England given in John Nix, *Farm Management Pocketbook* (University of London, Department of Agricultural Economics, November 1966).

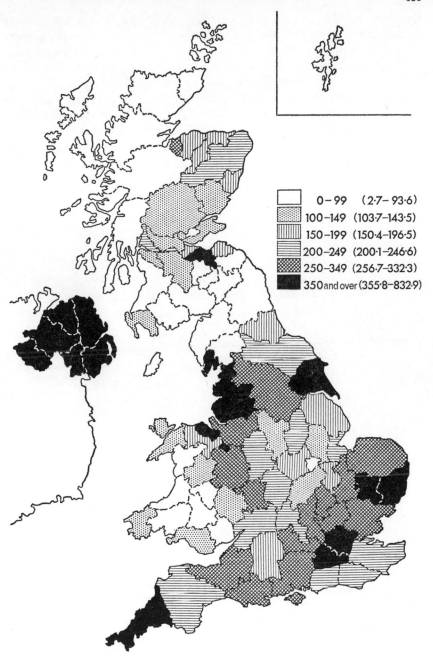

☐	0-99 (2·7-93·6)
▨	100-149 (103·7-143·5)
▥	150-199 (150·4-196·5)
▤	200-249 (200·1-246·6)
▩	250-349 (256·7-332·3)
■	350 and over (355·8-832·9)

10. Pigs in the UK (excluding Isle of Man)

Per 1,000 acres of crops and grass, Ø 1964–66. For 1964 Middlesex figures have been used for Greater London. Figures for Northern Ireland are for that area as a whole.
(Source: UK Agricultural Statistics)

therefore be free to sell as much bacon as it liked in the UK, export subsidization would be forbidden. As has already been shown the general level of efficiency of pigmeat production in the UK, though much improved, is still slightly inferior to that of Denmark, where the greater availability of skimmed milk will continue to be an important advantage. Denmark already has a large share (over half) of the UK bacon market and it will very probably be able to make further inroads. This will not be so disastrous for the home producer as might at first appear because the total UK demand for pigmeat should expand satisfactorily under EEC conditions, the rise in pigmeat prices being less than in beef prices.

10. Eggs

In the UK eggs at present account for an appreciably larger percentage of gross agricultural income than in the EEC. In 1965/66 it was about 18 per cent, compared with 7 per cent in Germany, where home production was still expanding to meet an unsatisfied demand, and between 4 and 5·5 per cent in the other member countries. This difference is to some extent due to the higher producer price of eggs in the UK relative to that of cereals and milk. A British farmer gets the same return from selling 180 dozen eggs as from selling a ton of wheat, and the German farmer has till now been in much the same position. But at recent price levels a French farmer would have had to sell over 220 dozen and a Dutch one nearly 300 dozen. The different price structure has meant that traditionally cereals do not occupy the same importance on small farms in the UK as they do on the Continent. In the UK eggs have therefore come to constitute a major secondary source of income after milk and their production has for political and social reasons enjoyed a measure of government support unknown in EEC countries. At the same time guaranteed producer prices at a relatively high level have, combined with low cereal feed costs, encouraged technical innovation and the development of large production units on a far wider scale than in the EEC. As can be seen from Table 19 the UK, with a laying flock a fifth the size of the Community's in 1965 had a total production equal to two-fifths, a disparity in average yields greatly influenced by the large proportion of barn-yard fowls still existing in France and Italy.

THE UNITED KINGDOM

The national laying flock is concentrated in five main regions (see Map 11). The first, in the south-east, with roughly 18 per cent of all layers, and the second, Lancashire, the West Riding of Yorkshire and the west and north Midlands, with about 28 per cent, are closely related to the major concentrations of human population (see Map 2). The other three, Northern Ireland (12 per cent), south-west England (12 per cent) and north-east Scotland (3 per cent), are more remote from urban markets, though the last two enjoy access to a substantial tourist trade. A proportion of Northern Irish supplies finds its way to Glasgow and the Lowland industrial area of Scotland.

The structure of production is changing rapidly. The number of producers sending eggs to packing stations fell from 300,000 in 1960 to under 110,000 in 1966, a reduction only marginally due to a switch by

TABLE 19. EGGS: PRODUCTION AND CONSUMPTION, 1965

	Laying hens[a] UK=100	Comparative production: UK=100	Percentage of total production: the Six	Percentage of total production: the Ten	Average yield per bird	Comparative yield UK=100	Degree of self-sufficiency %	Consumption per head[b] per year kg.
Germany (FR)	115·8	82·9	32·4	22·1	191	94·6	86·8	13·4
France	130·4	62·5	24·4	16·7	132	65·3	100·1	11·0
Italy	175·0	60·3	23·6	16·0	92	45·5	93·0	9·7
Netherlands	33·7	29·3	11·5	7·8	202	100·0	139·3	12·6
Belgium	22·7	20·3	8·0	5·4	221	109·4 }	120·0	14·8
Luxemburg	0·6	0·3	0·3	0·1	150	74·3		
The Six	478·4	255·5	100·0	68·1				
United Kingdom	100·0	100·0		26·7	202	100·0	98·5	14·9
Ireland	5·5c	5·4		1·4	140[d]	69·3[d]	100·2	15·2
Denmark	13·8	10·4		2·8	194	96·0	130·6	12·4
Norway	6·1	3·9		1·0	157e	77·7e	99·1	8·4
The Four				31·9			100·8	
							99·0	

a End of year except for Norway (June).   b 1964/65.   c Fowls over 6 months only.   d Estimated.   e 1964.

Sources: EEC, Agricultural Statistics, 1967, No. 2. FAO/ECE: Review of the Agricultural Situation in Europe 1966. Food Consumption in OECD Countries, 1962/63–1964/65. Norway: Jordbruksstatistikk 1965. UK Trade Statistics.

producers to direct sales. Although these increased by about 18 per cent, packing station throughput also went up by nearly 12 per cent during the period. The British Egg Marketing Board's producer surveys also reveal a remarkable shift in flock size. In 1961 about 30 per cent of eggs reaching packing stations came from producers with 1,000 or more birds. By 1966 the proportion had risen to nearly three-quarters. Whereas in 1960 79·5 per cent of commercial flocks were sending six cases (of 360 eggs) or less a week to packing stations, six years later the proportion had fallen to 33 per cent, and of the other two-thirds well over half were sending over 40 cases a week. The shift is reflected in changes in the system of management during the same six years. In October 1966 8 per cent of flocks were kept on free range compared with 24 per cent in 1960; the proportion of deep-litter flocks had been more than halved during the period; and 67 per cent were housed in battery cages compared with 17 per cent in 1960.

Since 1957 all producers with more than 50 head of poultry have been required to register with the British Egg Marketing Board. This statutory body is elected by registered producers, voting power being proportionate to the number of layers kept by each producer. The Board is the purchaser of all eggs offered for sale through packing stations (about 66 per cent of eggs produced for human consumption). Registered producers may also sell direct to consumers or, under 'B' licence from the Board, to retailers. About 10 per cent, or just over a quarter of eggs not sold through packing stations, are, according to returns made by licence holders to the Board, sold under licence. The Board sells the first quality eggs which it has purchased either to the packing stations at which they have been graded or to other packing stations or wholesalers. First quality eggs for which the Board can find no buyer, and all second quality (and extra small) eggs, are broken out by processers working under contract to the Board. Egg products for which there is no market at home or abroad are stored at the Board's expense.

The possibility of disposing of surplus shell eggs by exporting them is restricted to a few small traditional markets such as Malta and Gibraltar, Kuwait, and the Argentine. Exports to about 50 countries, including all the major industrialized ones, are virtually excluded under the spirit if not the letter of the GATT. The placing on these markets, many of them in a state of near over-supply, of quantities of eggs produced under subsidized conditions, and by a country not a traditional exporter, could cause major perturbations.

The Board's administrative costs, as well as expenditure on advertising and sales promotion and on market and technical research are met out of a levy of 0·5d. per dozen on all eggs sold through packing stations and of 0·25d. per dozen on those sold direct to retailers under 'B' licence.

Packing stations

Packing stations, all independent private or co-operative enterprises, are remunerated by the Board as its collecting agents, mainly on the basis of the number of cases collected, but with some allowance made for the number of different points at which eggs have to be picked up.[1] In May 1967 there were 425 authorized packing stations, operated by 328 packers, in the UK (compared with 593 in 1960), with an average weekly throughput of about 1,020 cases. Average throughput varies considerably from one part of the country to another, as can be seen from the figures in the Table below, which themselves conceal an even greater spread between the largest packing stations and the smallest.

TABLE 20. UK THROUGHPUT OF FIRST QUALITY[a]
EGGS, WEEK ENDING 20 MAY 1967
('000 cases)

	No. of packing stations	Total cases	Per cent of total	Average cases per station
England	277	316·8	72·9	1·14
Wales	25	13·6	3·1	0·54
Scotland	39	26·6	6·1	0·68
N. Ireland	84	77·6	17·9	0·92
UK	425	434·6	100·0	1·02

a Total throughput of eggs includes an additional 7·7 per cent of extra smalls and seconds.
Source: BEMB.

Of the Board's twelve administrative regions, Northern Ireland (six counties) had 17·9 per cent of throughput, SW England (six counties) 16·2 per cent, NW England (three counties) 12·7 per cent, and East Anglia (seven counties) 12·7 per cent. These proportions remain fairly constant.

Something over 40 per cent of the throughput of English packing stations is believed to be in the hands of the 18 producer co-operatives dealing in eggs, with a combined turnover of £33·8 mn. in 1965, of which the two largest account for well over half. Yorkshire Egg Producers, with a turn-over of £12·3 mn. occupy a strong position in the north, and Thames Valley (£7 mn. turnover) and United Suprema Farmers (£8·1 mn. turn-over, of which about £3·9 mn. is due to eggs) in the southern half of the country. A distinctive distributive pattern has been established by the major co-operatives in contracting with supermarkets and other chains to deliver direct to, and regularly supply, each store or branch shop instead of supplying central depots for subsequent redistribution by the chains. A number of the national chains, however, operate their own packing stations.

Although the Board, as the central purchaser of all eggs reaching packing stations, fixes the weekly prices for all grades of eggs which it will pay producers, packing stations are at liberty to attract a larger throughput by means of additional inducements in the way of bonuses relating to either

[1] For every case declared weekly by a packing station the Board pays 7s. 5d. into a central pool. Out of this pool an initial payment of 2s. 0d. per pick-up is made regardless of the number of cases picked up. The balance is then distributed on a per case basis, usually amounting to about 6s. 8d. In addition packing stations receive from the Board 1s. 6d. per case towards the cost of Keyes trays, and a rebate of 8d. on each case retained for re-sale.

size of pick-up or to value of eggs sold. For producers sending away 50 or more cases a week these may amount to 2·0d. a dozen and upwards. Uneconomic use of transport is gradually being eliminated by the disappearance of small pick-ups, two cases a week now being considered for this purpose the bare economic minimum; some packing stations are already disinclined to collect less than five cases from a single point. A packing station is in theory bound to accept on behalf of the Board all eggs offered to it by a registered producer, but this obligation to collect has not, so far, been seriously tested.

Over a third of home-produced eggs sold now by-pass the packing stations. With more townspeople owning cars each year the volume of direct egg sales on farms is inevitably increasing, but there is also evidence of growing purchases of unstamped eggs at retail. These are preferred to eggs graded and stamped at packing stations, and command a price premium, in the often mistaken belief of the purchasers that they are fresher, have been produced out of doors, or are more likely to have been laid by pullets reared without antibiotic prophylaxis.

The British Egg Marketing Board receives an exchequer subsidy, in the form of a basic deficiency payment and a supplementary payment, on each dozen eggs sold. The basic payment is equal to the difference between the guaranteed price and either the Board's estimated average selling price (including the equivalent price for products) per dozen for first quality eggs or an 'indicator' price, whichever is the higher. The indicator price (3s. 1d. per dozen for 1967/68) represents what the Board might be expected to receive from a market that is not over-supplied. If the average selling price is lower than the indicator price (which it usually is) the Board receives 40 per cent of the difference as a supplementary payment. This proportion is due to be reduced by 10 per cent a year from 1968/69. The guaranteed price fixed annually by the government is adjusted during the year for changes in a feed price index and applies only to first quality eggs. The subsidy is distributed by the Board through the payments which it makes to producers for eggs sold to it through the packing stations. Eggs sold by producers direct to consumers or retailers therefore receive no part of the subsidy.

In an attempt to win over a proportion of the eggs by-passing the packing stations, as well as to encourage more level deliveries from producers, the Board in 1966 introduced a contract scheme. Producers taking part in the scheme (a total of 92,000 in 1967/68) receive a premium of 4·0d. per dozen (above the current basic weekly price announced by the Board for each grade of eggs) for a quantity of eggs per quarter not exceeding one-eighth of their total previous two years' deliveries to packing stations. Supplies reaching packing stations in excess of the contracted maxima only qualify for the basic price (which is itself reduced from what it might otherwise have been owing to retention by the Board of funds out of which to distribute premiums to contracting producers). Since entitlements are allotted on a quarterly and not an annual basis producers who, mainly for veterinary reasons, prefer to replace their laying flocks on an 'all in—all out' basis find themselves at a disadvantage. In the quarter during which buildings are being cleaned out and replacement pullets are coming into lay they are unable to fulfil their quota. Officially recognized consortia, each consisting of not more than 36 producers, may, however, pool their entitlements and thus maximize premiums to all members, each gaining some advantage from the entitlements of those clearing out their birds which are not being taken up.

In its first year the contract scheme by no means achieved its objective and substantial numbers of eggs continued to by-pass the packing stations. The Board therefore decided to seek powers enabling it to offer a much larger incentive by paying to non-contracting producers making casual sales to the Board a lower price than the basic price paid to contracting producers.

THE EEC

Germany (Federal Republic)

Germany is still by far the largest egg importing country of the Six. Both numbers of layers and gross egg production have risen, the latter at a slightly increasing annual rate, since 1958. The cyclical reduction which has been apparent in the other countries since 1965 has not therefore occurred in Germany. Between 1962 and 1966 numbers of laying birds rose by 16 per cent in the Federal Republic as a whole, the biggest increase (23 per cent) being in Lower Saxony, which contains just over a quarter of the total layer population. North Rhine-Westphalia has 23 per cent of the German national flock and Bavaria comes third with 20 per cent. Egg production has been traditionally concentrated in the north-west and in the south-east. Since the war the layer population of the north-west has more than doubled, the region being accessible both to imported supplies of grain through the North Sea and Rhine ports and to the expanding industrial populations of the Ruhr and the Middle Rhine. In the south-east, cut off from its traditional grain supplies along the Danube and from the East German market, the egg industry has expanded by no more than 20 per cent since 1945. This has been largely due to a marked cost/price disadvantage. For the five-year period 1957/58 to 1961/62 the average number of grammes of layers' mash to be bought for the price of one egg was 308 in Bavaria, compared with 347 in Lower Saxony and between 354 and 400 in North Rhine-Westphalia.[2]

There are no published figures of flock size more recent than 1963, when flocks of 1,000 birds or more comprised 16 per cent of the national flock,[3] an increase of 4 per cent over 1961. It seems likely that the proportion is now at least 25 per cent. There are a number of 10,000-bird flocks, about 20 units of between 50,000 and 300,000 and one of 500,000 in West Berlin.

[2] F. Hülsemeyer, *Die Erzeugung und Vermarktung von Eiern und Geflügelfleisch in der BR Deutschland* (Kiel, 1966), p. 69.

[3] H. Gocht, *Marktstruktur und Preisbildung bei Eiern und Eiprodukten in der BR Deutschland* (Bonn, 1966), p. 11.

It seems doubtful whether a draft bill restricting the sizes of agricultural enterprises for social reasons (10,000 being the proposed maximum in the case of layers) will ever obtain enough support to become law. In any case large-scale expansion is likely to be limited by its high capital cost. If production has expanded on what are by German standards medium and larger holdings (25 to 125 acres) rather than on the very small family farms it is because for a 5,000-bird unit the cost is about 60s. 0d. a bird for buildings, equipment and point-of-lay pullet.

It is estimated that only a third of eggs sold off farms passes through private or co-operative packing stations. Of the balance sold direct by producers (either at farm-gate, from door-to-door, or to retailers and caterers) nearly 20 per cent are bought by itinerant dealers, often on a barter basis, who re-sell to retail shops or to consumers. This volume of direct off-farm sales is highest (about 80 per cent of all sales) in country districts, but still represents between 35 and 40 per cent of all sales even in cities of 100,000 inhabitants and above. The premium enjoyed by un-stamped 'farm' eggs (ranging from 2·5d. to 8·0d. a dozen according to season and area) on a market which taken as a whole has only been just over 80 per cent self-sufficient is the main reason for the slow development of packing stations. These exist mainly in the intensive production areas, but out of 81 in the Federal Republic with a weekly throughput of over 50 cases (of 360 eggs) a week in 1964, only 16 were sending away 1,000 cases or more. This compares with an average for the whole UK at that time of 923 cases from 532 packing stations. Although four packing station groups in the north and north-west had by 1966 made contracts with a number of large retail outlets, supermarkets and other chains have, due to the atom-istic nature of home supplies, had to rely, both for quality and quantity, mainly on the purchase of imported eggs on the wholesale market.

The unified EEC market will deprive German producers of the sub-stantial degree of protection which they have enjoyed since 1962 from intra-Community levies, and before that from government subsidies. An increase in imports, and the impetus likely to be given to larger-scale domestic production by a simultaneous fall in prices of both cereals and eggs after July 1967 should lead rapidly to a saturation of the German market. In the consequent shake-up numbers of medium-sized laying units and most of the smaller packing stations look like disappearing over the next two or three years, and the pattern of concentration familiar in other countries will begin to emerge. Whether direct sales will continue on their present scale, particularly of those to travelling dealers, depends largely on the nature of the common marketing regulations adopted by the Com-munity, but the dealers are bound in any case to lose by the disappearance of the smaller producers of whom they are the main customers.

France

Poultry are not included in the producer returns which form the basis of French agricultural statistics. Total numbers can therefore only be very roughly estimated. The geographical pattern of egg production, if not its actual volume, can be seen from the concentration of hatcheries, all of which make compulsory returns of throughput. Of the 1,360 hatcheries making returns in 1965[4] the 220 (17 per cent) with an incubator capacity of 50,000 and over accounted for 65 per cent of total capacity. Nearly 60 per cent of all day-old chicks of laying breeds (18·7 mn. hatched in 1965) are hatched west and north of a line Toulouse-Poitiers-Mézières (on the Belgian frontier) coinciding almost exactly with the 600-foot contour of the south-eastern upland two-thirds of France. Within the lowland north-western third of the country output is heavily concentrated in Brittany (24 per cent) and in the Parisian and central regions (21 per cent), with much smaller nuclei in the south-west, upper Normandy and along the Belgian frontier. In south-eastern France, round Lyon, an outlying area accounts for just under 10 per cent of total hatchery output.

Very little is yet known about the structure of egg production within these major geographical groupings. In addition to the 19 mn. day-old pullet chicks of laying breeds produced by hatcheries, about half the 39 mn. 'as hatched' day-olds of unspecified breeds might be presumed to become layers, and possibly another 15–20 mn. are still hatched by natural means. In France as a whole farmyard hens, estimated to have been declining at the rate of about 2 mn. a year since 1963, are still believed to comprise at least two-thirds of the national flock, with the remaining third in commercial units. In the main areas served by the large hatcheries these proportions would probably be reversed. Efforts have been made from time to time, for social and political reasons, to set an upper limit to flock size. Although these have never been rigorously applied, and can in any case be circumvented, very large laying units are still exceptional. They are less likely to develop in Brittany, essentially a region of family small-holdings, and the south-east, than round Paris, where relatively large arable farms are close to a mass market. Restrictions on entry into farming by 'non-professionals' provide another check to the investment of outside capital in large-scale commercial egg production.

Until now the farmyard egg has played a key role in the pattern of French egg prices. About 50 per cent of all eggs reaching the market during a year are reckoned to have been laid by the hens of uncertain age and breeding who scratch for their livelihood in peasant *basses-cours*. Since virtually no costs of production are imputed to them they are often disposed of at a price equivalent to the feed-cost of commercially produced eggs, usually as payment in kind to local grocers making deliveries to the farm. The grocers, having themselves a relatively small retail outlet for eggs, thus become willy-nilly collectors of eggs for one of the 4,000 licensed packing stations (*centres de conditionnement*) existing in France. For most of the year farmyard eggs represent not more than 10 per cent of arrivals on the central market of les Halles at Paris, but the highly seasonal

A. Canguilhem *et al.*, *Etude de la production de poussins d'un jour par les accouveurs en 1965* (Ministry of Agriculture, Paris, January 1966).

nature of this type of production has always resulted in their having a particularly strong marginal effect on market prices in the spring, when they may form as much as 25 per cent of supplies. Following a stringent tightening up of quality standards by the veterinary authorities in Paris, however, this depressing effect is likely in future to become increasingly smaller. The known poor keeping quality of farmyard eggs has, in any case, begun to eliminate them from les Halles in the warmer months.

The authorized packing stations include a number established on farms by producers themselves, and about 20 per cent of production is sold direct to retailers in this way. A regulation forbidding the direct sale to consumers or retailers of more than five dozen ungraded eggs a week appears to be fairly effectively policed through inspection of wholesale markets, packing stations, and farms where commercial production is carried out. Since country grocers are by tacit agreement exempt from inspection a proportion of farmyard eggs consumed locally escapes this net, but, as most of the eggs which they collect find their way on to the wholesale market through packing stations, evasion of the five-dozen rule is by no means as widespread as might at first seem likely. In any case the *œuf fermier* has a quite opposite reputation for freshness from its English counterpart and invites no kind of price premium.

Co-operatives control about 30 per cent of packing station throughput, all but a very small proportion of which is sold at retail. There are no large co-operative packing stations and only one small breaking-out plant. The private sector, on the other hand, has traditionally sold to the wholesale market or to the manufacturing trade, though a trend towards direct sales to retailers is now becoming noticeable. About half a dozen exceptionally large private packing stations, with a throughput of between 6,000 and 8,000 cases a week, have emerged very recently, some equipped with their own breaking-out plants.

The approach of the unified egg market caused considerable alarm among French producers, more experienced than most in the effects of seasonal and cyclical surpluses. Taking advantage of the 1962 *Loi d'Orien-tation Agricole*, certain of whose provisions encouraged the formation of producer groups and the association of these groups under regional committees (*comités économiques régionaux*), four such associations had already been constituted, covering all France, in 1965, with a national federation to co-ordinate their activities. Early in 1967 each *comité* obtained authority to impose certain obligations on all producers in its region with 500 or more layers, whether members of producer groups or not. Although in principle this so-called *extension des règles de discipline* should be subject to a producer referendum, an accelerated procedure allowed under the 1962 Law in case of urgency was adopted. Objectors had the chance to put their views to local independent courts of inquiry, though no effective opposition appears to have been raised. Some of the obligations thus extended to all producers were the same as those already adopted voluntarily by the *comités* (provision of statistical information on

M

production and marketing, uniform standards for grading and packaging, central payment, etc.), but the two most important aspects were new: fixing of a buying-in price (*prix de retrait*), and setting up of a market fund financed out of producer levies for the purpose of intervention.

The job of administering these new mandatory rules, and of operating the market intervention fund, falls to the *Société Interprofessionnelle des Produits Avicoles* (SIPA-ŒUF—there is a parallel organization for poultry meat—SIPA-VOLAILLE). This includes representatives of the national federation of regional economic committees, of the national association of egg-packing stations, and of the egg products industry. Producers have a 50 per cent vote on the SIPA's executive council and general assembly, and the interests of private enterprise and co-operatives among both producers and processers are carefully balanced.

The success of an experimental intervention on the Paris market during the 1967 spring flush, before the SIPA had become fully operational, led to considerable optimism among its sponsors about the possibilities of the new scheme. On that occasion the removal of a relatively small quantity of shell eggs from the market is said to have been sufficient to raise prices again to a tolerable level. This was carried out at the expense of the egg breakers since no form of producer levy had yet been introduced. On 1 July, 'vesting day' for the unified market in eggs, a number of major problems still faced the SIPA. No decision had yet been taken on the amount of the levy and the basis on which it should be raised. A charge levied at hatcheries on day-old chicks as well as one on eggs passing through packing stations seemed the most likely means of obtaining the widest coverage. These charges would inevitably be felt by many producers with 500 birds and less even though they were nominally exempt from the *extension des règles*, but considering the large contribution still made to the market, and especially to the spring flush, by small producers such an arrangement could hardly be thought inequitable. The amount of the levy would depend on the level of intervention envisaged. The intention has been that this should be set relatively low, the object of intervention being merely to prevent a serious collapse of the market. It would not therefore be very costly.

This optimistic view rests on two premises. First it is assumed that there will continue to be a ready market for broken-out eggs so that the SIPA will not have to bear on top of any marketing loss that it may incur the very high cost of storing surplus egg products. Second, the arrival on the French market of substantial imports from other member countries has been largely discounted. Neither assumption seems in the long run justifiable. *Pasta* manufacture will continue to absorb a substantial proportion of egg products in Italy and Germany, but in the EEC as a whole, where plant bakeries are still the exception, demand for frozen or liquid egg by the bread and confectionery trade is likely to expand very slowly. As far as imports of shell eggs into France are concerned, French producers are militant to the point of paranoia about the possibility of dumping by the

Dutch, which they are determined to oppose by every means. They would properly expect, and no doubt obtain, swift redress from the Commission if eggs were in fact being offered below cost of production, which, in the case of the Netherlands, is known from officially published costings. It seems that the Commission took a very long hard look at a Dutch scheme for forming export groups before eventually agreeing to it for a limited period. French producers seem far less concerned by the much more likely risk that member countries like Belgium and the Netherlands with relatively low production costs and large export surpluses will simply take advantage of the SIPA's intervention arrangements to unload on to the French market eggs at low, but not dumped, prices at around intervention level. The SIPA, with no control over imports, will find itself trying to keep afloat a leaking boat which fills up as fast as intervention measures bale it out.

The Netherlands

The total of 18·1 mn. layers given in official statistics excludes backyard hens (about 1·5 mn.) but includes breeding stock (3 mn.). Non-commercial production is therefore relatively small, about 5 per cent of total. Commercial output has been traditionally directed to export. Over 70 per cent of Netherlands production comes from the south-eastern provinces of Gelderland, Noordbrabant, and Limburg. Units of 1,000 birds or over are rare (3 per cent of all commercial flocks in 1966) and 80 per cent of all flocks have fewer than 200 layers.

Hatchery returns show a notable levelling out of seasonal demand for day-old chicks of laying breeds during the past five years. This, and a steady rise in average yields per hen, are indications of the efficient state of the Netherlands industry, which has remained to a large extent competitive in the export market while absorbing rising costs, especially of feed. These went up by over 20 per cent, largely due to the adjustment of cereal prices upwards towards the common EEC level, between 1960 and 1965.

As is to be expected from the small scale of production, distribution, including export, is mainly through co-operative packing stations. The 10 to 15 per cent of output sold direct to consumers mostly originates outside the three poultry provinces. Owing to intra-Community levies protecting Germany, the Netherlands' major export market, since 1962 total production has been falling steadily. By 1966 there were 40 per cent fewer producers than in 1961. There has also been some concentration of packing stations in response to the official encouragement of exporting groups that aroused French suspicions. The unified market will provide an opportunity for the export machine to move into higher gear.

Belgium

A considerable divergence is evident between poultry statistics derived from the twice-yearly returns and those based on Ministry estimates from chick placings and imports and exports of day-old chicks. Although, with the switch from farmyard to commercial production, the divergence continues to decrease from year to year, census returns still appear to under-declare numbers by anything up to one-third. This is no doubt due to a widespread but unfounded suspicion on the part of farmers that statistics and taxes are collected by the same authority. Sample surveys of producers now in hand should help further to increase the reliability of the Ministry's estimates. The census figures can, however, be used as a guide to the geographical distribution of the national laying flock, just over half of which is in Flanders (roughly speaking between Brussels and the North Sea), and another 15 per cent in the adjoining northern province of Antwerp. Over 80 per cent of Belgium's 14 mn. laying birds are believed to be in commercial units, but no reliable information is yet available about their distribution by flock size. As in the Netherlands, egg production is generally linked to small farm enterprises, and very large units are exceptional. About 75 per cent of the eggs marketed pass through packing stations.[5]

Italy

Information about the Italian poultry industry is sparse, unreliable, and out of date. Distribution costs, like those of most foodstuffs, are high, especially in the centre and south of the country. Commercial egg production, some of it on a fairly large scale, is concentrated in the north, in the Po valley and in the Veneto. Elsewhere demand is mainly satisfied by the farmyard hen. Particularly in the far south consumption is still low compared with the rest of the Community and there are long-term prospects for egg production going beyond a closing of the present 7 per cent gap between supply and demand. Enforcement of uniform EEC regulations on grading and packing should help to get rid of some of the barnacles on the distributive system. Eventually this will raise demand by lowering prices and improving quality.

EEC Regulations

It is not intended that there should be any direct internal price support for shell eggs. Protection by external levies against imports from third countries will, however, be substantial,[6] and help to mitigate the effects of seasonal surpluses within the Community, especially once it becomes self-sufficient. This seems likely to occur by 1969. The egg-cycle, which has already to a great extent become harmonized during the transition period, will become fully integrated once the intra-Community levies have disappeared. The summer of 1967 having been a price trough in each of the

---

[5] See also R. Goffinet and A. Ledent, *Production, commerce extérieur et consommation d'œufs, Belgique—CEE, 1950–64*, Cahiers de l'IEA (Brussels, May 1966).

[6] Regulation 122/67 applies equally to egg products, levies on which are calculated by means of fixed co-efficients (e.g. the levy on dried whole egg is 4·3 times that on shell eggs). Imports which are to be re-exported in processed form are subject to special conditions and exemptions (*régime du trafic de perfectionnement actif*).

six countries, the first proper Community peak should begin to appear in the autumn of 1968.

Levies consist of two components:

(a) a variable component (per kg. of eggs or hatching eggs) equal to the difference in the feed cost of producing one kg. of eggs (or hatching eggs) inside the Community and outside it, due to the difference in the price of feed grains in the Community and on the world market. For the purposes of calculating this component Community prices are deemed to be the threshold prices fixed annually on 1 August and subject to monthly increments. World market prices are calculated quarterly from 1 August (and fixed for a quarter ahead) on the basis of prices over the previous six months, but remain unaltered on the last three quarter days if no change is being made in the sluice-gate price (see below).

(b) a fixed component equal to 7 per cent of the average sluice-gate price for shell eggs (or hatching eggs) for the four quarters up to 1 May preceding the 1 August on which the component is fixed. It is fixed for a period of twelve months ahead.

The close interlocking of variable levies with sluice-gate prices is evident. These minimum import prices are an additional form of protection against abnormally low offers from third countries. When import prices c.i.f. or free-at-frontier fall below the sluice-gate level a supplementary levy is imposed on all imports equivalent to the difference between the offering price and the sluice-gate price. Goods are thus prevented from entering the Community at a price which when raised by the amount of the variable levy alone could still cause disturbances on the internal market.

At a fairly early stage of the transition period it was found that the sluice-gate mechanism was being evaded by various means. Eggs would, for instance, be invoiced at the full sluice-gate price, thus attracting no supplementary levy at the frontier, but rebates would subsequently be credited to the importer's account in the exporting country. As a result it was decided to make application of supplementary levies automatic, though any country prepared to sign an undertaking that none of its exports will be offered at below sluice-gate price can obtain exemption. This has been done by South Africa, Poland, and Finland.

Sluice-gate prices are fixed quarterly in advance, taking into account changes in feedgrain prices on the world market during the preceding six months. The conversion factor per kg. of eggs has, as in the case of the variable component of the basic levy, hitherto been based on the hypothesis of an average annual yield of 215 eggs per bird, a proportion of 85 per cent of pullets, and a proportion of 80 per cent of maize in the feed, and it allows for feeding up to point of lay.

The free-at-frontier or c.i.f. price which forms the basis of the supplementary levy is determined by the lowest current offer on the world market. However, should abnormally low offers arise on one or more markets a second free-at-frontier price is determined, on which the supplementary levy applicable to those countries' exports is then based.

To give some idea of the practical effect which these regulations would have on imports into the UK, basic levies and sluice-gate prices operative during the first six months of the unified market have been applied in the following Table to c.i.f. prices of imports into the UK during the same period. It is evident that inside the EEC the degree of protection for UK producers

TABLE 21.   UK/EEC: ESTIMATED IMPORT PRICES OF LARGE EGGS (16½ lbs per 120)

(pence per dozen)

Date	Country of Origin	c.i.f.[a] price	s.g. price	Supp. levy	Basic levy	Total levy	Duty paid price EEC	UK[b]
25.7.67	Denmark	22·8	32·8	10·0	7·8	17·8	40·6	24·6
1.8.67	S. Africa	24·0[c]	32·8	8·8	7·8	16·6	40·6	24·0[d]
26.9.67	Finland	25·8[c]	32·8	7·0	7·8	14·8	40·6	27·6
16.1.67	Denmark	35·3	38·2[e]	2·9	9·1[e]	12·0	47·3	37·1
23.1.67	Sweden	26·4	38·2	11·8	9·1	20·9	47·3	28·2
30.1.67	Finland	28·8[c]	38·2	9·4	9·1	18·5	47·3	30·6

a Quoted on London Egg Exchange.
b Import duty of 1s. 6d. per 120 eggs.
c Would not be offered below sluice-gate price c.i.f. EEC ports.
d Preferential nil duty.
e Allowance made for devaluation.

Sources: *The Grocer. CEE Informations, Marchés Agricoles.*

against imports from non-EEC countries would be substantially greater than at present.

Export restitutions may be granted on eggs and egg products. They are uniform throughout the EEC, but can be varied according to the country of destination.

Although there is to be no form of direct intervention a number of Community measures are envisaged to 'adjust the volume of supply to the requirements of the market'. They specifically exclude any official buying-in policy and are to be such as to (a) encourage producers to improve, on their own initiative, the organization of production, processing and marketing of eggs; (b) improve quality; (c) establish short- and long-term production forecasts; and (d) help make available market intelligence on price trends.

These steps towards a better ordering (*régularisation*) of the market are to be the subject of detailed regulations during the course of the next year or two. The first of the four objectives was touched on in the draft regulation on producer groups and their unions submitted by the Commission to the Council of Ministers in February 1967.[7]

It should not be supposed that all the decisions on a unified market for eggs were taken at the marathon of June 1964. The acceptance by the Council of Ministers of the Commission's proposal for stamping, grading, and packaging, and for the licensing and inspection of packing stations, submitted in May 1967, could involve a great deal of bargaining and compromise among the Six. The Commission's proposal has already been returned to them once by the Council. Its main features were that

7 See pp. 67-68.

(a) except that a producer may sell on the farm up to five dozen eggs at a time to a consumer for his personal needs, all shell eggs (other than hatching eggs) must reach the consumer by way of a licensed packing station;

(b) all shell eggs sold wholesale or retail must have been first graded by size and quality; this (including the regrading of stale eggs) may only be carried out at a licensed packing station;

(c) eggs which have been subjected to any cleaning process (wet or dry) do not qualify as Grade 'A';

(d) stamping of Grade 'A' eggs is optional, but may be enforced by the government of any member country for eggs produced within its territory. They may carry the trade mark of a packing station. Stamping of Grade 'B' and Grade 'C' eggs is obligatory throughout the Community.

Controversy on these issues has tended to become polarized round the *dirigiste* outlook of the French on the one hand, and the *laisser-faire* attitude of the Germans on the other. But aside from this philosophical consideration French producers have already had some experience of the undesirable results of uncoordinated supplies of eggs reaching a saturated market. In Germany protection against imports and absence of an internal surplus have so far lessened the urgency for orderly marketing. Dutch producers, though traditionally disciplined in their attitude to agricultural marketing, are as exporters mainly concerned that the new regulations should not impede the free flow of eggs within the Community, or require stamping of eggs with country of origin. This view is shared in Belgium. The French have objected to the incorporation of their 'extra-fresh' grade (minimum size of air-cell 4 mm.) distinct since 1939 from 'fresh' (6 mm. minimum) into a communal Grade 'A' (also 6 mm.) category. The Commission by making stamping of Grade 'A' eggs optional evidently hopes to reduce the premium obtainable on unstamped eggs in some member countries, and to provide an economic incentive towards channelling the bulk of eggs through licensed packing stations. Inspection and penal sanctions may not always prove adequate to achieve this and would be difficult to enforce in country districts. The French experience, however, suggests that the farmyard egg, because of its poor quality, will tend to disturb the market less and less and that commercial production is relatively easy to police.

THE UNITED KINGDOM AS A MEMBER OF THE EEC
The outlook for producers

Adoption of the EEC regulations for eggs will involve the disappearance of the deficiency payment and of any form of guaranteed price. Not only will this result in lower average returns to producers, but the absence of any central purchasing agency to remove surplus eggs from the market would expose them to much severer fluctuations in price, both seasonally and between one year and another. The extent to which the element of government guarantee and intervention by the Board have cushioned producers from more cyclical price movements during recent years can only be conjectured. The more violent price oscillations which have occurred in EEC countries where these factors have been absent, especially in France, during the same period, suggest that it has not been negligible.

Wider price differences in space as well as in time can also be expected from the establishment of a free market in eggs. The BEMB's weekly published prices (basic prices since April 1966, to which is subsequently added the 4·0d. per dozen premium due to those taking part in the contract scheme) have all along been payable to all producers regardless of geographical location. To the extent that this has encouraged the production of eggs surplus to local demand, in Northern Ireland or Lancashire for instance, the cost of moving them to deficit areas is borne directly by the Board.[8] The cost is of course borne ultimately by the producers closer to the deficit areas, through the general lowering of the Board's prices which financing of the transport subsidy inevitably involves. Dissatisfaction with this state of affairs, especially in the south-east, with its higher wages, rates and other overheads, has provided a strong incentive to many producers to by-pass the Board and the packing stations and try to obtain on the free market the price advantage of their location. Under the EEC system this equalization of transport costs could no longer occur.

By the time the UK becomes a member of the EEC the present Community will be virtually self-sufficient in eggs. It can be assumed that imports from third countries are unlikely to cross the sluice-gates in significant quantities, and that internal prices, at any rate at times of seasonal surplus, will be generally just above sluice-gate level. They will certainly be no higher to producers than recent levels in the Netherlands and Belgium, the member countries with the highest average of productive efficiency and with cereal prices in 1966/67 already closest to the unified 1967/68 level. Between January and November 1966 BEMB monthly average prices for standard eggs paid to producers in the contract scheme coincided remarkably closely to those quoted on the Belgian and Dutch *wholesale* markets during the same period. Entry into the EEC then might therefore have meant a general lowering of producer prices in the UK by something approaching the wholesale margin, say 25 per cent. During 1967, however, prices in the Low Countries being a little higher and UK prices somewhat lower, the immediate effect of entry would have been less catastrophic, and devaluation would have further redressed the balance. The downward trend in UK producer prices is likely to continue, though there will be cyclical fluctuations on both sides of the Channel. Nevertheless, at whatever moment entry into the EEC eventually takes place, some reduction in price for UK producers seems inevitable.

Besides this unfavourable prospect the higher cost of compound feed must be taken into account in order to get some idea of the challenge facing the UK egg producer in the common market. Depending on his managerial

---

[8] Above a distance of 40 miles the Board pays some part, and eventually up to the whole, of the cost, according to a fixed mileage/load scale, of moving eggs from one wholesale warehouse to another.

efficiency a rise in layers' mash of £9.10s.0d. per ton might cost between 6·3d. and 7·5d. a dozen (for birds with hen-house averages of 240 eggs and 210 eggs over 52 weeks respectively and allowing 24 lbs. of mash per bird for rearing to point of lay).[9] Gross margins per bird could therefore be cut by as much as 13s. 0d., leaving the prospect of a greatly reduced profit to even the most efficient converter, and none at all to the inefficient. It is worth noting that in France, where feed prices are likely to rise by between 5 and 10 per cent with the coming of the unified feed market, wholesale prices for eggs have been about 20 per cent higher than in the Netherlands for the past two years. French producers look like facing a period of even more painful adjustment.

The regulation restricting farm-gate sales to 5 dozen eggs per purchaser could, and no doubt would, be evaded, either openly or by the exercise of a number of easily imaginable legal fictions. It could, all the same, sub-stantially reduce the volume of direct sales from farms to retailers, who would be obliged to display eggs graded according to quality and to one of six different weight grades, and would be subject to inspection. The regulation is of course mainly aimed at the travelling dealers, who often give a poor service to the consumer. In the UK it would involve the abandonment of the 'B' licence system, though producers now selling direct to the market would still be free to operate their own licensed pack-ing stations. The abolition of compulsory stamping of Grade 'A' eggs would also help to extinguish the present premium on unstamped eggs. Conversely a black market in *ungraded* eggs 'straight from the farm' might to some extent take its place.

The future for processers

Of the thirty UK firms engaged in egg processing nineteen are under exclusive contract to the Board, breaking only home-produced seconds (and some of them breaking first quality eggs as well when the Board is obliged to take them off the market). Only incubator clears from hatcheries in the UK and imported eggs may, on the other hand, be purchased for breaking by other firms. In these circumstances the Board has acquired a dominant position in the UK domestic and export trade in frozen and liquid egg. Its interest in the domestic market for sprayed dried egg remains a minority one, confined to two only of its contracted plants. An experimental accelerated freeze dried plant has been run in connection with Ranks. Owing to the decline in Chinese exports since the war British expansion on the world market for egg products, where Denmark and the Netherlands are not traditional exporters, has not met with the opposition

[9] This would be the increase to be expected for a top quality hybrid layers' mash at 'Duis-burg' levels of (1968/69) cereal prices. At 'Liverpool' levels the amount would be between 6·4d. and 7·6d. depending on hen-housed averages. For a lower quality intensive mash the additional cost might be between 5·2d. and 6·2d. ('Duisburg') or 5·3d. and 6·4d. ('Liver-pool'), again assuming averages of 240 or 210 eggs. It is interesting to note that feedgrain price increases approved for 1968/69 will raise egg producers' costs by between 0·6d. and 1·5d. a dozen, according to type of mash, conversion efficiency and assumption about inter-vention price derivation.

which would greet any attempt by the Board to enter the international shell-egg market. A considerable proportion of the Board's total sales of products, which rose in value from £2·7 mn. in 1958/59 to £6·8 mn. in 1965/66, therefore goes for export.

It would be a major interest of any association of producer groups or co-operatives which might take the Board's place inside the EEC to maintain these export outlets if it were to carry out an intervention policy that was to be effective and not too costly. With storage costs of liquid egg running at between 0·5d. and 0·75d. per lb. per month rapid disposal is essential. The Board's heirs are unlikely to be in a position to offer exclusive contracts for home-produced seconds to a minority of breakers as at present. Indeed, if SIPA-ŒUF were to be taken as a model, the breakers would themselves be directly associated as an industry with any 'interprofessional' attempt to regulate the egg market.

The future for packing stations

The British distributive network is in general better organized and equipped than any in the Six except the Dutch. Individual packing stations would already be up to the standards laid down, though only those in Northern Ireland, where a premium on naturally clean eggs has been operating since 1963, have so far had any experience of detecting artificially cleaned ones. The economic efficiency of a considerable proportion of packing stations, on the other hand, is questionable. With a single grading machine capable of dealing with 500 to 600 cases a week, a throughput of 1,000 cases is reckoned to be the minimum viable. Stations with a lesser throughput have not on the whole been considered by the larger operators worth taking over unless there were real possibilities for expansion. The low average throughput of the relatively large number of packing stations in Northern Ireland and north-west and south-west England suggests that there is room for reduction in these areas. In Scotland and Wales, however, where average throughput is not much more than half that of the English packing stations, combination of egg packing with other activities may allow it to continue precariously for a time in remoter districts. Compulsory grading might be expected, for a time at least, to slow up the process of concentration by increasing the total volume of business available to packing stations, at any rate in populated areas where the regulation is likely to be most widely enforceable. But in the long run the disappearance of the egg subsidy, especially the transport element, and of the BEMB's central purchasing role will expose packing stations, like producers, to the cold winds of the open market place. Competition for the output of the larger producers especially will become intensified. The situation in the EEC will undoubtedly present packing station co-operatives with an opportunity of consolidating their already considerable position in the market, especially if they cease to compete amongst themselves— quite apart from the wider role, discussed below, which might be open to them as part heirs to the BEMB.

Possible roles for the BEMB

Apart from winding it up altogether, there seem to be three possible future spheres of activity for the Board under the EEC system:

(i) to continue its work of publicity, market intelligence, and research and development for the egg industry as part of the Commission's plan for measures for 'the better ordering of the market';

(ii) to act as the body envisaged in each member country by the marketing order as responsible for inspection and enforcement;

(iii) to continue its marketing activities in the guise of a 'union of producer groups', the sort of super-co-operative discussed on page 68.

Prima facie it should be possible for either activities (i) and (ii) or (i) and (iii) to be combined without much difficulty. A combination of (ii) and (iii) would present problems, but probably no greater than those of the present Board, a producer-elected body responsible for disciplining its electors. However, those who framed the EEC regulations envisage the three roles as being quite separately exercised, so the choice is to that extent simplified.

Alternative (i) is the sort of anodyne activity into which the Board's present critics would, if it is to continue to exist at all, anyway wish it to be shunted as soon as possible. Under Community law a Board of this kind could even be financed out of the national budget, so long as its advertising promoted the consumption of eggs in general and not of Lion eggs in particular. Indeed the Commission has in mind a semi-official body for carrying out its proposed measures, so that the Board, if it took this on, would cease to be producer elected.

Curiously enough the Commission envisages activity (ii), policing, as being carried out by a professional and not an official body. To that extent, then, the Board would be better suited to take on the second alternative. Since it would be enforcing EEC regulations it would presumably be financed out of FEOGA.

Alternative (iii) is the most interesting of the three, particularly in the light of current controversy about the Board's future part in the existing UK support system. In egg production it is the packing station co-operatives which are most obviously suited to be transformed into officially recognized producer groups.[10] Their participation would therefore be essential if the Board were to assume the role of a union of producer groups (or *comité économique régional* in the French scheme of things). Packing stations operated by private firms or public companies, on the other hand, would clearly not be eligible for producer group status, though a public company in which producers held a majority holding of the shares (a former co-operative which 'went public' provides a well-known instance) might be seen as a border-line case. At all events the draft rules for EEC producer groups include both the right of each member to secede (after due notice given) and an obligation to sell his entire production through the

---

[10] The situation differs from milk production where the co-operatives are relatively weak and the Milk Marketing Boards are strongly established in the regions.

group. For those producers not already members of a packing station co-operative, therefore, the consortia formed in connection with the present contract scheme seem to offer the next best basis for the forming of producer groups. The administration of these consortia is in a majority of cases effectively carried out on their behalf by the packing station to which members have agreed to supply their eggs.

Given, then, that a sufficient number of producers could be induced to market their eggs through groups so as to give them collectively a dominating influence in the UK wholesale market, the BEMB could without much alteration be transformed into a union of producer groups. Such a transformation, involving a closer participation of producers, packing stations, and processers in its day-to-day transactions (on the lines of the French SIPA), would also meet the objections of those who have criticized it as excessively remote and olympian, not to say commercially incompetent. Grading being obligatory and stamping optional, these two pressures against opting out might well prove more effective for collective action than are the regulations under the present UK scheme for preventing eggs from by-passing the Board. The new Board-union would co-ordinate the groups' marketing activities, intervening on the market at periods of flush, breaking out surplus eggs of all grades as necessary, and marketing the consequent egg products on behalf of the groups. A major difficulty would be the condition that the combined throughput of a union may not in general exceed 5 per cent of the total throughput of the Community, though the proportion may be varied at the discretion of the Council for particular products. The UK's share of the total production of the Ten in 1965 was 27 per cent (see Table 19). Although, with the expansion of production in the Six, the proportion may have decreased somewhat by 1970 it is unlikely to be less than 20 per cent, of which at least three quarters will be English. As such a situation would seem inevitably to require a number of regional unions (at least three in England, and one each in the other countries of the UK), it becomes arguable that these would be better set up *ab initio*, based in England at any rate on the strong position of the egg co-operatives, and the BEMB be left at the centre to assume role number (ii).

Whether or not it were decided that the Board was worth perpetuating in a regionalized form, a condition for the success of any producer union scheme would be that once an appropriate majority of producers had assented to joint marketing in any region, the principle of the *extension des règles de discipline* should operate, obliging all other producers in the region who were not members of groups to conform to group practice. One essential power to be exercised by groups, or by a union centrally, over members and non-members alike would be that of raising a levy (based presumably, in the light of recent experience, on some criterion other than production) out of which to finance the union's market stabilizing activities. Buying-in arrangements of this kind by producers themselves on their own behalf are envisaged as the first stage of intervention for fruit and vegetables.[11] For eggs there is of course no intention of proceeding to a second, official stage. The present cost to the BEMB of breaking out is never officially announced, but can be estimated to have been running at an average of about £4·5 mn. a year recently, the equivalent of a levy of about 1s. 10d. per bird on total registered producers' flocks of laying birds, or 1·2d. per dozen on a 216-egg bird.

Besides its high cost the major problem facing anyone trying to operate a breaking-out policy is that of imports. Although egg imports into the UK from third countries would be effectively controlled during periods of surplus by the system of sluice-gate prices, those from other member countries would be unrestricted. The main threat could be from a cheap and efficient 'roll-on-roll-off' to south-eastern ports operated from Denmark and the Low Countries, reducing transport costs to below the present level of between 1·8d. and 2·0d. per dozen. Unions of producers attempting in isolation to steady the market in the UK would soon find themselves in an untenable position, attracting surpluses from abroad. In order to be successful non-official intervention would have to be co-ordinated across national frontiers, with agreements between unions mutually to refrain from taking advantage of each other's breaking-out policies at periods of general surplus.

Before concluding this somewhat speculative examination of the future of egg marketing in the UK under EEC conditions it is worth considering to what extent, if at all, the Board's latest proposals anticipate a move into Europe. After the 1967 Price Review four main points emerged for discussion between the Board, the National Farmers' Unions, and the Ministry of Agriculture, and were eventually referred to a reorganization commission under the provisions of the 1958 Agricultural Marketing Act. In the first place should there be a different basis for raising the funds needed by the Board for publicity, research, and support buying? The present levy of 0·5d. a dozen falls only on producers who market their eggs through the Board, although the Board's activities, particularly its support of the market, benefit all producers. Any step such as extending the levy to sales of day-old chicks from accredited hatcheries would, if French precedent is acceptable, seem to be compatible with EEC regulations. Second, a modification of the present egg marketing scheme which removed the obligation to stamp home-produced eggs would be in line with the Commission's proposal to make the stamping at least of Grade 'A'[12] eggs optional. As regards low-priced imports, the third matter for discussion, minimum import prices for eggs and egg products, would of course be in line with Community policy. If set so high as to exclude most imports, however, there is a strong risk of their giving UK producers a false sense of security. They might find themselves all the less well prepared

[11] See pp. 201–2.
[12] The criteria proposed for Grade 'A' eggs, are somewhat more stringent than for UK 'first quality'. Grade 'B' covers part of UK 'first quality' as well as the upper reaches of 'second quality'. In the same way the seven weight grades in general use in the Community, set at 5 gramme intervals, straddle the five current UK grades.

to face competition from Dutch and Danish producers when the moment came to enter an enlarged Community.

The fourth plank of the Board's reform platform, amendment of the contracts scheme to provide for a three-tier price structure, has already been mentioned. Given the Board's present position as sole buyer of all eggs offered to packing stations the amendment makes a good deal of sense. Once government support to the Board were withdrawn, however, and a nominally free market established such a system would be no longer workable. Although producer groups, or unions of groups, would be at liberty to offer their members seasonal premia or other inducements to level marketing and regular supplies, the contract scheme in its present form, based on the Board's power to fix a uniform basic price for the whole country, could not survive. Indeed, if the EEC regulation obliging all eggs to be marketed through packing stations were to be enforced, a contract scheme mainly designed to attract eggs into the packing stations would no longer have much point.

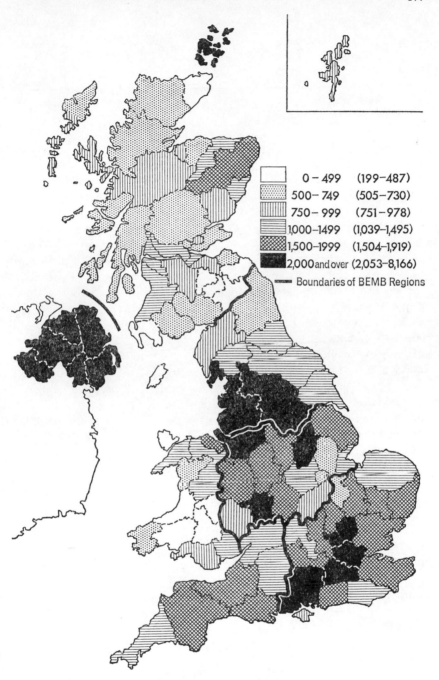

	0 – 499	(199–487)
	500 – 749	(505–730)
	750 – 999	(751–978)
	1,000–1499	(1,039–1,495)
	1,500–1999	(1,504–1,919)
	2,000 and over	(2,053–8,166)

Boundaries of BEMB Regions

11. Laying hens and pullets in the UK (excluding Isle of Man)

Per 1,000 acres of crops and grass, 1966 (Scotland 1965). Figures for Northern Ireland
are for that area as a whole.

(Source: UK Agricultural Statistics)

11. Poultry Meat

The chicken war broke out less than five years ago, but now it is part of history. The EEC's high tariff barrier has to be accepted as one of the disagreeable facts of life that broiler growers in other countries have to live with, like the UK's veterinary restrictions and its quota on Danish imports. Thus an agricultural activity so independent of the normal hazards of the weather (though not of disease) as to be regarded as an industrial one in its domestic context, and not therefore deserving of subsidy, is supported in the international sphere by a variety of protectionist devices even more effective than those accorded by most governments to the textile industry. In the UK, where broilers account for about two-thirds of poultry meat output, help of this kind can be given at no direct cost to the exchequer and does not have to appear on the annual bill for agricultural support presented to parliament. Since the housing, feeding, and eating of broilers are all emotive subjects, liable to arouse passionate feelings in many a constituent, it must be reckoned that MPs are, in this respect, being let off lightly. Perhaps the main reason why broiler growers have had to do without subsidies is simply that they arrived about ten years too late on the scene to make a bid for any share of the blessings of the 1947 Act. Nor are they by now in any political position to obtain any. The broiler man, whatever his contribution to import saving, has little appeal as the preserver of a way of life or of the English countryside, especially if he is thought to have sold his sturdy independence to the integrators, those hard-faced business men from between the lurid covers of American paperbacks.

That broiler production means agribusiness in the UK is in fact the result of, rather than the reason for, absence of government support. With no guaranteed prices from the state the producer had to look to other sources and methods of financing to obtain some kind of assured return: to forward contracts with firms supplying a mass market, and to hatcheries and feed compounders to finance output on a sufficient scale to fulfil them. In this process the small-scale producer has disappeared. In the EEC, paradoxically, any minimum guaranteed price for poultry meat, or for eggs, has been ruled out of the CAP precisely on the grounds that (quite apart from its potential cost to FEOGA) it would be assisting the development of large-scale industrial enterprises. There is something to be said for this view, though the likelihood is that they will develop in any case. In a few areas of the Community like the Netherlands, where small-holders have a traditional discipline in co-ordinating their supply on the market, the co-operative framework is likely to remain, but even in Holland the trend is towards fewer and larger flocks. How far groupings of small-scale producers, for all the official encouragement they receive, will be able to survive and flourish elsewhere is still an open question.

TABLE 22. POULTRY MEAT: PRODUCTION AND CONSUMPTION, 1965

	Comparative production UK = 100	Percentage of total production: the Six	Percentage of total production: the Ten	Degree of self-sufficiency per cent	Consumption[a] per head per year, kg.
Germany (FR)	38·7	12·8	9·05	42·8	6·0
France	114·5	38·0	26·8	105·7	11·0
Italy	84·5	28·1	19·8	98·7	7·3
Netherlands	38·7	12·8	9·05	315·4	3·8
Belgium/Luxemburg	24·9	8·3	5·8	123·1	7·8
The Six	301·3	100·0	70·5	95·1	
United Kingdom	100·0		23·4	97·0	7·5
Ireland	5·4		1·3	101·9	7·3
Denmark	19·6		4·6	202·6	4·6
Norway	0·8		0·2	97·0	0·8
The Four			29·5	105·8	
The Ten			100·0	98·0	

[a] 1964/65.

Sources: FAO/ECE *Review of the Agricultural Situation in Europe 1966. Food consumption in OECD countries 1962/63–1964/65.*

THE UNITED KINGDOM

Chicken meat accounted for 88 per cent of the total UK output of poultry meat of 400,000 tons in 1965/66, the rest being mainly turkey. Production is strongly concentrated around the main centres of demand, in south-eastern England, the west Midlands and Lancashire and Yorkshire (see Maps 12 and 13). Output of broiler meat (262,000 tons in 1965/66) expanded by about 10 per cent a year during the early sixties and it is from this source that any future increase in poultry meat will mainly come. Production of turkey meat almost doubled between 1959/60 and 1965/66, but at 39,000 tons still represents less than 10 per cent of the total. Meat from cocks and hens, whose volume is necessarily a function of the profitability of egg production, has oscillated between 90,000 and 100,000 tons a year during the past five years.

Poultry meat production has never received any form of direct government support, nor have buildings for poultry generally been eligible for grant under the Farm Improvement Scheme. Poultry farmers receive the normal tax investment allowances and grants available to all farmers. On the other hand broiler houses do not enjoy the same exemption from local rates as other farm buildings. A strong element of indirect support, however, exists in the shape of an import duty of 3·0d. per lb. on all dead poultry (fresh, chilled, or frozen) from non-Commonwealth sources,

N

and, more important still, in the virtual exclusion, on animal health grounds, of imports from the United States and from the rest of Europe except the Scandinavian countries and Iceland. Furthermore, Danish broiler imports are subject to a monthly quota of 625 tons. Imports of live poultry, including breeding stock, are permitted only from Ireland and Scandinavia, Australia, and New Zealand, and, exceptionally, grandparent stock of hybrid lines may be imported from North America.

The broiler industry is highly concentrated, just over half the market being shared about equally between Ross, Buxted, and Eastwood, and most of the rest of it between some dozen other firms. All these enterprises, except Eastwood, also enter into contracts, generally on a quarterly basis, with so-called independent producers, a form of partial integration under which either day-old chicks or feed, sometimes both, are supplied by the integrator. Payment to the producer normally consists of an agreed contract price plus a bonus related to actual realization price, which may turn out to be anything up to 50 per cent.

Latest available figures show a total of 2,790 holdings of over one acre with broiler enterprises. Units on smaller holdings may number another 300. Of the 2,790 well over half are small units of under 5,000 birds housing capacity, or 25,000-bird annual throughput. 301 holdings, with 20,000-bird capacity or more, account for 18 mn. birds, or 70 per cent of all broilers. There has been a big shake-out in the industry since 1960, the total number of units having more than halved while the total number of birds almost doubled.

In the turkey industry the proportion of smaller firms is much larger. Producers for the fresh market, mainly a Christmas market, remain particularly independent. Only 60 per cent of turkeys are frozen, compared with 80 per cent of broilers. There are four major firms, Bernard Mathews, the largest, British United Turkeys (which has links with one of the secondary broiler groups), Ross, and Buxted.

THE EEC[1]

In response to a demand mainly generated by rising incomes, production of poultry-meat expanded by over 250 per cent between 1955 and 1965, the main impetus having occurred since 1960. As in the UK this is largely attributable to the introduction of North American production techniques and breeding-stock, but continental agriculture, owing to its small-holding structure, has adapted itself more slowly to the integrating trends with which these technical changes are closely associated. The relative strength of co-operatives and the small scale of the private feed compounding industry have also discouraged the emergence of very large broiler units in major production areas like Brittany, or in the Netherlands where the vast scale of co-operative feed production provides some

[1] R. Goffinet and A. Ledent, *Production, commerce extérieur et consommation de viande de volaille, Belgique-CEE, 1950–64*, Cahiers de l'IEA, Brussels, May 1966, analyse international trade, production, and demand in the Community, but, for lack of statistical data, have little to say about trends in the structure of production.

countervailing power against potential integrators from the private sector. In Belgium, on the other hand, the major compounders are a strongly established integrating force. In Germany, where the private sector of the compounding industry operates more extensively than in any other member country, the larger firms have, with one notable exception, entered rather reluctantly into the competitive financial commitments which integration involves.

This is perhaps one of the reasons why German broiler production, despite an enormous potential local demand, has been rather a late developer. It still accounted for less than a third of German poultry meat production in 1964. Recently it has begun to make more rapid headway, output for the first half of 1967 being about 20 per cent higher than that for the first half of 1966. As in the case of eggs Germany provides the key to the unified EEC market and will be the main outlet for the first few years at any rate after the disappearance of the intra-Community levies for Dutch, Belgian, and French surpluses. Imports into Germany from within the EEC, especially from the Netherlands, will continue to expand at the expense of those from Denmark and from the United States, whose share declined from 23 per cent in 1964 to 14 per cent in 1966.

Italy, though somewhat unusual in that over half its imports are in the form of turkeys, provides a second large potential market for poultry meat. Consumption in Italy rose by a third between 1963 and 1965 alone, but in 1964 was still only 1·7 kg. per head in Puglia, Basilicata, and Calabria, the heel and toe of Italy, and 2·5 kg. in Sicily and Sardinia. Production, which increased by over 40 per cent in Italy between 1960 and 1964, is at present mainly located in the north. Broilers are produced in fairly large units and there is some integration, but as only 2 per cent of compounding plants in the country had an output of more than 10 tons an hour (say, 20,000 tons a year) in 1966, and over half the plants produced less than a tenth of that amount, the conditions for a widespread injection of working capital by the feed industry scarcely exist. The potential demand for poultry meat to be released by the gradual industrialization of central and southern Italy could be met from local broiler production and marketing organized co-operatively. Poultry, being a form of livestock not dependent on green fodder and relatively well suited to a hot climate, is seen by some as a welcome alternative to fruit and vegetable production for areas not suitable for irrigation, as well as providing export possibilities to eastern Mediterranean countries.[2] Adoption of uniform EEC standards would be especially useful in improving Italian distribution methods and weeding out sub-standard production.

In France, whose share of EEC poultry meat production fell from half in 1960 to under 40 per cent in 1965, output of broilers has nevertheless been increasing rapidly. Nearly 400,000 tons in 1965, it has already exceeded forecasts made for 1970. Poor standards of presentation and high unit

[2] See G. Zucchi, *Problematica di sviluppo dell'avicunicoltura meridionale in rapporto alla situazione nazionale*, address to Foggia Poultry Conference, April 1967.

costs of transport and of freezing (due to the French housewife's un-compromising preference for fresh meat) are factors contributing to the very sharp decline in French exports to the German market since 1965. The statistical inquiry into French hatcheries already referred to indicates that although a proportion of table poultry production is conveniently located either along the Belgian frontier, in the Paris area, or, for export to Switzerland, in the south-east, the major concentration is, like that of egg production, in Brittany. In this remote region the majority of producers are small-holders with an annual throughput of about 25,000 birds. In 1967 eight of the 27 recognized producer groups in the region were also legally constituted co-operatives, with an average of over 270 members each. The remaining groups consisted on average of 105 producers each, the smallest having only 22. In the rest of France, of 21 groups spread over three regions 11 co-operatives had an average of 70 members each. The remain-der averaged 140 members each. The ten largest groups are believed to control over a third of integrated broiler output, but the co-operatives less than 20 per cent. Organized, like the egg producers,[3] into regional *comités économiques* whose federation is represented on SIPA-VOLAILLE, French poultry meat producers, having likewise accepted the *extension des règles de discipline* to all units of 3,000 birds and over, are hoping to be in a stronger position to face the rigours of the unified market. The SIPA, it should be remembered, is an 'inter-professional' body on which poultry breeders and packers are also represented.

The most spectacular expansion in poultry meat production, one, in relation to the place of agriculture in the economy, more striking even than that which occurred in Italy, has been in the Low Countries, where it more than doubled between 1959 and 1965. Output of broilers in Belgium almost trebled, reaching about 59,000 tons, or two-thirds of the total, by 1964. In the Netherlands the proportion was just under 70 per cent, or 87,000 tons, in 1964 compared with 40 per cent four years earlier. Both countries are highly geared to exporting poultry (90 per cent of it chicken meat), Belgium sending virtually 100 per cent of its exports, and the Netherlands all but 10 per cent, on to the German market.[4] Since dom-estic consumption in Belgium is already high (8·0 kg. per head in 1964) future expansion is particularly dependent on exports, which increased by over 20 per cent in 1966. The Netherlands industry, on the other hand, although equally dependent on exports, still has a considerable potential home demand to help cushion any recession in the export market, and of the additional 23,000 tons produced in 1964 19,000 were absorbed at home. In both countries the structure of production is essentially one of family small-holdings, many of them part-time in Belgium,

[3] See p. 163.

[4] Export marketing in the Netherlands has, with government encouragement, been concen-trated into four selling organizations whose membership is confined to producers with a minimum output of 50 tons of poultry meat a year (about 30,000 birds). Financial aids to this end were declared by the Commission to be compatible with the Treaty and not distort-ing to competition.

selling on a contract basis and mostly integrated in one way or another. There are no Belgian statistics of flock size. In the Netherlands the median size group increased from 1,000–2,499 birds in 1964 to 5,000–9,999 in 1966, a quarter of the 37,000 flocks being of that size. The number of flocks of over 10,000 bird capacity (50,000-plus annual throughput in view of the smaller, 53-day, bird generally favoured) increased from 300 to 630 during the same period.

The basic EEC regulation for the unified market in poultry meat which came into force (subject to a transition period of three months for Germany) on 1 July 1967 being in its essentials the same as that for eggs and egg products[5] requires no detailed examination here. With the introduction of the CAP for poultry in 1962 measures of protection against imports, including live poultry and day-old chicks, from third countries by means of levies, reinforced by minimum import (sluice-gate) prices, were from the outset sharp and effective. Only imports of poultry livers, and certain kinds of preserved meat and offals are limited to lower rates of duty bound in GATT. From 1 Nov. 1966 to 31 Jan. 1968 the levy on poultry, plucked, eviscerated, without head or feet, but with heart, liver and gizzard, was the equivalent of 6d. per lb., with a sluice-gate price of 3s. 0d. per lb. As in the case of eggs, uniform EEC regulations for standards of hygiene and presentation in the grading, packing, and retailing of poultry meat are also being laid down.

THE UNITED KINGDOM AS A MEMBER OF THE EEC

In the absence of any government support for poultry production no organizational problems would arise from UK entry into the EEC. Duty on imports from third countries, would be, on the whole, higher than at present and would, in addition, apply to those from the Commonwealth. Effectively, however, adoption of the CAP would expose UK producers of poultry meat, and of broilers in particular, to a competition such as they have never had to face before, even during the years of over-supply of the domestic market in the early sixties from which the industry emerged with its present relatively streamlined figure and healthy muscular tone. Any lingering fat or flabbiness would be rapidly eliminated after the first few rounds in the open ring with producers from Denmark, no longer restrained by quota, and the Low Countries, whose outlets to Germany and France are likely to have become circumscribed by the improvements in economic efficiency forced on producers in those countries over the next five years. Standards of hygiene and animal health have, it is true, not yet been harmonized among the Six, and it has even been possible for Dutch and Belgian exports to be largely excluded from the French market by a national regulation on evisceration. But it is hardly conceivable, and certainly not to be relied upon, that the present discriminatory hygienic barrier protecting the UK broiler industry from non-Scandinavian imports would be allowed to continue much beyond a transition period.

[5] See pp. 166–8.

Current projections confidently predict a continued rise in demand for poultry meat both in the EEC and in the UK up to 1970. In the EEC as a whole consumption per head in '1962' (i.e. a three-year average of 1961/62, 1962/63, and 1963/64) was, at 6·5 kg., estimated to be 20 per cent above the trend anticipated in the Commission's original projections for '1970' (average of 1969/70, 1970/71, and 1971/72).[6] According to these it was expected to reach 8·5 kg. per head, or a total of 1·6 mn. tons. With consumption already up to over 1·3 mn. tons by 1965 this estimate seems very likely indeed to be exceeded, though probably not by the full 20 per cent recorded in the earlier years of the decade, which would imply a demand of nearly 2 mn. tons by the beginning of the seventies. 1·8 mn. might be nearer the mark. In the UK the National Plan envisaged an increase in domestic production by 1970 to 465,000 tons (100,000 tons above the 1964 level). Warley's estimate of 461,000 tons by 1970,[7] assuming the UK remained outside the EEC, represents an increase of 47 per cent over his base period, compared with one of 33 per cent had the UK entered the Community. Unilever on the other hand are more optimistic, anticipating increases in home production of 73 per cent and 50 per cent in the course of their ten-year period for the 'out' and 'in' alternatives respectively.[8] Warley's estimate of an almost threefold increase (44,000 tons) in imports into the UK were it inside the EEC, seems, however, a good deal more realistic than Unilever's 25 per cent or 3,000 tons. He also takes a somewhat more pessimistic view of the future level of producer prices, anticipating some fall (about 2 per cent) in nominal prices to the British producer even inside the EEC.

To the extent that prices are comparable, given local variations in specification for the finished product, gross producer returns per lb. on broilers seem on average since 1965 to have been a little higher in the Netherlands than in the UK, around 1s. 9d. at the new rate of exchange. With UK entry into the EEC, on the other hand, feed costs would become substantially higher. Averaging out seasonal increments on intervention and threshold prices and assuming the basic price levels proposed by the Commission for cereals for 1968/69, the cost of broiler food might be expected to go up by about £10 or £12 per ton, depending on whether UK wheat prices were derived from Duisburg or from Liverpool. At a conversion rate of 1:2·35 this implies an additional cost of raw materials alone (assuming no increase in compounders' margins) per 4·1 lb. liveweight broiler of either 10·5d. or 12·5d. a bird, or say 2½d. or 3d. per lb. liveweight. Given an average return of 1s. 9d. per lb. such a cost increase, even at the lower level of cereal prices, could make a very substantial inroad indeed into present profit margins. How do broiler growers in the Netherlands manage, at rather similar levels of both feed and chicken prices, to derive a reasonable livelihood from their production? As may have been observed from earlier chapters any idea that the cost of credit

[6] *Informations internes sur l'agriculture*, No. 7 (EEC, Brussels, June 1966), pp. 130–40.

[7] Warley, op. cit., Table IX.   [8] CBI Report, pp. 30–31.

or of labour are lower in the Netherlands can be dismissed. It is of course arguable that family labour may, at its best, provide a higher level of management. The small scale of production in the Netherlands and elsewhere makes the industry more resilient to cyclical falls in prices. But these factors would hardly of themselves make acceptable a return over 10 per cent lower than the average at present received by the UK producer.

One possible answer, suggested in an investigation carried out for the British Chicken Association,[9] lies in the relatively high cost of day-old chicks in the UK. The prices of the Dutch Euribrid Hybro, which includes immunization in the egg against PPLO (*mycoplasma gallisepticum*) by the hatchery, was in 1966 some 30 per cent lower than that of equivalent chicks in the UK, and if the additional cost to the British producer of antibiotic treatment against PPLO is taken into account, the disparity was over 35 per cent. The requirement for the export market to Germany of a smaller type of broiler might account for some difference in the price of the chick, but as wide a discrepancy as that observed by the authors of the BCA report in their view 'warrants close investigation', including experimental imports of Dutch breeding stock.

[9] Tristram Beresford and Peter Tolson, *The broiler industry in France, Belgium and Holland* (London, December 1966).

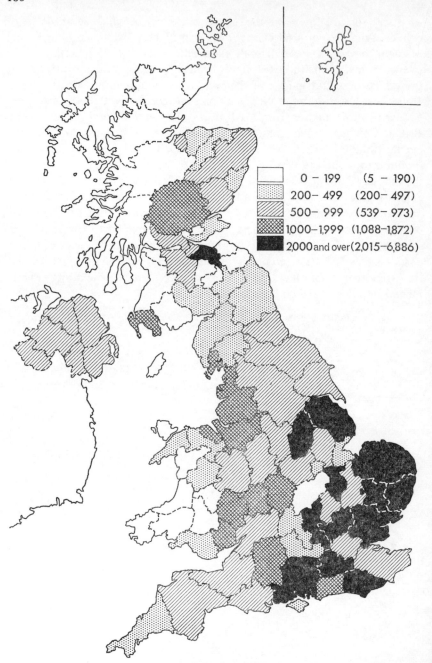

0 – 199 (5 – 190)
200– 499 (200– 497)
500– 999 (539– 973)
1,000–1,999 (1,088–1,872)
2,000 and over (2,015–6,886)

12. Table chickens[a] in the UK (excluding Isle of Man)

Per 1,000 acres of crops and grass, 1966 (Scotland 1965). Figures for Northern Ireland
are for that area as a whole.

[a] Broilers plus other table fowls. The latter represented 4·8 per cent of all table chickens in
England and Wales in 1966.

(Source: UK Agricultural Statistics)

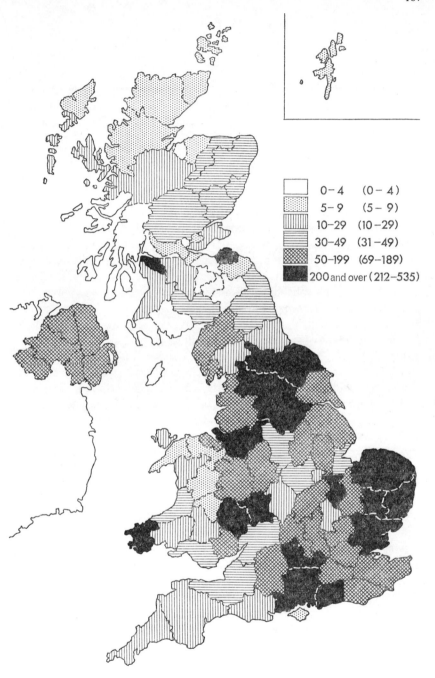

	0 – 4	(0 – 4)
5 – 9	(5 – 9)
10 – 29	(10 – 29)
30 – 49	(31 – 49)
50 – 199	(69 – 189)
200 and over	(212 – 535)

13. Turkeys in the UK (excluding Isle of Man)

Per 1,000 acres of crops and grass, 1966 (Scotland 1965). Figures for Northern Ireland are for that area as a whole.

(Source: UK Agricultural Statistics)

12. Sugar

Sugar is the only agricultural product for which there are two entirely separate sources of supply: sugar cane and beets. The former is grown mostly in the tropics, Spain being the only European cane sugar producer. The biggest beet sugar producers are the USSR, nearly 10 mn. tons, and the USA (about 3 mn. tons). Total world production in 1965 was about 27 mn. tons. Cane sugar production amounted to about 37 mn. tons, of which Cuba (6 mn. tons), Brazil (4·5 mn. tons), India (3·5 mn. tons), and Mexico and Australia (2 mn. tons each) were the biggest producers.

In Europe sugar presents the problem of differences of interest between 'the outsiders', the cane sugar industry, established in some parts of the world with the assistance of European capital, and the 'insiders', the sugar-beet industry which in many countries is well organized as a pressure group. Which type of sugar can be more cheaply produced? There are such wide variations between countries and also between farms and plantations that it is impossible to give a clear answer to this question. Both cane and beet sugar production costs are greatly influenced by the size and structure of the industry. For example, labour-saving resulting from mechanization of the beet harvest would not be possible unless the total size of the industry were large enough to justify the development of special machinery. Until recently the cost advantage of cane sugar has largely depended on the payment of very low wages in a relatively labour-intensive activity. Throughout Europe production is controlled by quotas. If these were removed average costs might well decline.

Cost comparisons are of rather limited interest. Beet sugar production was established and protected in Western Europe for reasons other than a cost advantage compared with cane sugar. In addition to the political influence of the farm vote, defence arguments have been used. In the two world wars these have looked very compelling.

The sugar industry consists of three related activities. The first stage is the production of sugar beet or cane; the next is the extraction of the raw sugar; this is followed by refining into whatever form the consumer requires. Ownership often overlaps these activities. The refiners own sugar plantations as well as factories for extraction. In Britain the British Sugar Corporation, which has a monopoly in the production of raw sugar from sugar beet, also has capacity for refining most of its output. Many of the continental sugar producers are similarly placed.

Governmental influence is very strong in the sugar industry, particularly through decisions on prices and quotas. In the UK the centralized

ABLE 23. SUGAR: PRODUCTION AND CONSUMPTION, 1965

	Comparative acreage UK=100 (sugar beet)	Comparative production UK=100 (sugar beet)	Percentage of total production: the Six (sugar beet)	Percentage of total production: the Ten (sugar beet)	Average yield per hectare (sugar beet) 100 kg.	Comparative yield UK=100	Degree of self-sufficiency[a] per cent	Consumption per head per year[c] 1965/66 kg.	Comparative production UK=100 (white sugar)	Percentage of total production: the Six (white sugar)	Percentage of total production: the Ten (white sugar)
Germany (FR)	163·4	160·6	25·4	20·8	366	98·4	68	32·2	167·5	25·4	21·0
France	215·9	249·0	39·3	32·3	429	115·3	136	31·1	250·4	38·0	31·4
Italy	154·1	133·3	21·1	17·3	322	86·6	91	24·3	132·3	20·0	16·6
Netherlands	49·7	52·4	8·3	6·8	394	105·9	95	46·4	63·6	9·6	8·0
Belgium/Luxemburg	35·5	37·2	5·9	4·8	388	104·3	131	30·7	45·9	7·0	5·7
The Six	618·6	632·5	100·0	82·0	381	102·4	97	30·5	659·7	100·0	82·7
United Kingdom	100·0	100·0		13·0	372	100·0	31[c]	46·3	100·0		12·5
Ireland	14·8	11·1		1·4	281	75·5	82[d]	48·5[e]	12·7		1·6
Denmark	32·8	27·6		3·6	314	84·4	85[c]	47·8	25·7		3·2
Norway[b]								39·8			
The Four				18·0							17·3
The Ten				100·0							100·0

a In terms of white sugar.
b No sugar beet is grown in Norway.
c Including unrefined.
d Estimated.
e 1963.

Sources: EEC Agricultural Statistics, 1967, No. 1. FAO, Monthly Bulletin of Agricultural Statistics, February, 1967. Food Consumption in OECD countries, 1963/64–1964/65.

character of the refining industry led the post-war Labour government to plan to nationalize it. This was fought off by Tate & Lyle Ltd. in a long and expensive campaign. The less concentrated sugar industry in EEC countries has not been threatened in this way. But its freedom of action is curtailed by price controls, quality standards, and the quota system.

As both the UK and the EEC operate a quota system it is worth commenting on the practical problems of its administration. The main difference between the two is that the British method uses acreage control whereas EEC quotas are by tonnage. The British Sugar Corporation divides up among its factories the total contract acreage, which is decided by the government at the Price Review. Factories apportion their quota among farmers, the quotas being usually attached to the farm and passing with ownership. The contract acreage has varied very little over the past twenty years from its current level of 443,000 acres.

The methods in the EEC are rather more complicated as the quotas are based on tonnage, and the sugar manufacturer has to translate his sugar quota into the necessary tonnage of beet. There is no established way of doing this and the sugar manufacturer does not have to furnish any justification for the figure finally arrived at. Two factories with the same quotas may contract for different quantities of beet. This may be due to different extraction rates or different assessments of farmers' tendencies to over- or under-deliver. Farmers thus have to calculate what acreage of beet they should sow and there are bound to be different degrees of optimism about yields. The division of the quota is decided between the factory and the farmers' organizations. In France, for instance, a protocol its drawn up and agreed each year, and the division is superintended by a committee of representatives from the factory and the farmers, usually three of each. The normal procedure is for the protocol to include a provision for retaining each year 2 per cent of the quota for division among farmers starting beet-growing, the remainder being shared out on the basis of previous allocations.

On theoretical grounds the EEC system might be preferred to the British because output at the guaranteed price under the latter is at the mercy of seasonal variations in yield. But if the object is to exert an effective control on production the British system has distinct advantages. Under the EEC tonnage quota system farmers, being determined to fill their quota, are very likely to exceed it. The marginal price for quantities in excess of the quota may be low but farmers more often think in terms of average returns from their whole beet crop.

THE UNITED KINGDOM

Before the First World War the UK drew its supplies of sugar almost entirely from abroad, from the beet sugar industry of northern Europe and the cane sugar industry of the West Indies and elsewhere. The wartime sugar shortage and the education of farmers in the possibilities of sugar-beet culture led to the establishment in the twenties of a domestic industry supported by various forms of government intervention. These consisted of direct subsidies to the industry established under the Sugar Industry (Subsidy) Act 1925 coupled with duties on imports of refined sugar. Beet growing expanded rapidly and by 1930/31 accounted for about 350,000 acres, only about 20 per cent less than the present acreage. The original idea behind the 1925 Act was that the sugar industry should be able to stand on its own feet without subsidies or tariffs after a period of ten years. The depression, which hit all commodities including sugar in the thirties, made it quite certain that this object could not be achieved. Following a report from a Committee of Inquiry and a White Paper which revealed the government's intention 'to continue to assist the beet sugar industry without any specific limitation of the period', the Sugar Industry (Reorganization) Act 1936 was passed. This Act effectively determined the present structure of the British beet sugar industry, as it led to the amalgamation of all beet sugar factories into the ownership of the British Sugar Corporation which was given the sole right to produce home grown beet sugar. The refiners, now excluded from the domestic beet sugar industry, felt themselves threatened by the new corporation, which was permitted to produce both raw and refined sugar. In fact the British Sugar Corporation now refines most of the sugar which it produces, owning fourteen white sugar and only four raw sugar factories. Any factories built in the future will almost certainly be capable of producing white sugar.

This expansion of domestic sugar production could only occur at the expense of overseas producers. Government policy has consisted of maintaining the proportion of sugar supplied by British farmers at, or just under, one third of total requirements, excluding re-exports. Yields of sugar beet have tended to rise, the average for the years 1961 to 1965 being about 20 per cent higher than ten years previously. A rigid policy of acreage control has therefore been adopted in order to restrict total domestic production. The decision to leave available to outside sources about two-thirds of total British sugar requirements was made at least as much on political as on economic grounds, and is related to the fact that the main source of foreign supply has been Commonwealth countries where sugar plantations and factories have been developed by British capital and, in many cases, still remain in British ownership.

For many years before the last war Commonwealth countries and British colonies had enjoyed a privileged position in the British market through preferential duties. But they had no guarantee of access for certain quantities. Bulk buying on quotas began in the war and continued afterwards under the influence of the post-war dollar shortage. In 1951 negotiations for a formal long-term agreement which had been going on for some time were finally concluded. The Commonwealth Sugar Agreement, originally negotiated to last for eight years until December 1959, has been extended each year, sometimes with amendments, for a further year, and still has eight years to go. As the principal document governing British trade policy for sugar it deserves careful consideration.[1]

The Agreement consists of 29 Articles, the most important of which are Numbers 13 and 15. By these the United Kingdom government agrees to buy in each year, at prices which shall be reasonably remunerative to efficient producers, the following quantities representing the so-called Negotiated Price Quotas (revised to take account of the withdrawal of South Africa from the Agreement and the reallocation of St. Vincent's small quota and the addition in 1964 of India).

Australia	300,000 tons
West Indies and British Guiana	641,000 ,,
British Honduras	18,000 ,,
East Africa	5,000 ,,
Fiji	120,000 ,,
Mauritius	335,000 ,,
Swaziland	85,000 ,,
India	25,000 ,,
	1,529,000 ,,

In addition the United Kingdom is obliged to increase the quotas to take account of higher United Kingdom consumption by 'at least the same percentage as the percentage by which the unrestricted domestic consumption exceeds 2,550,000 tons'. This additional quantity, which varied from year to year, was consolidated in the arrangements for 1965 to give a total of 1,692,500 tons, or, after allowing for India's quota, 1,717,500 tons. There is no provision in the Agreement for any reduction in the Negotiated Price Quotas. The United Kingdom might feel that it was entitled to the pre-1965 arrangement (i.e. quotas unconsolidated), but this would make little practical difference to its purchasing obligations. The total of the basic Negotiated Price Quotas plus the additional quantities representing the percentage of increased domestic consumption is much the same as the total of Consolidated Price Quotas.

At first sight the provision for pricing—'reasonably remunerative to efficient producers'—appears to leave some flexibility to the United Kingdom, possibly to the extent of allowing the Agreement to lapse due to failure to agree a price. The Agreement is, however, very specific on what information is to be provided by the exporting countries for the price-fixing arrangement and includes an Appendix illustrating the method of price computation. Should the price negotiation, which in some respects is not dissimilar to the UK Annual Farm Price Review, fail to reach an agreed conclusion (as occurred in 1964) the previous year's price is carried forward until a new price agreement is concluded.

In the 1965 negotiations a Negotiated Price was set for the following three years instead of for one year only as had been the practice before.

[1] The text of the Agreement signed 21 December 1951, with amendments since then, is published by the Commonwealth Sugar Exporters' London Office.

The Agreement was modified to allow triennial reviews and minor alterations to the price-fixing arrangement were agreed. It was also decided that the less developed exporting countries would receive a special payment additional to the Negotiated Price, which would be highest (maximum £2. 10s. 0d. per ton) when the world price was low and would be phased out to *nil* when the world price reached £39 per ton, plus a fixed element of £1. 10s. 0d. a ton. The Negotiated Price for 1966–68 is £43. 10s. 0d. per ton.

From the United Kingdom point of view the Agreement is operated by the Sugar Board, which buys at the Negotiated Price and sells to the trade at the world price, both f.o.b. stored in bulk. The difference between the two prices is made up by a Surcharge or a Distribution Payment on sugar imported into the United Kingdom, which is assessed at the Sugar Board's discretion to take account of movements in market prices in relation to the Negotiated Price. The Board may sell the sugar while afloat but is not permitted to store it. The Sugar Board is also responsible for pricing arrangements for domestically produced raw sugar, and operates on behalf of the government a price equalization scheme with the British Sugar Corporation. The Board is obliged to balance its accounts taking one year with another.

As the Agreement has now been in operation for some fifteen years it might be possible to establish which side has done best out of it. Unfortunately this cannot be done except in very broad terms. The difficulty is that most of the sugar that enters world trade is subject to quotas and preferential arrangements. Both the other major importers, the United States and Russia, whose net imports in 1965 amounted to 3·7 mn. and 1·6 mn. tons, have agreements at fixed prices for the bulk of their imports. The free market for sugar is a residual one and as such liable to extreme price fluctuations. In the first half of 1967 with world sugar prices standing at around £15–£20 a ton the Commonwealth price looks generous. But there have been several occasions when the world price has been above the Negotiated Price, notably in 1963.

A more realistic question to ask is what sort of agreement the United Kingdom would now sign if the current Agreement expired. A term similar to that of the present Agreement would be regarded as suitable and the price-fixing arrangement would be acceptable. But the quota system would have to be altered to provide greater opportunity for expansion of home sugar production. The economics of production have moved in favour of beet-sugar growing, through higher yields and mechanization. On economic grounds there is no compelling reason why the United Kingdom should limit its production indefinitely to a third of consumption, necessitating imports costing some £80 mn. a year.

THE EEC

The difficulties which faced the EEC in adopting a common agricultural policy for sugar mainly arose from differences among the member countries in existing prices for sugar and in their respective trade situations. Prices in Belgium, the Netherlands, and France had been low compared with those in Germany and Italy. In 1965/66 the French price for sugar was about 30 per cent below the Italian. Germany, Italy, and the Netherlands have all needed to import sugar. Belgium and France have been exporters, the latter on a large scale. In recent years the EEC as a whole has tended to be in surplus, average net exports for the seven years 1959/65 being about 250,000 tons.

Draft sugar regulations and prices proposals were included in the Commission's package of March 1966. Agreement was reached by the Council of Ministers in July. After a transitional year (the 1967/68 campaign) the provisions for which need not concern us, the uniform price system starts from 1 July 1968, when the target and intervention prices for white sugar for the areas of greatest surplus will be respectively about £94 and £90 per ton. Derived intervention prices will be fixed for other areas including the French overseas departments, Réunion, Guadeloupe, and Martinique, which will take account of transport costs. The price will be implemented by levies, restrictions on exports, and intervention purchases. In the area of greatest surplus the intervention price for beet has been fixed at approximately £7. 3s. 0d. per ton, basis 16 per cent sugar content. Beet intervention prices in other areas will be related to the intervention prices for sugar.

Coupled with these prices are quota arrangements designed to ease the burden on FEOGA by limiting its open-ended commitment. In theory they are only operative until 1975, after which it is intended that there shall be a 'free market' in sugar on the same lines as that for grains. Presumably it is hoped to operate this within the framework of a new International Sugar Agreement. These quotas can be compared with the British standard quantities. The basic quota is divided among the member states as follows (white sugar equivalent):

	Quota	1965/66 Production
Germany (FR)	1,750,000	1,437,000
France	2,400,000	2,647,000
Italy	1,230,000	1,147,000
Netherlands	550,000	548,000
Belgium/Luxemburg	550,000	380,000
	6,480,000	6,159,000

These quotas are further distributed among individual manufacturers in the member countries on the basis of average production over the campaigns 1961/62–1965/66. In addition to his basic quota each manufacturer is also allocated a ceiling equivalent to 135 per cent of his quota. If Community production exceeds 105 per cent of consumption (calculated at 6,594,000 tons for 1968/69 or about 2 per cent more than the total quota) a levy is made on producers. This is intended to make up the cost of disposing of the surplus sugar. A maximum has been set to the production levy which will mean that the beet price cannot fall below £4. 4s. 0d. per ton for 1968/69. Quantities produced above the ceiling cannot be disposed of on the Community's market and will not attract export restitutions.

Italian sugar-beet production suffers from some special disabilities. Apart from the structural difficulties of agriculture in Italy, the mineral content tends to be high and the sugar content of the beet correspondingly low. The campaign usually has to be undertaken in only six weeks. These factors were given recognition through the permission to the Italian government to operate a national subsidy amounting to a maximum of about 9s. 3d. per ton for producers of sugar-beet and about £6. 3s. 0d. per ton for processers (both being about 6 per cent of the target price). The subsidies at this level are limited to 1968/69 to 1970/71. From 1971/72 the subsidies have to be phased out over a seven-year period.

The Council's decisions differed from the Commission's proposals in two important respects. All the prices were about 2 per cent higher than had been suggested and the total quota was raised in the negotiations by 200,000 tons or about 3 per cent. The Council, however, accepted the Commission's insistence on the need to limit by quotas the quantities which would be eligible for the high prices, and therefore the sums for which the Fund would be liable.

In harmonizing sugar prices the EEC has had to settle for a relatively high price. Only in Germany and Italy are the prices for beets and sugar coming down. In France, where production is anyway rising and where the potentialities are greatest, the beet price is being raised by about 30 per cent, a relatively larger increase than in the case of wheat. Forecasting production under the new pricing is extremely difficult. It seems likely that the EEC surplus will be at least 500,000 tons within a year or two and may soon be one million tons. The 35 per cent over consumption which the regulations provide for is equivalent to about 1·9 mn. tons.

The Commission's original proposals were based on the expectation that sugar consumption *per caput* would rise by about $1\frac{1}{2}$ per cent a year to a figure of 33·7 kg. in 1970, with a particularly strong tendency to increase in Italy and the Netherlands. An increase of at least this amount is likely to take place because it is only in France that the consumer sugar price will rise to any great extent. The projected EEC *per caput* consumption is only about 60 per cent of the UK's present *per caput* consumption. The UK price is of course lower but demand in EEC may continue to be more elastic to increases in income. Taking these figures into consideration a reasonable guess at the EEC's exportable surplus over the decade is that it will run at between half and one million tons of sugar.

THE UNITED KINGDOM AS A MEMBER OF THE EEC

The chief characteristic of the UK's sugar market is the large importation of raw sugar, much of which is produced in underdeveloped countries whose economies are very heavily dependent on sugar. The situation in the EEC is entirely different. The Community is more or less self-sufficient in sugar and with the addition of the French overseas departments, Réunion, Martinique, and Guadeloupe, has an exportable surplus. How can the two situations be reconciled?

Before turning to the Commonwealth Sugar Agreement the effects must be discussed of EEC sugar pricing on UK sugar-beet growers and sugar processers. The present sugar-beet price (1967 Review) is 133s. 0d. per ton, basis 16 per cent sugar. After allowing for differences on transportation and pulp arrangements the EEC price to the farmer would be about 164s. 0d. per ton. From the farmer's point of view, therefore, there is no difficulty over the price. The domestic quota the government would press for would largely depend on what arrangements were made to deal with the Commonwealth Sugar Agreement. Most probably the quota that the UK received would lead to increased domestic production. It is likely that this extra tonnage would be refined by the British Sugar Corporation and might not benefit the domestic refiners, who would also face competition from sugar refined in the EEC. But the size and efficiency of the British companies could enable them to gain more from increased sales in the EEC than they lose from tariff-free competition here. The more important effect on the UK companies is the improvement in the margin between raw and refined sugar prices which the EEC will bring.

The monopolistic position of the British Sugar Corporation might present difficulties under the provisions of the Rome Treaty, but there is no particular reason why the factories owned by the Corporation should not be offered for sale. Total fixed assets of the Corporation are shown on the Balance Sheet at about £37 mn. Actual value is presumably very much higher than this, as no revaluation has been published since 1948. Alternatively, it might be a question of terminating the monopoly. Other companies, including the refiners, would then be free to build extraction plants and compete with the British Sugar Corporation. The high cost of a new factory for processing beet would be a considerable deterrent.

It was shown earlier that an EEC sugar surplus of up to one million tons is to be expected in the fairly near future. The Commission claims that it can get rid of at least this amount on the domestic market, i.e. without dumping the sugar on the world market. This would be done by denaturing about 800,000 tons for animal feed and using the remainder (up to about 400,000 tons) in the chemical industry. Both would, of course, involve subsidies, but these would be less per ton than the cost of dumping the sugar abroad. Besides, the effect of a further million tons of sugar offered on the world market could be disastrous to prices. While these forecasts of sugar consumed outside the food sector are encouraging, they must be treated with some reserve. It is also as well to remember that denatured sugar will be competing with other feed ingredients.

The perfect solution from the narrowest point of view of existing EEC member countries would be for the CSA to lapse and for most of present and future EEC sugar surpluses to be sold at the Community price in the

UK. As the Agreement exists and there is no cancellation clause, this is not a possibility. The next best would be for no renewal whatever of the CSA to take place. Beginning from 1975 the EEC surplus would then flow into the UK to the great benefit of FEOGA, which would be spared the cost of restitutions. This might well amount to about £60 per ton on however many tons of surplus sugar the Community is unable to use for the other purposes mentioned earlier. The balance of the UK's requirements, reduced by the effects of higher sugar prices, would be met by the world market in which Commonwealth suppliers would compete. There would be no guarantee of either price or access. As the former French territories in Africa have found, the status of association is of no benefit when tropical products are in question for which temperate products can be substituted.

It is important to distinguish between the sugar problem over the next eight years, i.e. during the term of the existing CSA, and the problem after this period. In the former the UK will have to be permitted to provide access to the CSA basic quotas plus the quantities called for under Article 15 of the Agreement. The present surcharge could be retained in order to implement the Agreement. Levies raised in excess of the CSA price would be remitted in the usual way to Brussels. So far as the latter period is concerned, when the Agreement is reviewed again the Australian quotas (totalling 335,000 tons) for the year following the end of the Agreement should be considerably reduced and then phased out altogether over a three-year term. If market conditions are generally similar to those at present, French and Belgian sugar would then be substituted for the Australian. The quotas for the low-income countries should be geared to a proportion of total Community consumption on a diminishing scale. Future extensions of the Agreement would become Community responsibilities rather than being confined to the UK.

The total transition period for Commonwealth sugar producers might amount to sixteen years, eight of the current agreement which would be honoured, and eight when a gradual run-down of access and price commitments would take place. Such a term does not seem excessively severe. In the interim it might prove possible to conclude a new International Sugar Agreement. This would be a great deal better than nothing for Commonwealth and other sugar producers. But no International Agreement is likely to be as favourable as the terms of the CSA either on quantities or on price.

The two large refining companies, Tate & Lyle Ltd. and Manbré & Garton Ltd., have various worries connected with UK membership of the EEC. One has already been indicated. If UK beet production increases, the output of white sugar by the British Sugar Corporation will also rise, particularly as EEC policy is directed towards encouragement of refining by beet factories. In these circumstances the quantity of raw sugar available for the UK refiners will presumably fall, and might prove insufficient compared with their refining capacity. Another concern for the refiners is the level which might be set for intervention prices in the UK. These could be fixed so as to make it difficult for the refiners to compete in exports both to the EEC and to third countries. Finally, as food prices rise, the demand for cheaper, lower grade sugars may increase. This might well prove an advantage for French refiners who produce qualities similar to the 'plantation whites' available before the war, which are less highly refined, and therefore tend to be cheaper than granulated sugars produced by the UK refiners. Despite freight costs these sugars might be sold competitively in the UK market if tariff barriers were removed.

13. Horticultural Products

(i) FRUIT AND VEGETABLES

Horticultural products, largely as a result of their dependence on comparative climatic advantage, present, as will be evident from Table 24, an entirely different picture from the rest of those covered by the CAP. The Netherlands, it is true, and Belgium too, play their part as exporters in this as in other fields, but horticulture is chiefly notable for the predominance of Italy, whose growers earned just over 20 per cent of gross national agricultural income in 1965. Italian fruit and vegetables supply a large part of the considerable import needs of the German market, Germans being

TABLE 24. FRUIT AND VEGETABLES:
PRODUCTION AND CONSUMPTION, 1964/65

	Comparative production UK=100	Percentage of total production: the Six	Degree of self-sufficiency per cent	Consumption per head per year kg.
Fresh Fruit[a]				
Germany (FR)	236·8	19·3	51	60·6
France	232·2	18·9	97	48·0
Italy	637·4	52·1	119	74·4
Netherlands	81·8	6·7	126	40·4
Belgium/Luxemburg	36·3	3·0	83	34·4
The Six	1,224·5	100·0	91	
United Kingdom	100·0		42	35·6
Ireland	n.a.		34[b]	41·1[b]
Denmark	28·3		81	60·8
Norway	8·0		55	34·3
Fresh vegetables[c]				
Germany (FR)	62·8	8·9	62	48·6
France	226·1	31·9	95	132·1
Italy	327·8	46·2	114	149·1
Netherlands	57·1	8·1	166	50·9
Belgium/Luxemburg	35·0	4·9	115	88·1
The Six	708·8	100·0	102	
United Kingdom	100·0		80	61·4
Ireland	n.a.		100·1	65·4
Denmark	11·7		100·5	63·3
Norway	4·7		90	33·2

[a] Including preserved in terms of fresh fruit, but excluding citrus.
[b] 1963 only.   [c] Including preserved in terms of fresh vegetables, as well as tomatoes.
Sources: EEC, *Agricultural Statistics, 1966*, No. 2. *Food Consumption Levels in OECD Countries 1962/3–1964/5.*

second only to the Italians themselves as eaters of fresh fruit. Fruit consumption has been increasing in Germany at a rate of about 3 per cent a year since the early fifties. In the UK it has hardly risen at all. The British eat more vegetables, however, and in an enlarged Community the UK would run Germany a very close second as the main importer of horticultural produce.

THE UNITED KINGDOM

Output from horticultural crops in the UK, whose value has risen (at current prices) by just over half during the past ten years, accounted, at £188 mn., for 10·2 per cent of gross agricultural income in 1966/67, compared with 8·9 per cent in 1956/57. Its rate of expansion has thus been slightly greater than that of UK agriculture as a whole. The main part of this total of £188 mn. relates to production in England. It does not include that of the Channel Islands which, mainly of tomatoes, was valued at £17·2 mn. in 1966.

During recent years fruit and vegetable production has become increasingly concentrated, both structurally and geographically. The bulk of production comes from the larger units. About 12 per cent of orchards account for over 70 per cent of the top-fruit acreage; about 12 per cent of vegetable growers for two-thirds of the vegetable acreage. More than a third of the 4,000 acres of glasshouses in 1965 were concentrated on 200 holdings with 2·5 acres or more of glass. Given a current capital investment cost of some £30,000 an acre of glass this is scarcely surprising. With developments in road transport and more widespread use of selling by description, proximity to large urban markets is no longer the important factor which it used to be in the location of fruit and vegetable production. Market gardening in suburban areas has declined. As a result certain products have become even more closely associated with particular regions than in the past: cauliflowers in the Holland region of Lincolnshire, for instance, where 28 per cent of total UK acreage is now located compared with 15 per cent ten years ago; carrots in Norfolk, which now produces well over 40 per cent compared with 28 per cent in 1954; raspberries in the Angus area of Scotland (over three-quarters of the GB total, an increase of 18 per cent in ten years); and apples in Kent, whose proportion of the English crop has risen from under 30 to over 40 per cent. In the glasshouse sector, on the other hand, similar considerations have resulted in a wider regional dispersal, owing to the loss of the Lea Valley's former preponderance. This area on the northern edge of Greater London lost a third of its glasshouse acreage between 1954 and 1965, and a redistribution took place in favour of areas in Scotland and the north of England and round Worthing in Sussex chosen for their good light and freedom from urban smog. The movement has, however, to some extent been prevented from reaching its fullest possible extent by planning restrictions in green-belt areas, which hinder the erection of glasshouses in new regions at the same time as reducing the capital value of obsolete sites for other building.

Horticulture, unlike other branches of agriculture, has never received government support in the form of price guarantees or production grants (other than those such as the fertilizer and lime subsidies from which growers benefit equally with farmers). Direct assistance has been through investment grants towards buildings, plant, and equipment for production, storage, and preparation of produce. These amounted, for England and Wales alone, to nearly £4·5 mn. during the first five years of operation of the 1960 Horticulture Improvement Scheme. Indirect assistance has taken the form of tariffs and quotas, many of them varied seasonally, on imports of most horticultural products from non-Commonwealth sources. Commonwealth produce has entered free of tariff. The tariffs applicable to the main import crops are listed in Appendix D.

THE EEC

Producers of fruit and vegetables in the EEC also enjoy a substantial degree of tariff protection against imports from third countries. The common external tariff for the crops listed in Appendix D is given by way of comparison. Not only is the level of protection in general higher, but the Community system also allows for additional countervailing duties to be imposed in the case of abnormally low offers. For this purpose reference prices for all products are fixed by the Commission corresponding to the lowest market prices in the area of greatest surplus for each product. If import prices remain below the reference price for more than three consecutive days a countervailing duty is applied equivalent to the difference between the reference price and the import price. Effectively import prices are calculated at a number of main internal markets with due allowance made for transport costs from the frontier and customs duty.

Similarly the second aspect of EEC protection for fruit and vegetables, quality control, is also applied inland, either at wholesale or retail level, and not at the common frontier. Originally it had been considered by the Commission that tariffs and the strict application of grading would be sufficient support for growers. As a concession to particular Italian interests, however, the other five member countries agreed to introduce a measure of price support for fruit and vegetables as well, to be financed out of FEOGA. This is up to a total limit of $60 mn. for 1967–69, of which Italy is guaranteed a two-third's share, the remaining $20 mn. being shared between other member countries in proportion to their expenditure. The decision was part of the package deal reached by the Council of Ministers in December 1964 and a *quid pro quo* for the high level of the common price fixed for feedgrains, which was contrary to the interests of Italian livestock farmers. The support arrangements, eventually agreed upon in July 1966 after further lengthy negotiations and brought into force on 1 January 1967, are designed essentially as a safety net. Their principal objectives are to avoid giving any encouragement to the production of surpluses and to reduce to a minimum the liability of FEOGA.

Intervention in the market is to be in two stages. The first stage is left entirely to producers themselves, who may through their own organizations fix a buying-in price at which they will, in order to try to prevent a collapse of the market, enter the market and compensate those whose produce remains unsold. Such intervention must be wholly at the expense of the producers' associations by means of levies paid in by their members. Duly constituted and recognized groups may receive the usual investment grants (50 per cent of which are payable out of FEOGA) as well as loans of working capital. Official intervention by member governments marks the second stage should stage one fail to steady the market. Basic prices, representative of average prices over the previous three years in the surplus areas of the Community, are fixed annually by the Commission for each product covered by intervention.[1] Buying-in prices are then derived from these basic prices. Each buying-in price may, until the end of 1969, be fixed by member states at not more than 70 per cent of the basic price. Thereafter they will be confined within stricter limits.[2] If on three consecutive market days prices on representative markets are below the equivalent of the buying-in price plus 15 per cent of the basic price, the member government concerned will declare a state of crisis, during which official agencies for producers' organizations (where they exist) may start buying-in and be compensated out of FEOGA. A return to pre-crisis levels of market prices for three consecutive days automatically brings the crisis (and buying-in) to an end. If, however, prices continue to fall, a state of 'serious crisis' may be declared after prices have been below the buying-in price itself on three consecutive days. In that case full financial compensation, on an agreed scale, for unsold produce may be paid to producers out of national exchequers. After 1969 determination of a state of crisis or serious crisis will rest with the Commission alone. It may be noted that experience of the system during its first working summer has not been entirely satisfactory, the three-day rule tending to make markets operate by a series of fits and starts, and an amendment that would achieve a more long-term elimination of current surpluses before any attempt is made to return to normal market conditions is likely to be devised.

One further measure of assistance to EEC producers of fruit and vegetables is the granting of refunds on exports, equivalent to the duty under the common external tariff, plus any countervailing duty which may be applicable. Since internal EEC prices will not normally rise above those in third countries, export restitutions would probably be used only as a counter-measure against dumping.

THE UNITED KINGDOM AS A MEMBER OF THE EEC

Government measures of a general nature towards improving the efficiency of horticulture such as have been taken under the 1960 and 1964

[1] Cauliflowers, lettuce, endives, onions, tomatoes, oranges, apples, pears, apricots, peaches, plums, spinach, chicory, peas, beans, carrots, artichokes, lemons, table grapes, cherries, strawberries, asparagus, garlic, cucumbers and various types of cabbage.

[2] Cauliflowers and tomatoes: 40 to 45 per cent of the basic price; apples and pears: 50 to 55 per cent of the basic price; other products: 60 to 70 per cent of the basic price.

Acts would continue to find a place in the Community system. An especially favourable view would be taken of grants for co-operative marketing, but private firms and individuals would continue to be eligible for exchequer aids to capital investment as well. To the extent also that British growers have never received any form of direct price support or production grant, the EEC and UK systems are alike and there will be no need for major administrative changes. These resemblances are of course deceptive. In fact, growers of fruit and vegetables are far more vulnerable to entry into the EEC than other types of producer. Not only are they at more of a climatic disadvantage, but the home market will for the first time be exposed to all-year-round tariff-free imports from a number of major European exporters of horticultural products.

Not all sectors will be equally threatened. It seems likely that, at any rate until the opening of a Channel tunnel, producers of field vegetable crops (the value of whose output is about a third of the total for all crops) will still continue to enjoy a great deal of natural protection thanks to the bulkiness and perishability of potential exports from France and the Low Countries. Freight rates from Dunkirk to London are upwards of 9s. 0d. per cwt. The 20 per cent of field crops produced for canning and quick freezing do not in any case compete directly with imports, though competition from tariff-free processed produce from other member countries would tend to lower contract prices payable to farmers by British processers. The relatively large scale of production of field crops, and the increasing regional concentration already referred to, suggest that this sector would remain reasonably competitive at any rate for maincrop varieties. The marginal effect of imports will obviously be more serious for those specializing in early crops of broccoli, cauliflower, carrots, and asparagus, which at present enjoy a higher tariff.

Seasonal and climatic considerations would also weigh heavily with producers of soft fruit, particularly of strawberries, though they too might hope to enjoy the protection of high transport costs in the short run. Inasmuch as a Channel tunnel would bring the very large concentration of population of the south-east relatively closer to a greater number of French, Belgian, and Dutch growers than it would bring English growers to, say, the populated regions of the Rhineland, it could on balance (of the horticultural account at least) be a disadvantage. Early imports, a week or two ahead of the first home-grown earlies, would to some extent absorb local beginning of season demand for high-priced soft fruit, a market to which growers attach considerable, though possibly exaggerated, importance. Blackcurrant growers, mainly producing to contract, would be generally less vulnerable to imports.

Glasshouse production, having particularly benefited from the shot in the arm of the 1964 Horticultural Improvement Scheme, should be in a reasonably healthy state to withstand the cold winds of the CAP. These will be mainly blowing from the direction of the Netherlands, whose tomato and lettuce production is outstandingly efficient. The English, however, now probably make use of more up-to-date techniques of siting, construction, and light usage than the majority of Dutch growers, who were renewing their glasshouses during the fifties. To the extent that the glasshouse industry is still not as concentrated geographically as in the Netherlands, further rationalization will be forced upon it, and units which are too scattered to participate in any co-ordinated offer on the market are bound to suffer. Of the industry's two main variable costs, fuel and labour, there is no evidence that the Dutch enjoy any advantage on the first. Agricultural wages in the Netherlands, including social security contributions, are the highest in the Community and certainly higher than in the UK. It is often argued, however, that on the average Dutch horticultural holding, labour is to a great extent an imputed cost only. It is true up to a point that family labour, especially an owner-occupier and his wife, will work for a lower cash return than hired labour, but at a time when young people are leaving the land in large numbers for industrial employment much greater material inducements are needed even on a family holding than in the past. Probably the main advantage on the labour side to the Dutch glasshouse producer lies with overtime, part-time family members with outside jobs being prepared to work early and late on the holding for a relatively small monetary return. But whatever the balance of cost advantage between growers in the UK and the Netherlands, there is no doubt that the removal of the present UK tariff on tomatoes would present grave problems. According to one estimate it could lead to a doubling of Dutch imports (53,000 tons in 1965). This would raise potential supply on the home market to about 16 per cent above recent levels of consumption. Seasonal imports from Spain and the Canaries would attract a 1 per cent higher tariff from November to April but considerably lower rates than at present during May.

Of all the sectors of horticulture, top-fruit growing, especially apple growing, will have the least remedy against the effects of unlimited imports from EEC countries. Despite highly efficient production and packing methods and co-operative forms of marketing developed over recent years, apple growers will be at a certain natural disadvantage. An Italian orchard produces nearly three times as great a weight of apples to the acre as an English one. This involves higher picking costs per acre, and the English also benefits from a strong consumer preference for Cox's over Golden Delicious. But the Italians' higher yields would still give them a considerable edge on price on the UK market after allowing for transport charges. The same difficulty applies to finding export outlets for Cox's on the Continent, where a wider taste for the English apple could, given the right price, probably be encouraged. The EEC common external tariff, on the other hand, gives more protection against imports from third countries than does the present UK tariff which, apart from exempting the considerable Commonwealth imports from duty, only applies briefly (0·5d. per lb. from 15 April to 15 August) to those from other sources. The EEC tariff extends to the whole year, and is not less than 1·09d. per lb. from August to December.

The horticultural industry thus faces, if the UK adopts the CAP, a period of painful adjustment, but two points should be borne in mind. In the first place there has been plenty of warning. Growers have had considerable opportunity, of which many have taken advantage, of either modernizing their business with the help of government investment grants or of leaving the industry. For this reason it seems doubtful whether the idea of a special golden handshake, mooted by the NFU and others, for horticulture is likely to commend itself to any future government, though growers are of course as eligible as other farmers for the retirement pensions introduced by the 1967 Agricultural Act. Some case might possibly be made for compensating growers of top-fruit. Their livelihood and heavy capital investments would be prejudiced by their geographical disadvantage in the EEC rather than through any failure to be technically competitive. Second, it should be realized that UK growers would by no means be the only ones to suffer. Painful adjustments in horticulture are already taking place within the Community. In the face of Italian imports Belgian hothouse grapes are rapidly being driven from the market, and thousands of acres of French apple and peach orchards are being grubbed up that have only recently come into bearing.

Apart from having to face up to unpalatable decisions of this kind in face of long-term shifts in supply and demand, growers on the Continent, equally, cannot look forward to being completely insulated against the effects of seasonal fluctuations. During its first summer of full operation the CAP for fruit and vegetables seems to have brought some small relief to producers at moments of over-supply, at least if press reports of consumers' complaints about the deliberate destruction of surpluses are anything to go by. But withdrawal price levels, whether first or second stage, have been set purposely low by the Commission, representing little more than half the cost of production, and generally speaking rather less than Dutch producers have been used to expect over the years under their compulsory crop insurance schemes. Even at such a low level the grower is at least encouraged to keep off the market produce that would otherwise only serve further to depress prices and thus bring him a return which, although he might hope it would cover part of his production costs, often turns out barely to cover his marketing costs. All the same, the possibility cannot be ruled out that with the UK inside the EEC growers in other parts of the Community might, given very low buying-in prices, find it marginally more profitable to despatch part at least of their surplus to the UK than accept compensation locally from the intervention agency. If quantities of produce came in this way to be offered on UK markets at just above buying-in price British growers might find themselves obliged to intervene at their own expense, through their associations, to mop up other people's surpluses, with no immediate prospect of official intervention.

Of the 25-odd products covered by the EEC marketing scheme less than half, including cauliflowers, lettuce, tomatoes, apples, and pears, would be of sufficient importance in the UK to warrant the setting up of an inter-vention fund by producers' associations. Although such associations are not required to have the legal status of co-operatives, and are often groupings of private growers, this aspect of the CAP would present the co-operative movement in the UK with a considerable opportunity of extending the scope of its activity in horticulture. In 1965/66 the combined marketing turnover of English horticultural co-operatives amounted to £11·5 mn., of which about £8·5 mn. related to vegetables. The number of co-operative organizations involved went up from 40 to 60 between 1960/61 and 1965/66, and a further ten have been formed since. Turnover during the same period increased rather slowly, by about £3 mn., and in 1965/66 still represented only 6 per cent of the total gross value of UK horticultural output. From the moment that UK entry into the EEC appeared assured, co-operatives would have to increase their efforts towards concentration of supply among growers. This will be necessary if they are to be ready to compete with increasing pressure from mainly co-operatively marketed imports. There is still a good deal of traditional scepticism among UK growers about the possibility of co-operative action, especially when they are geographically scattered, but the rapidity with which patterns of retailing are changing suggests that the days of the isolated producer must in any case be numbered. He is already excluded from supplying the supermarkets and chain stores. His days could be brought to an even more rapid close once an unimpeded flow of imported produce began to reach local shops through private chains. Rising demand for cheaper and more readily available fresh fruit and vegetables of even quality could lead to a streamlining of their distribution as revolutionary as the one which has already affected less perishable foodstuffs. It is a revolution in which failure to co-operate can in the long run only land the small independent grower in the tumbrils.

Whatever the complaints of consumers about producer intervention on the market, there can be no doubt that they are intended by the Com-mission to benefit substantially from the second of the two complementary aspects of the CAP in fruit and vegetables, the enforcement of quality grades and standards, for home-grown as well as imported produce, right down to retail level. Some teething troubles will no doubt be experienced in adapting existing UK grades to EEC ones,[3] but the objection about the difficulty in recruiting and training sufficient inspectors to enforce the Community regulations, which was raised at the time of the 1962 negotia-tions, no longer applies. In 1967 a beginning was made in the UK to introduce national statutory grades for apples, pears, tomatoes, cucumbers, and cauliflowers. Adoption of the CAP should lead to the elimination of a still wider range of poor quality produce from British greengrocer shops.

[3] EEC standards are mostly identical with those laid down in the Geneva Protocol drawn up by the United Nations Economic Commission for Europe's Working Party on the standard-ization of perishable foodstuffs. The United Kingdom although represented on the Working Party has not accepted the Protocol.

(ii) NON-EDIBLE PRODUCTS

In January 1966 the Commission submitted to the Council its first draft regulation for non-edible horticultural products. This envisaged a system of Community standards for quality control, along the lines of the first regulation for fruit and vegetables. This draft was superseded by a second, submitted by the Commission in February 1967. The latter, which was of a more definitive character, has not yet been adopted. It provides for the establishment of a common organization of the market for flower bulbs, all kinds of live plants, regardless of the use to which they are put, cut flowers, and a wide variety of plant parts, including those used for bouquet and ornamental purposes. For the main products quality standards are suggested, covering size, packaging, marking, etc. These standards are designed to apply both in retail trade in the Community and in exports to third countries. Member countries are required to set up facilities for inspection of all products to which quality standards apply.

The draft regulations provide for the removal of all restrictions on intra-Community trade, including customs duties, which should be abolished from 1 July 1968. From that date the common external tariff on imports from outside the Community would apply. It is intended that duties on cut flowers and flower buds will vary according to the season. The draft proposes that from 1 June to 31 October the rate should be 24 per cent and from 1 November to 31 May, 18·8 per cent. The rate on dormant bulbs is to be 9·2 per cent and on bulbs in growth of orchids, hyacinths, narcissi, and tulips 16·8 per cent. All quantitative restrictions on imports are to be abandoned except for a safeguard clause which can be operated by the Commission at the request of a member country in order to keep out excessively low-priced imports. The Commission acting in conjunction with the Management Committee for non-edible horticultural products will fix minimum export prices for dormant bulbs.

Adoption of the CAP would provide UK producers of bulbs, plants, and cut flowers with adequate protection from imports from third countries. But competition comes mostly from member countries, particularly the Netherlands and Italy. Removal of all barriers to trade with EEC countries would expose UK producers to very severe competition from the Continent. But of course there would be some benefit to the consumer through lower prices. Adjustment to EEC quality standards might also prove a difficulty for producers unless it was spread over a transition period. The standards proposed by the draft regulation are in any case likely to be of a somewhat experimental character.

14. Potatoes

Potato production in the UK differs from that in the EEC in two respects. First, no potatoes are grown purposely for feeding to livestock. Second, none are processed for industrial uses. Over two-thirds of home-grown potatoes are sold for human consumption. Of the total of 4·5 mn. to 5·0 mn. tons, about 0·7 mn. are usually earlies. A further 0·3 mn. tons of earlies are imported, mainly from Cyprus, Spain, the Canaries, and the Channel Islands. Per head consumption has been almost stationary during the sixties. Apart from chats and seconds potatoes are only fed to stock in years of surplus. More than 40 per cent of the EEC's crop of about 40 mn. tons, on the other hand, is normally grown for stockfeed. Consumption of table potatoes, which has shown a sharp downward trend during the past decade, now accounts for only about one-third. Another 5 per cent, mainly in the Netherlands, is processed for starch.

THE UNITED KINGDOM

Potato acreage is mainly concentrated in the eastern half of England and Scotland, where there are extensive areas of flat, easily-worked, fertile soils and where attacks of potato blight occur less frequently, or at a much later point in the season, than in the more humid western half of Great Britain. Seed potatoes are traditionally produced in the aphid-free conditions of Scotland and Northern Ireland.

Government support for potato growers is channelled through the Potato Marketing Board in Great Britain and through the Northern Ireland Ministry of Agriculture. In England, Scotland, and Wales the Board receives from the government at the end of each potato year a deficiency payment per ton (representing the difference between the guaranteed price and average market realization price over the year) on the total tonnage of potatoes sold by producers for human consumption through licensed merchants. This lump sum is not distributed to producers but placed in a Market Support Fund for future use. All producers with one acre or more of potatoes are obliged to register with the Board,[1] which allots acreage quotas based on each producer's previous three years' plantings. The Board may raise a levy of up to £3 an acre on basic acreages and a further payment of up to £25 an acre on any excess acreage planted. In this way total acreage has been limited in recent years to around 700,000 acres. Half of the £3 levy thus provides the Board with about

---

[1] 58,000 in 1965, of whom two-thirds grew under 10 acres.

TABLE 25. POTATOES: PRODUCTION AND CONSUMPTION, 1965

	Comparative acreage UK=100	Comparative production UK=100	Percentage of total production: the Six	Percentage of total production: the Ten	Average yield per hectare, 100 kg.	Comparative yield UK=100	Degree of self-sufficiency per cent	Consumption per head[a] per year[b] kg.
Germany (FR)	261·0	238·7	47·4	36·5	231	91·3	97	118·0
France	210·0	155·9	30·9	23·9	188	74·3	104	104·6
Italy	116·0	46·8	9·3	7·2	102	40·3	97	44·5
Netherlands	41·3	42·9	8·5	6·6	262	103·6	120	92·2
Belgium	19·0	18·7	3·7	2·9	249	98·4	} 97	121·1
Luxemburg	1·3	1·0	0·2	0·1	182	71·9		
The Six	648·7	504·0	100·0	77·2			100·6	
United Kingdom	100·0	100·0		15·3	253	100·0	98	101·5
Ireland	23·7	21·7		3·3	232	91·7	103	151·5
Denmark	13·3	12·4		1·9	234	92·5	105	94·9
Norway	16·0	15·0		2·3	236	93·3	100	87·3
The Four				22·8			99	
The Ten				100·0			100·2	

a Human consumption only, includes dried potato where applicable. b 1964/65
Sources: *EEC Agricultural Statistics, 1966*, No. 6. *Food Consumption in the OECD Countries 1962/63–1964/65.*

£1 mn. a year towards the Market Support Fund, the other half being taken up in administration, sales promotion, and technical research.

Each season the Board announces the standard size for the riddle for both earlies and maincrop potatoes, and as the season advances may vary the riddle in the light of the current supply situation in order to let more or fewer potatoes through into the market. In the event of a narrowing of the riddle proving insufficient to prevent a glut the Board may intervene by undertaking to purchase all potatoes offered to it by producers at a price sufficient to raise market prices closer to the guarantee level. To help finance this intervention the government undertakes to contribute £2 for every £1 expended by the Board on support buying. It is calculated that the 700,000 acres is sufficient to satisfy domestic demand for maincrop potatoes (and about two-thirds of demand for earlies) except in years of abnormally low yields, and even in years of high yields will not normally result in surpluses greater than can be cleared at the cost of the Support Fund's assured income of around £3 mn. The amount of its additional income from deficiency payments naturally varies in inverse ratio to the success of the Board's intervention policy in keeping market prices close to the level of the guaranteed price. Should its reserves run out the Fund may borrow from the government, repayment being made out of future deficiency payments or unspent levy income. Imports of maincrop potatoes are, for obvious reasons, only authorized by the Board in seasons of scarcity. They bear a duty of 1s. 0d. per cwt. A duty of 9s. 4d. per cwt. on earlies, whose import is unrestricted, applicable between 16 May and 30 June, protects domestic producers during the early weeks of lifting. Cyprus and Channel Island earlies enter duty-free under the preferential tariff.

THE EEC

In the UK even if the majority of individual plantings of potatoes are fairly small they usually occur in the rotation of a, by Continental standards, comparatively large and mechanized holding. Potato-growing in the EEC is, on the other hand, like most other kinds of farming activity, mainly a small-holder's operation. For this reason the essentially labour-intensive practice of using potatoes for stock-feed has declined much less in recent years than might have been expected. The decline has been most marked in France, where domestic maize production has made rapid strides. In Germany the relatively high price of feedgrains has, on the other hand, helped to maintain the level of potato usage, particularly for pigs. In Italy, despite the fact that feedgrain prices have been lowest and movement of labour off the land highest in the Community, consumption of stockfeed potatoes has nevertheless risen substantially during the sixties, largely as a function of the country's greatly increased output of pigmeat.

The CAP does not at present cover potatoes, which are not included under the fruit and vegetable regulations. The nature and degree of government support therefore varies from one member country to another. In

Italy and Belgium, both exceptional in that well over half of production is sold for the table, there is none. France, where human and animal consumption each account for about one third of output, and Germany, where more than half is fed to stock, premiums are given on potatoes sold for industrial processing. Luxemburg, where guaranteed producer prices and maximum retail prices for potatoes are fixed, is permitted under the Protocol to the Rome Treaty to impose import quotas. Government support is most extensive in the Netherlands, which has a substantial export trade, particularly in seed. In years of surplus ware potatoes receive export subsidies or are diverted to stockfeed at the joint expense of the government and the commodity board (*Produktschap*) for potatoes. Surplus certified seed may also be removed from the market at the expense of the Seed Potato Fund, which is financed out of levies on producers and on exports.

The common external tariff applies a number of *ad valorem* duties, ranging from 9 per cent on potatoes imported for starch manufacture to 21 per cent on earlies in May and June.

THE UNITED KINGDOM AS A MEMBER OF THE EEC

In the absence of any EEC regulation it is difficult to foresee how much of the existing support arrangements would be allowed to stand. To the extent that they resemble those still current, and apparently permissible, in the Netherlands it would seem that they would not be wholly incompatible with EEC philosophy. The element of price guarantee, however, is a likely casualty. Its removal would of course mean somewhat greater uncertainty for the producer, but inasmuch as he does not actually see the deficiency payment in cash its disappearance might not make much psychological impact. In any case the Support Fund was set up in 1962 largely in order to limit exchequer liability for deficiency payments by preventing a collapse of market prices. It was reckoned that on balance the government's contribution of up to £2 mn. to the Fund would cost less, taking one year with another, than if there were no intervention. In effect this has proved to be so, the average annual cost to the exchequer during the first five years of the Fund's operation being well under half the average of the previous five years. Other than in a year of outstandingly high yields, such as 1965/66, deficiency payments on potatoes now play hardly any part in government support. The replacement of the guaranteed price by a target price on EEC lines, towards which it would be the object of intervention to guide market prices, would not therefore involve a major change of present practice.

The Potato Marketing Board, unlike other marketing boards, purchases only a fraction of its registered producers' output, and thus fails in a rather different respect from the other boards to measure up to the criteria of an EEC producer group: it does not trade. Probably an exception could be made in this case to allow member producers to continue trading direct, but as their total output would constitute about 12 per cent of that of an

P

enlarged Community the Board might have to be reconstituted as a federation of its own regions. This would present no great difficulty. Adoption of the principle of *extension des règles de discipline* would take care of the compulsory levy. It is doubtful, however, whether acreage quotas would be any longer permissible. Their abolition would no doubt be welcomed by liberal critics of the present system, and by a few cheerful anarchists among producers, though there is no conclusive evidence that controlled planting has either raised prices to the consumer or restricted the entry of a significant number of would-be producers. Individual applications for a new quota or an increase of an existing quota for rotational reasons are usually sympathetically considered by the Board. In fact the basic acreage was underplanted, sometimes by as much as 20 per cent, in each year between 1962 and 1966, all 100 per cent quota years. Abolishing quotas would be likely to lead to the development of a more pronounced cyclical, so-called cobweb, pattern of production, total acreage in any season becoming, to a much greater extent than at present, a function of the level of the previous season's prices. Even under a quota system year to year variations in supply due mainly to natural causes bring difficulties enough.

A much greater obstacle to the functioning of the potato scheme in its present form within the EEC, even allowing for the disappearance of deficiency payments, lies in the difficulty of operating an intervention policy with doors wide open to imports of maincrop potatoes from other member countries, whose exclusion would no longer be permissible. Three factors would, however, operate against entirely unrestricted imports. The first, quite fortuitous from one year to another, arises when climatic conditions result in the absence of an export surplus on the Continent. Experience indicates that levels of yields on both sides of the Channel do not necessarily coincide, even though in a common market the planting cycle would tend to get into phase. Conversely, in a season of scarcity imports of surplus potatoes from the rest of the Community could enter without unduly disrupting the UK market. When crops were large everywhere, however, the UK Support Fund could, failing a CAP for potatoes, and Community intervention arrangements, find itself ineluctably becoming the purchaser of everyone else's surpluses.

Second, the UK market would enjoy a measure of protection through transport costs, which, at current freight rates and handling charges for a bulky (and in winter highly perishable) commodity, might average about £5 per ton delivered on quayside. The average differential between prices in France and prices in the UK in February between 1962 and 1966 was 55s. 0d. per ton, and that between Dutch and UK prices only 35s. 0d. per ton.[2] Transport costs could, at certain seasons at any rate, prove a substantial deterrent to imports. Finally, although the EEC is aiming at an eventual harmonization of internal non-tariff barriers, the target is still a fairly distant one. National sanitary restrictions on potato imports, not

[2] *Agra-Europe* No. 209, 1967.

only those on seed, would have to be strictly maintained. At present only imports of washed potatoes are permitted from France as a precaution against Colorado beetle. Any extensive spread on the Continent of bacterial ring rot, an infection known to have been imported from North America within the last few years, could even result in a total stoppage of imports.

15. Vegetable Oils and Oilseeds

In principle the CAP covers all vegetable and fish oils and their by-products.[1] A majority of them are subject to bindings in GATT, ranging from duties of between 3 and 8 per cent on oils used for industrial purposes and of between 9 and 15 per cent on those for human consumption. There is a 25 per cent duty on margarine. The duty on oilseeds and fruits and on oilcakes is nil. This includes soya bean cake and meal, imports of which into the UK, it may be noted, bear a 15 per cent duty and those of other cakes 10 per cent. The UK duty on fishmeal (other than herring) is also 10 per cent, compared with the EEC common external tariff's 4 per cent. UK compounders once inside the Community would thus have access to vegetable and fish protein at lower prices than at present. While it is true that oilseeds and cakes from the Commonwealth enjoy the preferential *nil* tariff, in practice the present market situation usually enables suppliers from Commonwealth countries to sell c.i.f. at duty-paid prices.

Apart from the protection which the common external tariff gives to producers in the EEC of a number of products, such as olive oil and butter, for which vegetable oils provide direct substitutes, there are also separate market regulations for olive oil itself and for oilseeds.

OLIVE OIL

The regulation for olive oil, which is produced commercially only in Italy, operates in a manner similar to that for cereals, with a system of target, intervention, and threshold prices, seasonal increments, import levies and export restitutions. There is, however, one important difference in that there are two target prices: a producer target price, or norm price, fixed at a level 'fair to producers and with due regard to the need for maintaining the required volume of production'; and a market target price fixed at a level 'permitting a normal market flow of home production having regard to the prices of competing products'. Olive yields being by nature highly variable between one year and another, provision is made for the operation of an official buffer stock to help reduce excessive price fluctuations. If, despite this, the producer target price should, at the beginning of a season of over-production, have to be fixed at a level above that of the market target price, an aid or subsidy equivalent to the difference between the two is payable to producers. This is, in effect, a deficiency payment.

---

[1] Animal oils and fats are dealt with under the respective regulations covering the livestock products from which they are derived.

OILSEEDS

A form of deficiency payment is also provided for in the regulation on oilseeds which came into force in July 1967 for a trial period of one year. Although payable to the seed crusher its purpose is to support the domestic producer inside the EEC whose output of colza, rape, and sunflower seed only accounts for between 5 and 10 per cent of the Community's total demand for vegetable oils and fats. The payment, consisting of the difference between the Community target price and the lowest offer c.i.f. EEC ports as determined weekly by the Commission,[2] is made on all deliveries of home-grown seeds to crushing plants in the Community. In order to avoid fraud imported seeds are subject to strict inspection between port and plant.

The Community target price has been fixed at £85. 14s. 0d. per ton. With world prices currently around £51. 10s. 0d. the purpose of the subsidy is clear. Producers are guaranteed a minimum return by means of a basic intervention price (at Duisburg) of £83. 4s. 0d. per ton (with derived prices ranging down to £74. 4s. 0d.). The subsidy is designed to coax prices upwards in the direction of the target price. Buying at just above intervention level the crusher would be getting his seeds at a net price below that ruling on the world market, e.g. £83. 4s. 0d. *minus* subsidy of £34. 4s. 0d. (i.e. £85. 14s. 0d. *minus* £51. 10s. 0d.) equals £49. It depends on the strength of the producer's bargaining position how far he can edge the crusher up towards the target price, which is of course the crusher's break-even point, leaving aside transport costs, between home-grown and imported seeds. The producer may, however, if he prefers, sell direct to his national intervention agency and be paid the intervention price.

EEC production of colza and rape, the more important of the three types of seed, is expected to have reached a record level in 1966/67 of 480,000 tons. Of this over two thirds was grown in France and the rest, bar the 3 or 4 per cent of the Dutch and Italian crops, in Germany. Belgian producers have not yet entered the field, oilseeds not having enjoyed any subsidy in Belgium, or in the Netherlands, out of the national exchequer. Guaranteed prices have operated for a number of years in France and Germany, where production received a special boost at the time of the Korean war whose impetus was never lost. The argument for the high level of subsidy now being extended to the Community as a whole must be assumed to be mainly one of good husbandry. The EEC regulation merely states that its purpose is to 'ensure that the required volume of production is maintained in the Community'. The question of defining 'required' is not made any simpler if one considers that in 1963/64 and 1964/65 over half the French crop was exported to third countries. The regulation also provides for its eventual extension to other types of oilseeds. Existing national measures of support for linseed and raisin seed are to be allowed to continue until 1971/72.

---

[2] Or c.i.f. price of oil and oilcake adjusted for processing costs if offers of seed are insufficient.

No statistics of oilseed production are available for the UK since oilseed rape is not distinguished in the agricultural census returns from other forms of rape. Plantings are thought not to exceed 4,000 acres. Most of this is grown under contract, and prices have fluctuated around the £37 per ton mark. Given EEC intervention price levels production would undoubtedly expand considerably. With the rapeseed to wheat price ratio fixed at 1·9:1·0, the arable farmer's search for a profitable break crop would be at an end. At the rate of gross return per acre which that implies, not less than £59. 15s. 0d. assuming the lowest intervention price and the same average yield as on the Continent (16 cwt. per acre), the £5 an acre subsidy for beans, incompatible with EEC regulations, would scarcely be missed.

16. Wine and Tobacco

UK farmers, like those of Ireland, Denmark, and Norway, would, apart from drinking and smoking, have no direct interest in wine and tobacco. Nor is either commodity produced in Belgium or the Netherlands. But tobacco production in the EEC, about 133,000 tons of leaf, is worth $140 mn. a year, and the value of wine output in the four producer countries is more than half that of the Community's entire output of cereals. Their 7 mn. acres of vineyards, just under a third of the world's total, produce half the world's wine. The structure of wine-growing is highly fragmented, the average size of vineyard being no more than two acres. Although in Germany the proportion of gross agricultural output attributable to wine is now under 2 per cent, in Italy it rose from 8 per cent to 10 per cent between 1960 and 1965. In France where the value of output, as in Italy, increased by 50 per cent (at constant prices) during those five years, its proportionate contribution to total production actually fell from nearly 10 per cent to under 8 per cent. Yields have increased in both countries, particularly in Italy, where they were often very poor, through the abandonment of hill farms and increasing concentration of production and spread of know-how by means of co-operatives. French wine-growers, on the other hand, except for the minority producing first class wines, have felt themselves left even further behind in the struggle for income parity than most other farmers, and barricades have frequently appeared across roads in the poorer wine districts. Wine yields, being peculiarly susceptible to the weather, vary considerably from one year to another, producing seasons of local glut against a general background, taking the Community as a whole, of excess demand over supply. During the early sixties the EEC's annual import requirements averaged 300 mn. gallons. It is likely to become self-sufficient by about 1973. The French and Italians at present drink 240 and 220 pints of wine per head a year respectively.

Given these orders of magnitude of production and consumption wine inevitably falls under the CAP. Long-term intervention by means of aids for storage and premiums for distilling table wines for industrial purposes is envisaged for years when production exceeds foreseeable demand by more than a third. Local short-term market support, lasting as in the case of fruit and vegetables until market prices are re-established above intervention level, occurs when average prices for a given type of wine have remained below that level for two consecutive weeks. Intervention prices are fixed for a year ahead at not less than 75 per cent and not more than 90 per cent of the basic price for each type of wine. The basic price reflects average prices over the previous two years. No first-stage intervention by producers' associations is envisaged for wine. Imports are subject to the common external tariff reinforced by sluice-gate prices, and export restitutions may be granted in certain cases. The CAP also provides for the introduction by 1 September 1968 of harmonized measures for improving quality and for controlling the labelling and movement of grapes and wines. Finally, the structural and rural social problems associated with many of the Community's wine-growing areas ensure them special consideration for assistance from the Guidance Section of FEOGA.

No proposal has so far been made for any harmonization of national excise duties on wines or liqueurs derived from wines, which would be of considerable interest to British consumers in the event of UK entry into the EEC. The disappearance of the present UK tariff would result in only a modest reduction in retail prices, and any harmonization of excise rates, possibly at some level lower than those at present applied in the UK, seems unlikely to take place in the near future. In the case of tobacco, however, harmonization is considered by the Commission to be one of several measures urgently needed in order to introduce free trade in manufactured tobacco into the Community. This is essential if raw tobacco is to be included under the CAP. At present in the two main producing countries, France and Italy, whose growers supply about a third of the Community's total requirements of raw tobacco, state monopolies purchase all home-produced leaf at prices fixed by them in relation to estimated costs of production. Such arrangements thus cover almost 90 per cent of EEC output. In response to a resolution by the Council in May 1966 the Commission has submitted a draft proposal for the phasing out, between 1968 and 1970, of the two state monopolies. These control, to the direct financial benefit of the French and Italian treasuries, the manufacture, distribution, advertising, and import of all tobacco products in each country, besides acting as collectors of customs and excise. Their disappearance is necessary if a free trade in leaf tobacco is to be established within the common external frontier, all preferential excise rates and other discriminatory measures in favour of national tobacco products being eliminated and contract prices to growers being replaced by a Community-based system of deficiency payments. The disproportionately large contribution of tobacco to the incomes of the mostly very small holdings on which it is grown, in the south and south-west of France, on the upper Rhine, and in Italy, creates problems which, as in the case of wine, are largely structural and social. It will be remembered that a special grant of $15 mn. has been made towards structural improvement of Italian tobacco production from the Guidance Section of FEOGA.

PART III

Appendixes

Appendix A

EEC: Support arrangements under the CAP

Product	Threshold prices and variable levies	Sluice-gate prices	Customs duties	Quotas	Target price	Guide price	Intervention (price)[a]	Derived intervⁿ prices	Export restitutions	Deficiency payments	Production subsidies	Basic price	Buying-in price	Reference price	Quality standards	Production quotas	Consumer subsidies	CAP introduced	Single market stage begun	No. of basic regulation
Grains (except rice & durum)	×	—	—	—	×	—	×	×	×	—	—	—	—	—	—	—	—	1.8.62	1.7.67	120/67
durum wheat	×	—	—	—	×	—	×	×	—	×	—	—	—	—	—	—	—	1.8.62	1.7.67	120/67
rice[b]	×	—	—	—	×	—	×	×	×	—	—	—	—	—	—	—	—	1.9.64	1.9.67	359/67
Dairy products																				
raw milk	—	—	×	—	×	—	—	—	—	—	—	—	—	—	—	—	—	1.11.64	1.4.68	none[d]
butter	×	—	—	—	—	—	×	—	×	—	×	—	—	—	—	—	×[e]	1.11.64	1.4.68	13/64[d]
cheese	×	—	—	—	—	—	×[e]	—	×	—	×	—	—	—	—	—	×[e]	1.11.64	1.4.68	13/64[d]
skim milk	×	—	—	—	—	—	▬	—	×	—	×	—	—	—	—	—	—	1.11.64	1.4.68	13/64[d]
12 pilot products	×	—	—	—	—	—	—	—	×	—	—	—	—	—	—	—	—	1.11.64	1.4.68	13/64[d]
Beef and veal																				
fat cattle	×	—	×	—	—	×[f]	×	—	×	—	—	—	—	—	—	—	—	1.11.64	1.4.68	14/64[d]
veal calves	×	—	×	—	—	×[f]	—	—	×	—	—	—	—	—	—	—	—	1.11.64	1.4.68	14/64[d]
meat	×	—	×	×	—	—	—	—	×	—	—	—	—	—	—	—	—	1.11.64	1.4.68	14/64[d]
Mutton and lamb	—	—	×	—	—	—	—	—	—	—	—	—	—	—	—	—	—	no proposal so far		none
Pigmeat	×	×	—	—	—	—	×	—	—	—	—	×	—	—	—	—	—	1.8.62	1.7.67	121/67

	Threshold prices and variable levies	Sluice-gate prices	Customs duties	Quotas	Target price	Guide price	Intervention (price)	Derived interv. prices	Export restitutions	Deficiency payments	Production subsidies	Basic price	Buying-in price	Reference price	Quality standards	Production quotas	Consumer subsidies	CAP introduced	Single market stage begun	No. of basic regulations
Eggs	×	×	—	—	—	—	—	—	—	—	—	—	—	—	×	—	—	1.8.62	1.7.67	122/67
Poultry meat	×	×	—	—	—	—	—	—	—	—	—	—	—	—	×	—	—	1.8.62	1.7.67	123/67
Sugar																				
white sugar	×	—	—	—	×	—	×	×	×	—	—	—	—	—	—	×	—	1.7.67	1.7.68	1009/67
sugar-beet	—	—	—	—	×	—	—	—	—	—	—	—	—	—	—	×	—	1.7.67	1.7.68	1009/67
Horticulture																				
fruit and vegetables	—	—	×	—	—	—	×	—	×	—	—	×	×	×g	×	—	—	1.8.62	1.1.67–1.7.68	23/62 and 159/66
non-edible products	—	—	×	—	—	—	—	—	—	—	—	—	—	—	×	—	—	1.7.67	1.7.68	noneᵈ
potatoes	—	—	×	—	—	—	—	—	—	—	—	—	—	—	—	—	—	no proposal so far		none
Vegetable oils and oilseeds	×	—	×	—	×	—	×	×	×	×	—	—	—	—	—	—	—	1.7.67	1.7.67	136/66
Olive oil	—	—	×	—	×	—	×	—	×	×	—	—	—	—	—	—	—	1.11.66	1.11.66	136/66
Wine	—	×	×	—	—	—	×	—	—	—	—	×	—	—	×	—	—	1.11.69	1.11.69	24/62ᵈ
Tobacco	—	—	—	—	×	—	×	×	—	×	—	×	—	—	—	—	—	1.1.67	1.7.68	noneᵈ
Wool	—	—	—	—	—	—	—	—	—	—	—	—	—	—	—	—	—	not subject to the CAP		none
Hops	×	—	×	—	—	—	—	—	—	—	—	—	—	—	—	—	—	under consideration	none	

ᵃ In all cases at the discretion of the Commission.
ᵇ For non-producer countries (i.e. other than Italy and France) imports are subject to a fixed levy only.
ᶜ Till 1970 in Germany and Netherlands.   ᵈ New regulation due before single market stage.
ᵉ For Parmesan-type cheeses in Italy.
ᶠ On basis of which supplementary levy may be raised.
g On basis of which countervailing duty may be raised.
Source: EEC Regulations.

Appendix B

EEC: Official pricing arrangements for farm products[a] 1967/68

(£ per long ton and units of account per metric ton for each item unless otherwise stated)

Grains

	EEC					UK		
	Wheat[b]	Barley[b]	Maize[b]	Oats[b]		Wheat	Barley	Oats
Target price[c]	44·98	39·98	40·19	none	Guaranteed price[d]	25·93	24·75	27·43
	106·25	94·44	94·94			61·25	58·46	64·79
Threshold price[c]	44·19	40·00	39·20	35·41	Minimum import	22·50	20·00	20·00
	104·38	92·11	92·59	83·65	price	53·15	47·24	47·24
Basic intervention	41·71	37·24		none				
price[e]	98·75	87·97						

Dairy products

	EEC				UK		
	Milk[e]	Butter[e]	Cheese[ef]		Milk	Butter	Cheese
Target price				Guaranteed price[h]			
pence/gallon	45·60			pence/gallon	43·66	none	none
u.a./100 Kg	9·75[g]	none	none	u.a./100 Kg	9·33		
Threshold price	none	809·68	568·36				
		1912·50	1342·50				
Intervention price	none	746·17	none				
		1762·50					

Beef and veal

	EEC			UK		
	Fat cattle[e]	Veal calves[e]			Fat cattle	Veal calves
	(liveweight)				(liveweight)	
Guide price[j]	287·88	387·37	Guaranteed price[k]		189·00	none
	680·00	915·00			446·43	
Intervention price[l]	273·49	368·01				
	646·00	869·25				

Mutton, lamb, and wool

			Fat lambs and sheep (liveweight)	Wool
No arrangements		Guaranteed price	371·00[k]	497·00
			876·33	1173·95

Pigmeat

	EEC		UK	
	Fat pigs (deadweight)			Fat pigs (deadweight)
Basic price		Guaranteed price[m]		
sh./score	55·60	sh./score		45·92
u.a./m.ton	735·00	u.a./m.ton		607·41
Intervention price[n]				
sh./score	46·70			
u.a./m.ton	617·40			

Hen eggs

No arrangements	Guaranteed price[p]		
	sh./dozen		3·542
	u.a./egg		0·035

Sugar

	EEC			UK	
	Sugar beet[eq]	White sugar[e]		Sugar beet[q]	White sugar
Target price	none	94·62	Guaranteed price	6·65	none
		223·50		157·02	
Intervention price	none	89·88			
		212·30			
Minimum producer price	7·20	none			
	170·00				

Potatoes

No arrangements

Guaranteed price   14·50
                        342·50

Oilseeds

Target price	85·73
	202·50
Basic intervention price	83·19
	196·50
Minimum intervention price	74·72
	176·50

No arrangements

a Products of direct interest to UK producers only. UK production grants are not included in UK prices.

b Prices for 1968/69.

c July/August price, subject to ten monthly increments.

d Average price subject to seasonal variation and standard quantity/target indicator price arrangements.

e Prices are for 1968/69, when the unified market comes into force.

f Cheddar.

g 3·7 per cent fat content at farm-gate. Target price at dairy 10·30 u.a. (48·23 pence).

h Average price subject to seasonal variation and standard quantity arrangements. Actual farm-gate price estimated at about 40 pence (8·53 u.a.).

j The Commission has proposed the following guide prices for 1969/70

Fat cattle	Veal calves
£296·35/ton	£400·08/ton
u.a. 700·00/m.ton	u.a. 945·00/m. ton

k Average price subject to seasonal variation.

l Intervention price is within the range 93 to 96 per cent of guide price. Figures shown are 95 per cent of guide price.

m Average price subject to seasonal variation, to quality, and to flexible guarantee and feed formula arrangements.

n Intervention price is within the range 82 to 85 per cent of basic price. Figures shown are 84 per cent of basic price.

p Average price subject to seasonal variation and indicator price and feed formula arrangements. Actual farm-gate price to producers contracting to BEMB in 1966/67 was about 2·92 sh./dozen (0·029 u.a./egg).

q 16 per cent sugar content.

Appendix C

The CAP—A Glossary of Terms

The support arrangements listed in tabular form in Appendix A are described in detail in the course of Chapters 6 to 16. Since most of them are modelled, more or less closely according to circumstances, on the system adopted for the common market in grains, we have thought it useful, by way of glossary, to include here a 'plain man's guide' to the complexities of Regulation 120/1967.

Since 1 July 1967 the grain trade in the member countries of the European Economic Community has operated under a common price policy and with common regulations. Intra-Community levies, differences in national accounting years, etc., were then abolished.

Grain prices in the EEC are not (as in the UK) guaranteed to the producer. Instead prices are maintained above current world prices and, within limits, kept stable, by the application of import taxes in the form of variable levies on imports into the Communtiy, and by support buying of community farm produce. These measures are administered by official national agencies operating in each member country on behalf of the Commission in Brussels. Each year the Council of Ministers acting on proposals from the Commission decides for each particular type of grain a

Basic target or indicative price. This represents the level towards which it is intended that wholesale market prices should tend in the area of greatest deficit. To help keep prices at about this level the Council also fixes a

Basic intervention price, the wholesale market price level in the area of greatest deficit at which the national intervention agency is obliged to step in to support the market by purchasing all offers made to it. This level, providing a guaranteed minimum wholesale price, ranges between 5 per cent and 10 per cent below the basic target price. As there are many intervention points in the Community it has been necessary to fix

Derived target and intervention prices at a number of centres at varying distances from the area of greatest deficit (Duisburg). The level of these prices is, as a general rule (but see below), lower than that of the basic price by the amount of the lowest cost of transporting grain from the local to the basic intervention point. Similarly, in order to relate international prices to the basic Community price the Commission calculates transport (and handling) costs from the main ports so that the Council can fix a

Threshold price, or minimum duty-paid import price. Basic threshold prices for all grains are set for the months of July and August in each year. These are increased, as are target and intervention prices, by nine

Monthly increments (so-called *reports*) applied from September to May inclusive (eight, from October to May, in the case of maize) designed to encourage orderly marketing by compensating farmers for the costs of storing grain, including interest costs. Threshold prices of all grains take account of

Quality differences. For instance the threshold price for maize is based on US Nos. 1 and 2 Yellow Corn. An adjustment factor of 50 cents per ton for US No. 3 and of $1.00 per ton for US No. 4 is added to the c.i.f. price, i.e. deducted from the levy (see below). In the case of soft wheat, however, adjustment factors for North American varieties are all deducted from the c.i.f. price (added to the levy), ranging from $12.50 per ton for the highest quality, Manitoba I, down to $2.50 for Red Winter Garlicky I and II. English Milling and Swedish wheats, being close to EEC standard quality, are subject to no adjustment. For all types there are also appropriate adjustments for moisture content, sprouting, etc. These threshold prices are implemented by

Levies, import taxes fixed by relating the threshold price to the lowest offers of imported grain of the day. Levies, which, apart from weekends, may be altered daily, change to take account of (a) monthly movements and annual adjustments to the threshold price and (b) changes in offers of grain c.i.f. the Community. Assuming that threshold prices are constant, levies go up if c.i.f. prices fall and are lowered if c.i.f. prices increase. In order to assess the

Lowest offers the Price Information Office in Brussels receives by 2.15 p.m. each day between 600 and 1,000 quotations for spot and future shipment from national agencies (two in the case of Germany—the Hamburg market and the EVSt in Frankfurt). Small or non-representative offers are ignored in the processing of this data, which has to be completed in time for the Commission to approve the resulting lowest c.i.f. price by 4.30 p.m. Confirmation by each national delegation by 6 p.m. gives legal validity to the consequent levies, which are then operative from midnight. While world prices remain below threshold prices the Community's domestic market is therefore insulated from developments outside, apart from the relatively small variations permitted by the levy regulations. These regulations must be described in some detail because of their important

Effect on the trade. The effect of levies could have been to stifle trading. In fact it has been the opposite. Not only have import quotas for grains, such as were applied in Germany, been abolished, but the regulations leave considerable commercial flexibility and opportunities for speculative trading. Two features in particular should be mentioned. In the first place the regulations permit some

c.i.f. price variation with no levy change. For instance in the case of maize c.i.f. offers can rise or fall by $7\frac{1}{2}$ cents per 100 kg. (75 cents per metric ton) compared with the last levy fixation without the levy being changed. The c.i.f. price from which the levy is currently derived, however, remains the operative one for future changes. If, after a period of minor fluctuations within the permitted 15 cents bracket c.i.f. prices come to be assessed at, say, 9 cents below the last fixation, the levy would then be increased by the full 9 cents. The next possible change after that would then be based on the new c.i.f. price level, and so on. A second important feature is the permission to

fix levies for future imports. The rate of levy is fixed when an importer applies to his national agency, using telex or telegram, for permission to import a certain quantity of grain in a certain month. In order to obtain the levy announced for the day in question, the request has to be dispatched before 4 p.m. that day. The national agency then confirms back the licence, on which is stamped the appropriate levy. Levies can be fixed for shipment during the current month and the three following months. They are always the same for the current month and the next month. For the next two months levies may be different if the futures market and the threshold price (allowing for monthly increments) do not keep in step. If an importer wishes to fix the levy for these next two months he will have to pay a fixation premium representing the difference between current and future levies. This fixation premium is announced daily at the same time as are the levies for the current (and the following) month.

There are a number of

Penalties and charges affecting this trade. Levies are payable by the importer after the grain has been cleared through customs, when the exact quantities are established. A deposit amounting to $5.00 per ton has to be made at the time when the levy is fixed, but this is normally done by bank guarantee, the cost of which is under 1 per cent per annum. If a licence is not used there is anyway a penalty of 50 cents per ton. In addition, if at the end of the third month following the month of application the licence has not been used and the levy is then higher than that applicable to the licence, this difference has to be paid as well. The levy set on the last day of each month (being the day on which licences lapse) is therefore particularly important for the trade. Naturally it is also the day on which the Commission and the national agencies have to take particular care to make sure that the market is not being rigged. A similar penalty is payable when a vessel arrives after the end of the month in question and the levy applicable to the actual arrival date is higher, except when the delay is due to acts of God and strikes. For vessels discharging at Rotterdam, for instance, passing the Hook of Holland constitutes arrival, the date and time being officially certified.

Restitutions, or export subsidies, are granted to enable grains purchased on EEC markets, either by private traders, or by national agencies in the course of intervention, to be exported without financial loss on the world market. Rates of payment, which may be varied by the Commission, in agreement with the Management Committee for Cereals, according to the origin and destination of the exports, are normally the same as the current rate of levy.

Regionalization of prices. The original EEC concept involved only one basic indicative and intervention price, to be used in the area of greatest deficit, and from which all other prices would be derived. Two main objections were made to this: that it was unfair that the remotest regions which on social grounds might be entitled to special consideration should in fact be receiving the lowest prices; and that it was wrong to link areas such as the south-west of France and south-western Bavaria to a centre as remote as Duisburg. To go some way towards meeting these objections four points on the Rhine above Mainz (including Mannheim and Kehl) as well as Marseilles, Rome, and a number of markets in the south-east of Italy and the Islands have also been designated as basic intervention points.

Intervention levels. For an experimental period of the 1967/68 season a system of support for the grain market favoured by the French has been tried out for the whole Community. Instead of waiting invariably for prices to fall to intervention level before making any purchases agencies may, in order to attract grain to particular markets and prevent a general collapse of prices, enter a given market or markets at just above inter-vention point. This so-called type 'B' or preventive intervention, sometimes practised by ONIC, the French intervention agency, in the past, may only be undertaken with the agreement of the Commission.

Denaturation of soft wheat.   The principle followed in fixing the denatur-ation subsidy is to bring the price of wheat in line with barley but not lower in order not to depress barley prices. The subsidies are published in advance for the entire crop year and in 1967/68 range from $11.65 per ton in August to $14.20 for May/June/July plus $1.90 for the cost of denaturing. Alternatively a supplemental subsidy of $1 is granted when the wheat is incorporated into feeds without being denatured. Denaturation is naturally a source of concern for the importing trade since imports of feed grains will suffer. It is not believed, however, that the use of wheat for feed will be considerable. Because of minimum daily quantity requirements (it should be noted that an official must be present) only the larger compounders can incorporate or denature wheat. Moreover, since the price incentive is not great, even the larger compounders will probably not use large quantities of wheat.

Q

Appendix D

EEC: Imports and Exports of Agricultural Produce
Average 1963–1965

Countries of Origin and Destination	IMPORTS Tons	% of Total	$ '000	% of Total	EXPORTS Tons	% of Total	$ '000	% of Total
				LIVE CATTLE				
UK	73,756		32,862		22		109	
Ireland	30,408		15,435		12		77	
Norway	6		3		–		–	
Denmark	143,549		62,985		32		95	
Total	247,719	47·9	111,275	42·5	66	0·1	281	0·4
Intra-Community	80,792	15·6	52,239	19·9	85,807	83·3	55,293	78·7
Rest of World	188,480	36·5	98,428	37·6	17,155	16·7	14,697	20·9
World Total	516,990	100·0	261,942	100·0	103,028	100·0	70,271	100·0
				LIVE PIGS				
UK	1,837		1,045					
Ireland	571		244					
Norway	–		–					
Denmark	29,175		11,789					
Total	31,583	38·4	13,079	30·4	–	–	–	–
Intra-Community	38,905	47·3	24,475	57·0	37,939	95·9	23,699	95·9
Rest of World	11,782	14·3	5,407	12·6	1,619	4·1	1,001	4·1
World Total	82,262	100·0	42,952	100·0	39,558	100·0	24,700	100·0
				BEEF				
UK	5,435		4,461		3,326		5,716	
Ireland	14,739		10,535		–		–	
Norway	498		326		24		21	
Denmark	55,724		49,607		26		36	
Total	76,386	16·0	64,929	17·0	3,376	2·1	5,773	3·7
Intra-Community	126,872	26·6	122,908	32·2	129,196	80·0	126,076	81·7
Rest of World	274,161	57·4	193,813	50·8	28,933	17·9	22,479	14·6
World Total	477,419	100·0	381,641	100·0	161,505	100·0	154,329	100·0
			MEAT OF SHEEP AND GOATS					
UK	1,849		1,569		–		–	
Ireland	4,416		3,680		–		–	
Norway	–		–		–		–	
Denmark	–		–		–		–	
Total	6,265	28·0	5,248	25·9	–	–	–	–
Intra-Community	8,014	35·8	9,594	47·4	7,946	92·8	9,473	92·5
Rest of World	8,107	36·2	5,399	26·7	620	7·2	773	7·5
World Total	22,386	100·0	20,241	100·0	8,566	100·0	10,246	100·0
				PIGMEAT				
UK	5,372		4,183		248		218	
Ireland	2,322		1,954		–		–	
Norway	120		53		–		–	
Denmark	26,217		17,925		–		–	
Total	34,031	20·7	24,115	18·6	248	0·2	218	0·3
Intra-Community	89,831	54·5	73,506	56·8	93,492	93·5	75,577	94·4
Rest of World	40,876	24·8	31,832	24·6	6,267	6·3	4,266	5·3
World Total	164,738	100·0	129,454	100·0	100,006	100·0	80,061	100·0

Countries of Origin and Destination	IMPORTS				EXPORTS			
	Tons	% of Total	$ '000	% of Total	Tons	% of Total	$ '000	% of Total
SLAUGHTERED FOWLS								
UK	–		–		97		55	
Ireland	–		–		–		–	
Norway	4		3		–		–	
Denmark	25,819		16,343		6		5	
Total	25,823	13·3	16,346	12·0	103	0·1	60	0·1
Intra-Community	102,193	52·7	76,663	56·3	103,479	86·0	77,274	87·0
Rest of World	66,061	34·0	43,220	31·7	16,718	13·9	11,517	13·0
World Total	194,076	100·0	136,229	100·0	120,300	100·0	88,851	100·0
HORSEMEAT								
UK	2,261		1,185		117		23	
Ireland	3,030		1,733		–		–	
Norway	–		–		–		–	
Denmark	46		36		–		–	
Total	5,337	17·1	2,954	20·7	117	18·8	23	4·9
Intra-Community	812	2·6	581	4·1	477	76·8	415	89·2
Rest of World	24,994	80·3	10,751	75·3	27	4·3	27	5·8
World Total	31,144	100·0	14,286	100·0	621	100·0	465	100·0
EDIBLE OFFALS								
UK	417		151		1,525		518	
Ireland	854		327		–		–	
Norway	–		–		–		–	
Denmark	15,769		8,848		12		5	
Total	17,030	15·6	9,326	15·8	1,537	6·0	523	4·8
Intra-Community	18,001	16·5	9,149	15·5	22,522	87·5	9,480	87·0
Rest of World	74,133	67·9	40,668	68·8	1,687	6·6	897	8·2
World Total	109,165	100·0	59,144	100·0	25,746	100·0	10,899	100·0
PORK, DRIED, SALTED, EXCLUDING OFFALS								
UK	–		–		8,213		5,648	
Ireland	–		–		–		–	
Norway	–		–		–		–	
Denmark	25		32		–		–	
Total	25	0·6	32	0·5	8,213	60·1	5,648	42·2
Intra-Community	3,390	83·1	5,289	88·7	3,582	26·2	5,507	41·1
Rest of World	666	16·3	639	10·7	1,867	13·7	2,232	16·7
World Total	4,081	100·0	5,960	100·0	13,661	100·0	13,387	100·0
SAUSAGES ETC.								
UK	–		–		1,279		1,561	
Ireland	–		–		–		–	
Norway	–		–		–		–	
Denmark	467		501		3		4	
Total	467	6·3	501	5·3	1,282	8·5	1,565	7·3
Intra-Community	5,600	75·6	6,728	71·5	5,681	37·7	6,997	32·4
Rest of World	1,340	18·1	2,185	23·2	8,119	53·8	13,009	60·3
World Total	7,407	100·0	9,414	100·0	15,081	100·0	21,571	100·0
PRESERVED MEATS								
UK	240		228		38,567		45,207	
Ireland	44		44		4		8	
Norway	531		571		51		214	
Denmark	3,515		3,283		87		107	
Total	4,330	7·8	4,115	8·1	38,709	39·3	45,536	39·6
Intra-Community	18,141	32·6	18,913	37·3	18,835	19·1	19,685	17·1
Rest of World	33,261	59·7	27,657	54·6	40,834	41·5	49,641	43·2
World Total	55,724	100·0	50,685	100·0	98,378	100·0	114,863	100·0

	IMPORTS				EXPORTS			
Countries of Origin and Destination	*Tons*	*% of Total*	*$ '000*	*% of Total*	*Tons*	*% of Total*	*$ '000*	*% of Total*
CONCENTRATED LIQUID MILK								
UK	*398*		*160*		*4,825*		*1,370*	
Ireland	–		–		–		–	
Norway	–		–		–		–	
Denmark	*619*		*479*		*108*		*27*	
Total	1,017	3·8	639	7·8	4,933	1·2	1,397	1·1
Intra-Community	24,684	91·3	7,200	88·0	26,036	6·5	8,381	6·7
Rest of World	1,349	5·0	339	4·1	371,529	92·3	115,418	92·2
World Total	27,050	100·0	8,178	100·0	402,498	100·0	125,196	100·0
FULL CREAM MILK								
UK	*140*		*70*		*1,546*		*662*	
Ireland	*19*		*10*		–		–	
Norway	–		–		–		–	
Denmark	*1,170*		*644*		–		–	
Total	1,329	5·1	724	4·8	1,546	2·6	662	1·6
Intra-Community	15,941	61·4	8,820	58·5	15,340	25·4	8,297	20·1
Rest of World	8,696	33·5	5,531	36·7	43,581	72·1	32,356	78·3
World Total	25,966	100·0	15,075	100·0	60,467	100·0	41,314	100·0
SKIMMED MILK POWDER								
UK	*3,568*		*672*		*9,970*		*1,903*	
Ireland	*254*		*80*		–		–	
Norway	–		–		*19*		*5*	
Denmark	*1,889*		*645*		*3,576*		*651*	
Total	5,711	3·3	1,397	3·4	13,565	10·6	2,559	7·7
Intra-Community	61,301	35·5	16,178	39·6	77,208	60·5	20,187	60·8
Rest of World	105,547	61·2	23,314	57·0	36,895	28·9	10,435	31·4
World Total	172,559	100·0	40,890	100·0	127,669	100·0	33,180	100·0
FRESH MILK AND CREAM								
UK	–		–		*73*		*13*	
Ireland	–		–		–		–	
Norway	–		–		–		–	
Denmark	–		–		*32*		*4*	
Total	–	–	–	–	105	0·1	17	0·1
Intra-Community	76,674	93·1	6,094	91·8	135,286	75·0	15,951	74·5
Rest of World	5,646	6·9	542	8·2	44,928	24·9	5,427	25·4
World Total	82,320	100·0	6,636	100·0	180,319	100·0	21,398	100·0
BUTTER								
UK	*21*		*21*		*23,562*		*25,361*	
Ireland	*1,001*		*700*		–		–	
Norway	*358*		*418*		–		–	
Denmark	*2,659*		*2,661*		–		–	
Total	4,039	5·6	3,800	5·3	23,562	28·8	25,361	31·3
Intra-Community	32,817	45·8	38,711	53·9	38,900	47·5	32,513	40·1
Rest of World	34,868	48·6	29,375	40·9	19,427	23·7	23,183	28·6
World Total	71,723	100·0	71,886	100·0	81,889	100·0	81,057	100·0
CHEESE AND CURD								
UK	*408*		*340*		*11,030*		*15,796*	
Ireland	*54*		*41*		*53*		*63*	
Norway	*3,905*		*2,257*		*95*		*82*	
Denmark	*45,889*		*30,227*		*327*		*250*	
Total	50,256	20·0	32,865	16·3	11,505	6·1	16,191	7·2
Intra-Community	143,108	56·9	115,103	56·9	114,368	60·7	143,617	64·2
Rest of World	57,934	23·1	54,249	26·8	62,474	33·2	63,907	28·6
World Total	251,298	100·0	202,217	100·0	188,347	100·0	223,714	100·0

Countries of Origin and Destination	IMPORTS				EXPORTS			
	Tons	% of Total	$ '000	% of Total	Tons	% of Total	$ '000	% of Total
EGGS IN SHELL								
UK	225		292		1,441		2,276	
Ireland	2		3		–		–	
Norway	169		93		–		–	
Denmark	9,276		5,110		–		–	
Total	9,672	5·3	5,497	5·0	1,441	1·6	2,276	1·6
Intra-Community	120,848	66·8	78,303	71·2	80,540	87·2	124,937	86·4
Rest of World	50,383	27·9	26,110	23·8	10,393	11·3	17,362	12·0
World Total	180,903	100·0	109,911	100·0	92,374	100·0	144,575	100·0
EGGS WITHOUT SHELLS AND EGG YOLKS								
UK	2,308		1,214		570		518	
Ireland	–		–		–		–	
Norway	–		–		–		–	
Denmark	999		1,403		4		8	
Total	3,307	15·7	2,617	11·7	574	6·4	526	7·0
Intra-Community	6,270	28·8	7,713	34·4	7,533	84·4	6,285	83·6
Rest of World	11,463	55·5	12,065	53·9	823	9·2	706	9·4
World Total	21,040	100·0	22,396	100·0	8,930	100·0	7,516	100·0
WHEAT AND MIXED CORN								
UK	43,383		2,998		556,401		31,592	
Ireland	–		–		31,015		2,467	
Norway	161		11		52,969		2,941	
Denmark	14,384		914		41,337		2,362	
Total	57,928	1·4	3,923	1·2	681,722	18·3	39,362	16·4
Intra-Community	590,196	14·1	59,207	18·4	556,507	14·9	56,519	23·5
Rest of World	3,529,074	84·5	258,336	80·4	2,490,226	66·8	144,666	60·1
World Total	4,177,198	100·0	321,467	100·0	3,728,456	100·0	240,547	100·0
RICE—UNMILLED								
UK	–		–		3,716		500	
Ireland	–		–		36		5	
Norway	–		–		1,924		278	
Denmark	–		–		–		–	
Total	–	–	–	–	5,676	12·7	783	11·5
Intra-Community	17,821	12·5	2,907	14·7	17,380	38·8	2,777	40·6
Rest of World	124,952	87·5	16,805	85·3	21,683	48·5	3,279	48·0
World Total	142,774	100·0	19,712	100·0	44,738	100·0	6,838	100·0
RICE—HUSKED AND BROKEN								
UK	203		21		2,183		350	
Ireland	–		–		710		109	
Norway	–		–		1,819		284	
Denmark	–		–		2,921		426	
Total	203	0·1	21	0·1	7,633	6·9	1,169	6·6
Intra-Community	23,642	12·9	3,848	15·7	23,297	21·2	3,793	21·3
Rest of World	159,109	87·0	20,606	84·2	79,219	71·9	12,866	72·2
World Total	182,954	100·0	24,475	100·0	110,149	100·0	17,828	100·0
BARLEY								
UK	107,793		7,276		34,987		1,961	
Ireland	–		–		14,032		875	
Norway	–		–		14,093		796	
Denmark	120,453		8,214		134,039		7,407	
Total	228,246	9·5	15,490	9·2	197,151	8·9	11,039	8·7
Intra-Community	932,111	38·7	76,465	45·4	851,786	38·4	69,796	54·9
Rest of World	1,245,780	51·8	76,551	45·4	1,169,342	52·7	46,408	36·5
World Total	2,406,137	100·0	168,506	100·0	2,218,279	100·0	127,242	100·0

Countries of Origin and Destination	IMPORTS				EXPORTS			
	Tons	% of Total	$ '000	% of Total	Tons	% of Total	$ '000	% of Total
				MAIZE				
UK	344		23		160,050		9,514	
Ireland	–		–		2,153		132	
Norway	333		21		3,075		186	
Denmark	124		10		65,553		4,001	
Total	801	0·0	54	0·0	230,831	17·7	13,833	13·7
Intra-Community	702,973	7·7	64,142	10·8	708,556	54·2	63,563	62·7
Rest of World	8,475,097	92·3	528,478	89·2	367,104	28·1	23,932	23·6
World Total	9,178,871	100·0	592,674	100·0	1,306,492	100·0	101,328	100·0
				RYE				
UK	1,485		99		–		–	
Ireland	–		–		–		–	
Norway	–		–		–		–	
Denmark	26,676		1,788		1,142		81	
Total	28,161	9·0	1,887	9·5	1,142	2·6	81	2·4
Intra-Community	31,537	10·0	2,541	12·8	32,117	74·0	2,563	77·1
Rest of World	254,530	81·0	15,468	77·7	10,149	23·4	680	20·5
World Total	314,228	100·0	19,895	100·0	43,408	100·0	3,324	100·0
				OATS				
UK	872		48					
Ireland	–		–		484		31	
Norway	–		–		44		9	
Denmark	721		64		26,152		1,547	
Total	1,593	0·2	112	0·2	26,580	15·8	1,587	12·9
Intra-Community	99,121	12·4	8,018	16·1	98,662	58·8	8,010	65·3
Rest of World	701,438	87·4	41,715	83·7	42,612	25·4	2,678	21·8
World Total	802,152	100·0	49,845	100·0	167,854	100·0	12,274	100·0
			WHEATFLOUR OR MASLIN					
UK	389		41		39,281		1,796	
Ireland	–		–		16,229		715	
Norway	–		–		9,306		486	
Denmark	–		–		23,079		1,100	
Total	389	1·0	41	0·9	87,895	7·8	4,097	4·9
Intra-Community	16,433	41·2	2,305	52·2	17,183	1·5	2,348	2·8
Rest of World	23,058	57·8	2,068	46·9	1,017,618	90·6	76,548	92·2
World Total	39,879	100·0	4,414	100·0	1,122,696	100·0	82,993	100·0
			SEMOLINA OF WHEAT OR MASLIN					
UK	–		–		734		31	
Ireland	–		–		4,528		248	
Norway	–		–		700		45	
Denmark	–		–		1,220		135	
Total	–	–	–	–	7,182	32·5	459	25·9
Intra-Community	364	2·1	45	1·5	509	2·3	53	3·0
Rest of World	17,060	97·9	2,953	98·5	14,394	65·2	1,263	71·2
World Total	17,425	100·0	2,998	100·0	22,084	100·0	1,774	100·0
			FLOUR OTHER THAN WHEAT OR MASLIN					
UK	93		26		30,398		1,737	
Ireland	–		–		76		4	
Norway	–		–		–		–	
Denmark	–		–		10,641		530	
Total	93	3·0	26	8·6	41,115	72·6	2,271	70·7
Intra-Community	2,384	76·6	229	75·8	1,446	2·6	154	4·8
Rest of World	636	20·4	47	15·6	14,053	24·8	785	24·5
World Total	3,114	100·0	302	100·0	56,615	100·0	3,210	100·0

Countries of Origin and Destination	IMPORTS				EXPORTS			
	Tons	% of Total	$ '000	% of Total	Tons	% of Total	$ '000	% of Total
SEMOLINA GRITS OTHER THAN WHEAT								
UK	–		–		56,350		2,982	
Ireland	–		–		292		14	
Norway	–		–		–		–	
Denmark	–		–		36,683		2,013	
Total	–	–	–	–	93,478	68·2	5,009	59·5
Intra-Community	12,133	94·7	1,402	94·9	12,869	9·4	1,443	17·1
Rest of World	682	5·3	75	5·1	30,659	22·4	1,970	23·4
World Total	12,815	100·0	1,477	100·0	137,074	100·0	8,421	100·0
FLAKES, ETC., BROKEN RICE								
UK	38		12		28,020		1,471	
Ireland	–		–		11,854		599	
Norway	–		–		2,846		174	
Denmark	207		17		77,489		3,088	
Total	245	1·1	29	1·1	120,209	50·0	6,332	37·9
Intra-Community	19,911	87·5	2,401	90·8	18,329	7·6	2,240	13·4
Rest of World	2,600	11·4	213	8·1	101,894	42·4	8,150	48·7
World Total	22,757	100·0	2,643	100·0	240,432	100·0	16,723	100·0
MALT								
UK	18,615		2,411		1,109		113	
Ireland	1,691		203		–		–	
Norway	–		–		536		53	
Denmark	2,608		359		–		–	
Total	22,914	12·1	2,973	11·7	1,645	0·7	166	0·5
Intra-Community	108,928	57·3	15,785	61·9	106,684	43·4	15,636	49·0
Rest of World	58,268	30·6	6,736	26·4	137,300	55·9	16,095	50·5
World Total	190,110	100·0	25,494	100·0	245,630	100·0	31,897	100·0
PASTA								
UK	–		–		6,800		1,618	
Ireland	–		–		–		–	
Norway	–		–		63		16	
Denmark	–		–		231		66	
Total	–	–	–	–	7,094	13·1	1,700	14·2
Intra-Community	12,116	66·9	3,486	67·7	12,401	22·8	3,345	28·0
Rest of World	6,006	33·1	1,663	32·3	34,849	64·1	6,894	57·7
World Total	18,123	100·0	5,149	100·0	54,344	100·0	11,938	100·0
ORANGES								
UK	375		58		2,770		238	
Ireland	–		–		68		10	
Norway	–		–		387		56	
Denmark	–		–		359		54	
Total	375	–	58	–	3,484	1·8	358	1·2
Intra-Community	70,818	4·3	11,852	4·9	85,457	44·0	12,795	43·9
Rest of World	1,564,748	95·6	229,452	95·1	105,287	54·2	16,006	54·9
World Total	1,635,941	100·0	241,363	100·0	194,228	100·0	29,159	100·0
CLEMENTINES AND MANDARINS								
UK	–		–		137		26	
Ireland	–		–		–		–	
Norway	–		–		65		16	
Denmark	–		–		243		47	
Total	–	–	–	–	445	1·3	89	1·5
Intra-Community	19,148	8·6	3,368	6·1	23,608	67·4	4,017	66·2
Rest of World	203,627	91·4	52,256	93·9	10,981	31·3	1,957	32·3
World Total	222,775	100·0	55,624	100·0	35,034	100·0	6,064	100·0

Countries of Origin and Destination	IMPORTS Tons	% of Total	$ '000	% of Total	EXPORTS Tons	% of Total	$ '000	% of Total
				OTHER CITRUS INCLUDING LEMONS AND LIMES				
UK	–		–		15,503		2,132	
Ireland	–		–		249		30	
Norway	–		–		60		11	
Denmark	–		–		3,692		479	
Total	–	–	–	–	19,504	6·6	2,682	6·1
Intra-Community	133,397	56·5	23,663	53·4	136,954	46·1	21,116	47·6
Rest of World	102,571	43·4	20,665	46·6	140,522	47·3	20,526	46·3
World Total	235,969	100·0	44,328	100·0	296,980	100·0	44,323	100·0
				FRESH BANANAS				
UK	–		–		–		–	
Ireland	–		–		–		–	
Norway	–		–		–		–	
Denmark	–		–		–		–	
Total	–	–	–	–	–	–	–	–
Intra-Community	10,978	0·9	1,381	0·7	6,453	63·5	1,055	56·1
Rest of World	1,212,093	99·1	193,653	99·2	3,717	36·6	827	43·9
World Total	1,223,070	100·0	195,267	100·0	10,169	100·0	1,882	100·0
				FRESH APPLES				
UK	1,684		134		33,437		3,576	
Ireland	–		–		436		51	
Norway	–		–		2,318		255	
Denmark	1,278		200		97		9	
Total	2,962	0·4	334	0·3	36,288	5·5	3,891	4·7
Intra-Community	513,623	72·8	68,267	61·6	524,205	79·0	64,752	77·5
Rest of World	188,660	26·8	42,285	38·1	102,920	15·5	14,861	17·8
World Total	705,244	100·0	110,885	100·0	663,414	100·0	83,504	100·0
				FRESH GRAPES				
UK	85		41		6,196		2,108	
Ireland	–		–		226		141	
Norway	–		–		1,309		287	
Denmark	–		–		2,882		550	
Total	85	–	41	0·1	10,613	4·6	3,086	8·1
Intra-Community	174,681	67·5	33,132	65·1	179,416	77·3	27,795	72·7
Rest of World	83,983	32·5	17,727	34·8	42,091	18·1	7,348	19·2
World Total	258,749	100·0	50,899	100·0	232,120	100·0	38,229	100·0
				PEARS AND QUINCES				
UK	32		7		19,221		3,776	
Ireland	–		–		751		146	
Norway	–		–		1,428		276	
Denmark	–		–		1,207		191	
Total	32	–	7	–	22,607	10·4	4,389	12·4
Intra-Community	159,745	76·1	26,712	70·9	163,052	74·8	25,286	71·7
Rest of World	50,023	23·8	10,963	29·1	32,390	14·9	5,580	15·8
World Total	209,800	100·0	37,682	100·0	218,049	100·0	35,254	100·0
				STONE FRUIT				
UK	8		3		23,774		6,371	
Ireland	–		–		119		29	
Norway	–		–		282		83	
Denmark	110		32		2,470		621	
Total	118	–	35	0·1	26,645	7·7	7,104	10·2
Intra-Community	238,936	73·3	51,489	74·8	248,754	72·1	47,738	68·8
Rest of World	86,878	26·7	17,354	25·2	69,590	20·2	14,547	21·0
World Total	325,932	100·0	68,878	100·0	344,989	100·0	69,388	100·0

Countries of Origin and Destination	IMPORTS				EXPORTS			
	Tons	% of Total	$ '000	% of Total	Tons	% of Total	$ '000	% of Total
SOFT FRUIT								
UK	126		39		672		341	
Ireland	–		–		–		–	
Norway	7		4		3		4	
Denmark	106		41		60		17	
Total	237	0·5	84	0·4	735	1·7	362	2·1
Intra-Community	32,505	67·7	14,403	71·7	33,273	77·8	13,549	76·8
Rest of World	15,256	31·8	5,593	27·9	8,779	20·5	3,728	21·1
World Total	47,997	100·0	20,080	100·0	42,786	100·0	17,639	100·0
PRESERVES WITH SUGAR								
UK	1,151		514		143		41	
Ireland	75		30		–		–	
Norway	–		–		–		–	
Denmark	–		–		–		–	
Total	1,226	6·7	544	9·8	143	1·3	41	1·1
Intra-Community	7,092	39·0	2,105	38·1	7,970	71·9	2,266	63·4
Rest of World	9,879	54·3	2,877	51·2	2,969	26·8	1,269	35·5
World Total	18,198	100·0	5,526	100·0	11,082	100·0	3,576	100·0
PRESERVES WITHOUT SUGAR								
UK	13		13		139		34	
Ireland	–		–		–		–	
Norway	–		–		–		–	
Denmark	–		–		–		–	
Total	13	0·3	13	1·3	139	11·1	34	7·2
Intra-Community	1,210	23·8	281	27·2	842	67·1	267	56·8
Rest of World	3,869	76·0	739	71·6	273	21·8	169	36·0
World Total	5,091	100·0	1,032	100·0	1,254	100·0	470	100·0
FRUIT AND VEGETABLE JUICE								
UK	345		108		13,143		2,834	
Ireland	–		–		45		10	
Norway	–				122		66	
Denmark	76		12		1,282		252	
Total	421	0·2	120	0·3	14,592	13·1	3,162	13·6
Intra-Community	70,973	41·1	12,857	30·8	75,691	67·8	13,297	57·1
Rest of World	101,498	58·7	28,718	68·9	21,313	19·1	6,820	29·3
World Total	172,891	100·0	41,696	100·0	111,595	100·0	23,278	100·0
POTATOES								
UK	13,808		328		66,198		5,337	
Ireland	–		–		–		–	
Norway	–		–		888		53	
Denmark	13,560		621		7,312		674	
Total	27,368	2·4	949	1·3	74,398	5·1	6,064	6·8
Intra-Community	841,068	72·6	52,235	69·9	875,103	59·8	52,467	59·2
Rest of World	290,842	25·1	21,540	28·8	514,793	35·2	30,089	34·0
World Total	1,159,278	100·0	74,724	100·0	1,464,308	100·0	88,620	100·0
DRIED PULSES								
UK	14,766		1,526		18,271		3,495	
Ireland	37		55		1,472		278	
Norway	–		–		3,821		714	
Denmark	2,450		334		363		95	
Total	17,253	3·4	1,915	2·7	23,917	20·1	4,582	19·1
Intra-Community	65,082	13·0	13,010	18·3	66,069	55·6	13,020	54·2
Rest of World	419,124	83·6	56,093	79·0	28,843	24·3	6,426	26·7
World Total	501,459	100·0	71,018	100·0	118,830	100·0	24,027	100·0

Countries of Origin and Destination	IMPORTS				EXPORTS			
	Tons	% of Total	$ '000	% of Total	Tons	% of Total	$ '000	% of Total
FRESH OR CHILLED TOMATOES								
UK	–		–		50,715		19,021	
Ireland	–		–		1,000		593	
Norway	–		–		414		240	
Denmark	–		–		266		178	
Total	–	–	–	–	52,395	18·8	20,032	24·6
Intra-Community	190,797	44·4	54,592	50·8	195,920	70·4	53,180	65·2
Rest of World	238,444	55·6	52,948	49·2	30,043	10·8	8,369	10·3
World Total	429,241	100·0	107,539	100·0	278,358	100·0	81,582	100·0
FRESH OR CHILLED VEGETABLES								
UK	366		35		112,122		18,807	
Ireland	–		–		958		170	
Norway	–		–		5,637		1,141	
Denmark	2,600		647		2,946		689	
Total	2,966	0·3	682	0·3	121,663	10·5	21,807	10·4
Intra-Community	839,343	74·1	156,562	76·8	863,142	74·4	153,107	72·7
Rest of World	290,838	25·7	46,529	22·8	174,961	15·1	35,674	16·9
World Total	1,133,147	100·0	203,772	100·0	1,159,766	100·0	210,588	100·0
FROZEN VEGETABLES AND PLANTS								
UK	36		7		2,680		973	
Ireland	–		–		34		12	
Norway	–		–		–		–	
Denmark	1,331		345		–		–	
Total	1,367	6·9	352	6·3	2,714	12·7	985	14·6
Intra-Community	11,122	56·2	3,005	54·0	2,617	12·2	836	12·4
Rest of World	7,286	36·8	2,203	39·6	16,103	75·1	4,910	72·9
World Total	19,775	100·0	5,560	100·0	21,433	100·0	6,731	100·0
PRESERVED VEGETABLES AND PLANTS								
UK	49		8		12,586		2,747	
Ireland	–		–		57		24	
Norway	–		–		204		55	
Denmark	–		–		73		9	
Total	49	0·4	8	0·2	12,920	50·6	2,835	43·5
Intra-Community	4,523	36·4	1,378	27·8	4,417	17·3	1,258	19·3
Rest of World	7,842	63·2	3,577	72·1	8,174	32·0	2,422	37·2
World Total	12,414	100·0	4,963	100·0	25,510	100·0	6,515	100·0
HOPS								
UK	98		189		138		279	
Ireland	–		–		9		19	
Norway	–		–		78		205	
Denmark	–		–		170		360	
Total	98	1·2	189	1·2	395	5·1	863	4·7
Intra-Community	2,273	28·4	5,211	32·2	2,565	33·3	5,661	30·8
Rest of World	5,624	70·3	10,807	66·7	4,755	61·6	11,839	64·5
World Total	7,995	100·0	16,206	100·0	7,714	100·0	18,364	100·0
UNREFINED SUGAR								
UK	2,379		232		12,239		990	
Ireland	–		–		6,660		849	
Norway	–		–		1,229		352	
Denmark	–		–		2,637		646	
Total	2,379	0·3	232	0·2	22,765	5·4	2,837	4·8
Intra-Community	40,876	5·6	5,599	6·7	152,505	36·5	19,481	32·8
Rest of World	692,372	94·1	114,391	95·1	243,073	58·1	36,986	62·4
World Total	735,627	100·0	120,222	100·0	418,343	100·0	59,304	100·0

Countries of Origin and Destination	IMPORTS				EXPORTS			
	Tons	% of Total	$ '000	% of Total	Tons	% of Total	$ '000	% of Total
			SUGAR OTHER THAN RAW					
UK	94,771		17,907		3,917		733	
Ireland	–		–		–		–	
Norway	–		–		4,405		843	
Denmark	25,316		3,102		405		89	
Total	120,087	22·9	21,009	23·1	8,727	1·8	1,665	2·0
Intra-Community	182,876	34·9	27,639	30·4	105,131	21·2	14,564	17·3
Rest of World	220,971	42·2	42,209	46·5	382,423	77·1	67,851	80·7
World Total	523,933	100·0	90,857	100·0	496,281	100·0	84,079	100·0

Source: Statistical Office of the European Community, *Foreign Trade of the EEC.*

Appendix E

Details of the 'Departmental' Calculation of Net Income for 1965/66 (revised) and for 1966/67 (forecast)[a]

	1965/66 (revised) £ mn.		1966/67 (forecast) £ mn.	
Farm Sales[b]				
Grain: Wheat	91		82½	
Barley	123½		136	
Other grain	7½		7½	
Total grain	222		226	
Potatoes	84		94½	
Sugar beet	39½		40	
Other crops	13½		13	
Total farm crops		359		373½
Fat cattle and calves	272		274½	
Fat sheep and lambs	85		84	
Fat pigs	211½		203	
Poultry and other livestock	87½		92	
Total livestock		656		654
Eggs: for food and for hatching	179½		173	
Milk and milk products	412½		422½	
Wool (clip)	16½		16½	
Total livestock products		608½		611½
Vegetables	95		101	
Fruit	47		46½	
Flowers and nursery stock	39½		40	
Total horticulture		181½		188
Sundry output		23½		24½
Total value of output		1,828½		1,851½
Farming grants, subsidies and sundry receipts[c]		99		108
Total receipts		1,927½		1,959½
Farm Expenses				
Labour	312½		305	
Rent[d]	120½		129½	
Interest[e]	25½		28½	
Machinery: Depreciation	90½		95	
Repairs	73½		76½	
Fuel and oil	50		50	
Other	24		24	
Feedingstuffs	476½		463½	
Seeds[f]	28		32	
Fertilizers[g]	120		128	
Livestock[g]	72½		77	
Other expenses[h]	113½		116½	
Total expenses		1,507		1,525½
Change in the value of growing crops, livestock and farm stocks		+48		+38
Net income		468½		472

a Because of individual roundings, the figures will not necessarily add to the totals shown.
b The value of farm sales includes deficiency payments.
c Farming grants and subsidies exclude grants for landlord type functions.
d Including imputed rent for owner occupied farms.
e Interest on credit for current farming purposes.
f Comprises the full cost of imported seed and store livestock plus merchants' margins on purchases of homegrown.
g Total cost excluding subsidy, which is credited under Receipts.
h 'Other expenses' comprise maintenance charges and miscellaneous expenses.
Source: Ministry of Agriculture, Fisheries, and Food.

Appendix F

UK: Index of Agricultural Net Output

Average 1954/55–1956/57 = 100

Years beginning 1 June

1953/54	103
1954/55	95
1955/56	98
1956/57	107
1957/58	105
1958/59	102
1959/60	112
1960/61	119
1961/62	115
1962/63	125
1963/64	127
1964/65	137
1965/66 (provisional)	136
1966/67 (forecast)	135

Source: Ministry of Agriculture, Fisheries, and Food.

Appendix G

UK: Estimated Cost of Exchequer Support to Agriculture, £mn.

Financial years beginning 1 April.

	1958/59	1959/60	1960/61	1961/62	1962/63	1963/64	1964/65	1965/66	1966/67 (Latest Forecast)	1967/68 (estimates)
I. Implementation of price guarantees										
Cereals—										
Wheat and rye	19·3	20·4	18·1	22·0	16·6	30·3	15·9	14·2	13·9	13·5
Barley	23·5	25·2	33·6	33·2	36·3	36·8	37·4	21·6	29·4	39·3
Oats and mixed corn	9·8	12·8	11·7	18·1	11·0	10·0	10·0	7·3	6·9	7·3
	52·6	58·4	63·4	73·3	63·9	77·1	63·3	43·1	50·2	60·1
Potatoes	6·9	1·0	5·7	8·0	0·4	0·4	0·7	6·8	3·5	1·1
Eggs, hen and duck	33·7	33·1	22·5	16·2	21·5	20·2	32·3	18·2	17·3	18·0
Fatstock—										
Cattle	12·5	3·4	12·3	46·4	30·5	40·8	9·8	5·0	21·2	35·8
Sheep	11·7	25·3	13·9	30·7	18·9	13·3	5·7	5·3	9·9	10·3
Pigs	20·9	22·2	20·0	36·2	51·7	26·5	32·0	39·5	7·2	14·3
	45·1	50·9	46·2	113·3	101·1	80·6	47·5	49·8	38·3	60·4
Milk	10·1	8·5	10·8	11·8	—	—	—	—	—	—
Wool	6·3	2·8	2·6	2·9	3·2	0·6	2·3	3·8	3·7	3·2
Total I	154·7	154·7	151·2	225·5	190·1	178·9	146·1	121·7	113·0	142·8
II. Farming grants and subsidies										
Fertilizers	25·8	29·4	32·2	33·0	33·9	33·6	31·3	29·6	30·0	31·1
Lime	9·2	11·0	8·7	8·8	10·0	8·0	9·9	8·1	6·8	6·6
Ploughing	9·2	9·4	10·9	11·5	11·3	9·9	8·1	7·6	6·1	3·8
Field drainage	1·9	2·6	2·7	2·7	3·0	2·6	3·1	3·1	3·2	3·6
Water supply	0·8	0·7	0·8	0·8	0·8	0·7	0·7	0·6	0·5	0·5

Livestock rearing land	1·5	1·5	1·5	1·6	1·5	1·4	1·4	1·3	1·1	1·1
Hill land	—	—	—	—	—	—	—	—	—	0·5
Marginal production assistance	2·2	1·7	1·0	0·8	0·7	0·7	—	—	—	—
Tuberculosis eradication	8·5	9·0	9·0	7·2	5·2	3·2	1·5	0·6	—	—
Calves	14·3	16·5	17·6	17·8	17·7	19·4	20·4	22·7	25·2	25·5
Beef cow	3·1	4·1	4·6	5·0	5·4	5·6	5·7	6·7	2·7	3·2
Hill cow	—	—	—	0·8	1·4	2·4	6·0	4·4	7·5	7·8
Hill sheep	—	—	0·7	—	—	—	2·5	3·4	8·1	1·6
Winter keep	1·0	1·4	0·9	0·8	0·6	0·3	0·3	0·2	3·6	3·7
Silos	—	—	—	—	—	—	—	—	0·2	0·2
Farm improvements	3·3	6·6	7·8	9·2	10·3	10·2	11·5	11·6	11·5	13·2
Farm structure	—	—	—	—	—	—	—	—	—	0·1
Investment incentives	—	—	—	—	—	—	—	—	—	9·6
Small farmers	—	1·1	5·9	7·1	7·2	5·6	4·8	3·4	2·2	2·2
Farm business records	0·1	0·1	0·2	0·4	0·4	0·5	0·5	0·5	0·1	0·4
Other grants	—	—	—	—	—	—	—	—	0·5	0·6
Total II	80·9	95·1	104·5	107·5	109·4	104·1	107·7	103·8	109·3	115·3
Totals I and II	235·6	249·8	255·7	333·0	299·5	283·0	253·8	225·5	222·3	258·1
Administrative expenses estimate	5·0	5·9	6·1	8·7	9·0	9·4	9·7	9·8	10·2	10·8
	240·6	255·7	261·8	341·7	308·5	292·4	263·5	235·3	232·5	268·9
III. *Other services* Payment from U.K. Exchequer for the benefit of agricultural producers in Northern Ireland	0·8	1·2	1·1	0·9	1·1	1·5	0·8	1·3	1·7	1·7
Total estimated cost of agricultural support	241·4	256·9	262·9	342·6	309·6	293·9	264·3	236·6	234·2	270·6

Source: Ministry of Agriculture, Fisheries, and Food.

Appendix H

UK/EEC: Trade in Agricultural Engineering Products

Exports	1956		1963		1966	
1. Total UK exports of tractors and agricultural machinery (£mn.):	73·6		164·8		178·9	
of which Complete tractors		47·0		114·9		111·5
Tractor parts		9·1		24·9		37·0
Combine harvesters		2·7		3·5		4·3
Other agricultural machinery		14·8		21·5		26·1
2. UK exports of tractors and agricultural machinery to EEC (£mn.):	12·5		34·5		30·3	
of which Complete tractors		7·8		22·8		10·7
Tractor parts		1·6		3·5		9·7
Combine harvesters		1·1		2·1		1·4
Other agricultural machinery		2·0		6·1		7·5
3. 2 expressed as a percentage of 1 Total:	17·0		20·9		16·9	
Complete tractors		16·6		19·8		9·6
Tractor parts		17·2		13·9		26·1
Combine harvesters		42·7		58·6		31·8
Other agricultural machinery		13·5		27·9		23·2
4. UK exports of tractors and agricultural machinery to individual EEC countries, per cent of total:						
Germany (FR)	15		25		22	
France	44		42		29	
Italy	13		13		6	
Netherlands	19		13		12	
BLEU	9		7		31	
	100		100		100	

Imports	*1956*		*1963*		*1966*	
1. Total UK imports of tractors and agricultural machinery (£mn.):	4·5		14·5		30·0	
of which Complete tractors		1·1		2·2		1·7
Tractor parts		0·9		2·8		15·9
Combine harvesters		0·5		4·7		5·4
Other agricultural machinery		2·0		4·8		7·0
2. UK imports of tractors and agricultural machinery from EEC (£mn.):	1·7		6·9		19·9	
of which Complete tractors		0·2		0·1		0·8
Tractor parts		0·2		0·5		11·1
Combine harvesters		0·3		3·9		4·7
Other agricultural machinery		1·0		2·4		3·3
3. 2 expressed as a percentage of 1 Total:	37·2		47·7		66·5	
Complete tractors		13·7		5·8		44·2
Tractor parts		24·0		16·0		70·0
Combine harvesters		67·9		84·0		87·0
Other agricultural machinery		50·0		50·0		47·0
4. UK imports of tractors and agricultural machinery from individual EEC countries, per cent of total:						
Germany (FR)	65		47		21	
France	9		15		10	
Italy	6		3		3	
Netherlands	16		14		6	
BLEU	3		21		60	
	100		100		100	

Source: The Agricultural Engineers Association.

R

Appendix J

EEC: Common Threshold Prices for Milk Products by Groups, 1968/69 (u.a. ($) per 100 kg. and sh. per cwt)

Group No.	Pilot product	u.a./100 Kg.	sh./cwt
1	Powdered whey	21·50	91·0
2	Powdered whole milk	103·25	437·1
3	Powdered skimmed milk	54·25	229·7
4	Condensed milk, unsweetened	46·00	194·7
5	Condensed milk, sweetened	61·75	261·4
6	Blue-veined cheese	132·25	561·0
7	Parmesan	204·00	863·6
8	Emmenthal (hard cheese)	149·25	631·9
9	Gouda (medium-hard cheese)	123·50	522·8
10	Butterkäse	119·75	507·0
11	Camembert (soft cheese)	123·50	522·8
12	Lactose	43·00	182·0

Appendix K

UK/EEC: Selected Rates of Duty on Horticultural Produce

Tariff heading		UK Season (where applicable)	UK Rate (shillings per cwt. or per cent)	EEC Season (where applicable)	EEC Rate (shillings per cwt. or per cent)
07.01	Asparagus	1 Apr.–30 Jun.	56s.		16%
		1 July–15 Apr.	10%		
	Broccoli and	1 Mar.–30 Jun.	8s.	15 Apr.–1 Nov.	17% (min. 8s. 6d.)
	cauliflowers	1 July–28/29 Feb.	6s.	1 Dec.–14 Apr.	12% (min. 5s. 11d.)
	Carrots	1 May–30 Jun.	20s.		17%
		1 Jul.–30 Apr.	10%		
	Cucumbers	1 Mar.–30 Sept.	20s.	16 May–31 Oct.	20%
		1 Oct.–28/29 Feb.	10%		
	Green peas	1 Jun.–31 Jul.	18s. 8d.	1 Jun.–31 Aug.	17%
		1 Aug.–31 May	10%	1 Sept.–31 May	12%
	Lettuce and	1 Mar.–31 Mar.	20s.	1 Apr.–30 Nov.	15% (min. 10s. 8d.)
	endive	1 Jun.–31 Oct.	16s.	1 Dec.–31 Mar.	13% (min. 6s. 9d.)
		1 Nov.–28/29 Feb.	10s.		
	Mushrooms	1 Oct.–30 Apr.	20%		16%
		1 May–30 Sept.	10%		
	Potatoes	16 May–30 Jun.			
		(a) new	9s. 4d.	1 Jan.–15 Apr.	15%
				16 Apr.–30 Jun.	21%
		(b) other	1s.		18%
		1 Jul.–31 Aug.	2s.		
		1 Sept.–15 May	1s.		
	Tomatoes	1 May.–31 May		15 May–31 Oct.	18% (min. 14s. 10d.)
		(a) of a value exceeding £7	37s. 4d.		
		(b) other	10%		
		1 Jun.–31 Aug.	37s. 4d.		
		1 Sept.–31 Oct.	18s. 8d.		
		1 Nov.–30 Apr.	10%	1 Nov.–14 May	11% (min. 8s. 6d.)
	Dry-bulb onions and shallots	31 Aug.–30 Nov.	4s. 8d.		12%
		1 Dec.–31 July	10%		
07.02	Vegetables (whether or not cooked), preserved by freezing		10%		19%
08.02	Oranges	1 Apr.–30 Nov.	3s. 6d.	1 Apr.–15 Oct.	15%
		1 Dec.–31 Mar.	10%	16 Oct.–31 Mar.	20%
08.06	(A) Apples	16 Apr.–15 Aug.	4s. 6d.	1 Aug.–31 Dec.	14% (min. 10s. 2d.)
		16 Aug.–15 Apr.	Free	1 Jan.–31 Mar.	10% (min. 7s. 2d.)
				16 Apr.–31 July	8% (min. 5s. 11d.)
	(B) Pears	1 Feb.–31 Jul.	4s. 6d.	1 Jan.–31 July	10% (min. 6s. 5d.)
		1 Aug.–31 Jan.	3s. 0d.	1 Aug.–31 Dec.	13% (min. 8s. 6d.)

R*

Tariff heading		Season (where applicable)	UK Rate (shillings per cwt. or per cent)	EEC Season (where applicable)	Rate (shillings per cwt. or per cent)
08.07	(A) Cherries	1 Jun.–15 Aug.	37s. 4d.	1 May–15 Jul.	15% (min. 12s. 8d.)
		16 Aug.–31 May	10%	16 Jul.–30 Apr.	15%
	(B) Peaches and nectarines	1 Apr.–30 Nov.	10%		22%
		1 Dec.–31 Mar.	14s. 0d.		
	(C) Plums	1 Jul.–31 Oct.	16s. 9d.	1 Jul.–30 Sept.	15% (min. 12s. 8d.)
		1 Dec.–31 Mar.	9s. 4d.	1 Oct.–30 Jun.	10%
		other times	10%		
08.08	(A) Bilberries		Free		9%
	(B) Currants	16 Jun.–31 Aug.	37s. 4d.		12%
		1 Sept.–15 Jun.	10%		
	(C) Gooseberries	1 May–31 Jul.	18s. 8d.		
		1 Aug.–30 Apr.	10%		12%
	(D) Strawberries	1 Jun.–9 Jun.	37s. 4d.	1 May–31 July	16% (min. 12s. 8d.)
		10 Jun.–31 Jul.	56s. 0d.	1 Aug.–30 Apr.	16%
		1 Aug.–31 May	10%		
	(E) Other		10%		12%

Appendix L

UK/EEC Conversion Factors

To convert			*Multiply by*
Areas			
Hectares	to	Acres	2·4711
Acres	to	Hectares	0·40468
Yields			
Quintals (100 kg.)/			
Hectare	to	Hundredweights (112 lb.)/Acre	0·79657
Cwt./Acre	to	Qls/Ha	1·25538
All commodities by weight			
Units of Account ($)/			
metric ton (1,000 kg.)	to	£/long ton (2,240 lb.)	0·42336
£/long ton	to	u.a./m. ton	2·36207
u.a./100 kg.	to	shillings/hundredweight (112 lb.)	4·2336
sh./cwt.	to	u.a./100 kg.	0·236207
Milk			
sh/gallon	to	u.a./100 kg.	2·56283
u.a./100 kg.	to	sh./gall.	0·390194

£1   = 2·40 u.a.
1 u.a.   = £0·4166 (= DM 4·00).
1 kilogram   = 2·2046 pounds
100 kg.   = 220·462 lb.
1 long ton   = 1·016 metric tons
1 metric ton   = 0·9842 long tons
1 gallon   = 4·54596 litres
1 litre   = 0·21997 gallons
1 gallon milk weighs 10·3 lb.
1 litre milk weighs   1·028 kg.

Appendix M

The Other Applicants: A Note on Ireland, Denmark, and Norway[1]

Of the three other applicants for EEC membership Ireland and Denmark both have a strong agricultural incentive to enter the Community. As far as farming is concerned Norway is in a special position, analogous in some respects to that of the UK. Denmark, as can be seen from Appendix D, has the greatest volume of trade in agricultural products with the EEC. The CAP has, however, caused a serious decline in Danish exports to the Community, from a total of $737 mn. in 1961, before the first common levies came into force, to $633 mn. in 1966. The value to Denmark of coming within the wall of the common external tariff needs no stressing, but the importance of its agricultural exports to other markets, notably those of the EFTA countries, and of the UK in particular, have made its application to join the EEC dependent on that of the UK. Exports to EFTA rose from $627 mn. in 1961 to $1,160 mn. in 1966, of which nearly half were to the UK. Ireland's entry into the Community is even more closely linked to Britain's: 80 per cent of its exports, mainly agricultural, go to the UK. Irish farmers, like the Danes, also stand to benefit from the CAP quite apart from the British connection. Norway's motives in applying for membership, on the other hand, are in no way connected with its agriculture, which would gain little or nothing from adopting the CAP and could indeed be seriously disadvantaged, at any rate in the short run.

IRELAND

Like the Six, Ireland is mainly a country of small family farms. There are only 35,000 male employees among 250,000-odd persons working on the land. The proportion of farms of over 50 acres (20 hectares), around 30 per cent, is, however, higher than in any EEC country, and about the same as in Denmark. Labour productivity is still relatively low, the 30 per cent of the working population engaged in agriculture accounting for only 20 per cent of GNP. Farm produce makes up nearly two-thirds of Ireland's exports—nearly three-quarters if industrial exports mainly derived from agriculture are included.

Membership of the EEC would thus present a considerable opportunity to Ireland. The Anglo-Irish Free Trade Area Agreement, signed at the end of 1965, cannot provide a complete solution to its export needs. Although now double what they were in 1965/66 Ireland's butter exports will continue to be subject to quota. Imports of store cattle into the UK, partly owing to the doubly depressing effect of the credit squeeze and of

---

[1] For a detailed description of recent policy developments in each of the three countries, see *Agricultural Policies in 1966*, OECD, Paris, 1967.

EEC levies on English markets, declined steadily from the 1964 peak level of 638,000 which the Irish government had, as part of the Agreement, undertaken to make available annually. The shortfall was to some extent compensated by additional exports of finished cattle and of beef, and the store trade in 1967/68 improved considerably. If Ireland were inside the Community, however, there would be unrestricted access for butter to the UK and for cattle to the Continent. The CAP would have other advantages for Irish agriculture. EEC producer prices would help to raise farm incomes, even in the depressed 'congested districts' of the west. Except for wheat and sugar-beet, whose production is not of outstanding importance to most Irish farmers, prices within the Community would be higher than present ones. The improvement would be especially favourable for beef and dairy produce (mainly butter), which account for 60 per cent of total gross farm output. The present price for milk is one of the lowest in Western Europe and the butter support price, 469s. 0d. per cwt. would go up to 746s. 0d. Output of mutton and lamb (5 per cent of total) would also benefit. It is thought that the higher cost of home-grown barley (there is at present a guaranteed producer price of £22. 10s. 0d. a ton) and imported grains would be more than compensated, for efficient producers at any rate, by some rise in the present rather modest prices of eggs, poultry-meat, and pigmeat (which account for 20 per cent of total gross output). The Irish poultry industry is still relatively undeveloped. In 1966 less than 20 per cent of laying hens were in flocks of over 1,000 birds. There were under 400 broiler units, of which only 17 per cent had a capacity of over 10,000 birds. Only horticulture, accounting for 3 per cent of gross output, would, with the removal of tariff protection, find itself in a rather exposed position.

The disappearance of a number of production subsidies inadmissible under the CAP, such as those for mountain sheep and fertilizers, would not be enough to outweigh the advantage to most Irish farmers of the higher prices, and funds saved to the exchequer could be redeployed to the greater advantage of the economy as a whole. Additional farm income would be obtained from the market rather than from the pocket of the taxpayer. Levies on imports from third countries should, in the government's view, be more than compensated by improved export earnings. Great hopes are placed on the spur of the agricultural common market to raise farmers' efficiency and productivity, Mr. John Lynch, the prime minister, summarizing the impact of the CAP on Irish farming as 'better prices with increased competition'.[2]

DENMARK

Even Denmark's farm structure and organization, widely recognized for many years as a model of its kind in Western Europe, has been found during the past decade to be no longer proof, without substantial government assistance, against the customary economic pressures. 40 per cent

[2] Statement in the Dáil, 25 July 1967.

of holdings are still under 10 hectares (25 acres). But whatever the need for further increasing the average size and the viability of their farms, Danish farmers are better equipped than most to compete in international markets. Denmark exports about two-thirds of its agricultural output. Half goes to the EFTA countries and about a third to the EEC. Entry into the Community will not only restore easy access for beef and veal to Italy and for cheese, fatstock, poultry, eggs, and barley to Germany, but provide an outlet for bacon, butter, and poultry to the UK no longer restricted by the present market-sharing agreement and quotas. Meat production, including poultry, accounts for about 60 per cent of Denmark's gross farm output, of which nearly two-thirds is in the form of pigmeat.

In addition to these trading advantages adoption of the CAP and of Community prices is likely, in the view of the EEC Commission[3] and others, to result in higher incomes for most Danish farmers, even allowing for a rise in feedgrain prices and the abolition of various subsidies. A report by a committee of Danish civil servants has estimated a net increase in aggregate farm income for 1968/69, taking 1967/68 EEC prices, of between 16 per cent and 28 per cent,[4] depending on certain assumptions, should Denmark join the EEC. Minimum import prices for all grains are at present fixed at around $74 (£31) per ton. Import levies on grains (and on skimmed milk powder) are paid into a fund for subsidizing small farmers' purchases of feedgrains and dried skim. Producers receive world market prices for livestock products which are exported, but the value of their sales on the home market is boosted, at the consumer's expense, by means of a tax, the proceeds of which are distributed *pro rata* to producers in the form of supplementary payments. The incidence of the tax, or levy, represents the difference between a target price, fixed annually for each main product (except liquid milk and cheese), and its current average weekly export price. This mechanism would disappear under the CAP. The prices which it aims at are at present lower than EEC intervention prices for veal and butter, but somewhat higher than those for beef and pigmeat. The element of price guarantee involved for eggs and poultry-meat under the existing Danish system would of course also disappear. Though it seems unlikely that the protection afforded by the present veterinary ban on imports would be allowed to continue in the long run, exporters from other parts of an enlarged Community would with difficulty compete with Danish producers and co-operatives on their own domestic market. Renewed access to the markets of the Six and the lapse of the poultry-meat quota to the UK should compensate them for higher feed costs and loss of price support at home. But competition will be fierce; total production will probably not return to its pre-1962 level; and the trend towards larger scale production will continue in Denmark as elsewhere.

[3] *Opinion on the application for membership received from the United Kingdom, Ireland, Denmark, and Norway, for submission to the Council*, Brussels, 29 September 1967, p. 38.
[4] *Danmark og de Europæiske Fællesskaber*, Vol. II, Copenhagen, 1967, p. 216.

NORWAY

Considering that Norway has few large industrial cities the proportion of its resources devoted to farming is surprisingly small. Agriculture as a whole accounts for only about 9 per cent of GNP, of which almost half is attributable to forestry and fishing. On the other hand between 40 per cent and 50 per cent of the country's export earnings are in the form of shipping services. Official agricultural policy aims (without conspicuous success) at giving farm people a level of income comparable to that in other sectors, but is also closely concerned with preserving rural social life over wide areas of sparsely populated countryside (the so-called 'settlement' problem), as well as with national defence. The country is reckoned to be broadly self-sufficient in food except for wheat and feedgrains, between 80 per cent and 90 per cent of which are imported. Exports consist mainly of the surplus dairy products arising from a heavy subsidy on milk, and of occasional seasonal or cyclical surpluses of beef and pigmeat. In addition to export subsidies these products, like most others, are assisted by direct price support and by control of imports. This is carried out by a State trading monopoly in the case of cereals and feeding stuffs, by an 'inter-professional' Import Council for fruit and vegetables, and, for a number of other products, by the government in association with semi-public marketing boards. Of the £60 mn. spent in 1966 on aid to agriculture about £42·5 mn. was directed towards cereals and dairy produce, about £25 mn. of it in price support and the rest in production grants and in transport and hill-farming subsidies. Fertilizer subsidies and acreage payments for potatoes together amounted to a further £3·25 mn. Over £5 mn. was received by farmers in remote areas in the form of direct cash payments, not linked to any form of production, on a variable acreage basis.

From this brief summary it will be evident that Norwegian agricultural policy involves a number of major features that are incompatible with the CAP: import controls, State and producer monopolies, and production grants of various kinds. It has been officially estimated that the less stable and much lower EEC prices (about 20 per cent lower for cereals and dairy produce) combined with removal of inadmissible grants and subsidies could result in a reduction of £25 mn., or one third, in Norwegian farmers' aggregate net income.[5] The calculation is of course a static one and makes no allowance for adjustments to new circumstances, but it is difficult to see how most of the adjustments could be anything but painful. In its White Paper the Norwegian government recognizes that the transition to the CAP could to some extent be mitigated by structural improvements, by re-equipping holdings and adapting them to new techniques of production and marketing. Unfortunately, as OECD has reported,[6] the recommendation of an official committee, made as long ago as 1960, that the subsidy system be simplified and aid concentrated on investment grants rather than general price support was not followed up. In fact the pro-

[5] *Om Norges forhold til de Europeiske Felleskap*, Government White Paper. No. 86, 1966/67.
[6] *Agricultural Policies in 1966*, p. 414.

portion of aid to investment fell from 12 per cent of total government support to 6 per cent between 1960 and 1965. Any fundamental change of policy is likely to remain difficult so long as the two farmers' unions retain their strongly entrenched position as statutory parties to the series of Agricultural Agreements that regulate all support measures. These have been re-negotiated from time to time since the original General Agreement of 1950. Entry into the EEC would provide the occasion for a break with this tradition.

Inside the EEC structural improvements would of course assume much greater prominence, whether grant-aided by the government or by the Guidance Section of FEOGA. Of the 130,000 holdings of over 2 hectares (5 acres) only 20,000 are more than 10 hectares (25 acres). The scope for further amalgamations of farms is, however, often limited by their remoteness. Re-training of farmers and their families for other types of employment would be eligible for assistance from the European Social Fund. As it is, only three-quarters of the 177,000 farm operators in Norway are occupied full time on their holdings, and in predominantly forestry or fishery districts between 70 per cent and 85 per cent of those engaged in farm work have a secondary occupation. Unfortunately only about 10 per cent of farms are situated within daily reach of industrial employment.

The measures hitherto devised in the EEC for assisting problem farming areas appear inadequate to fit the case of Norway. The Commission in its report to the Council recognizes that 'Norwegian agriculture is carried on under particularly unfavourable natural and structural conditions (the area of the average farm is 5 ha.); it could not survive in the northern part of the country without substantial support from the State. In its efforts to maintain a minimum of population in these areas, Norway has not yet been able to dispense with aid of this kind.'[7] The Norwegian government's White Paper holds that these unfavourable conditions would warrant 'more extensive arrangements' for the country as a whole than are necessary in other EEC countries. Arrangements 'of a permanent nature', they believe, could be justified by the Rome Treaty provided they were subject to periodic scrutiny by the Commission. The special measures applying to North Norway, the mountains and the western fjords, should be allowed to continue in their present form, such as the incentives needed to secure supplies of liquid milk for these remote areas. The White Paper concludes, treading delicately between the susceptibilities of the Six and those of the Norwegian farmers' unions:

Norwegian agriculture will not derive any direct concrete advantage from entry, at least not on a short-term view. However, it is recognized that agriculture is dependent on the general economic growth and development of a country. Indirectly, therefore, farming will benefit from the economic progress of other industries resulting from membership. Provided that arrangements can be achieved which will mitigate the agricultural difficulties involved in Norwegian membership it is possible that the industry will in the somewhat longer term stand to gain from an expanded market.[8]

[7] *Opinion*, p. 38.   [8] White Paper, op. cit.

The UK's fellow applicants for membership are thus faced with a variety of problems and opportunities. It is worth noting in conclusion the concern shared by all three of them on three particular issues. First, official statements in each country have referred to the possible effects for farming of the 'right of establishment' under the Treaty of Rome. In Denmark, mention of 'acquisition of farm holdings for commercial purposes',[9] and in Norway of the importance of holdings not being taken over by 'outside interests', underlines a deep distrust, also felt in many parts of the EEC, on the part of farmers of the invasion of their industry by outside capital and the acquisition of farm land by 'non-professionals'.

Second, adoption of the CAP would involve for all three countries a rise in retail food prices, and consequently in the cost of living. For Denmark an increase in food prices over and above the present 'home market' levels of about 12 per cent would, it is estimated, lead to a rise of between 2 per cent and 3 per cent in the cost of living.[10] Mr. John Lynch, cautious about the actual effect on food prices, suggested that the Irish cost-of-living index might go up by about $3\frac{1}{2}$ per cent.[11] No specific mention is made of food prices in the Norwegian White Paper. Official thinking has all along tended to discount any rise, presumably owing to the general fall in farm-gate prices which would occur. The Commission in its report,[12] however, takes the view that 'the lowering of producer prices in Norway would not mean a reduction in consumers' expenditure. On the contrary, the removal of consumer subsidies and the rise in prices for imported goods would lead to a certain increase in consumer prices.'

Finally, all three governments stress the importance to them of the UK's negotiations on agriculture. The Norwegians would like to know in advance the problems to be raised. Ireland's benefits from the CAP 'may well be affected by the length of any transitional period that Britain may negotiate for changing over to the Community system'.[13] The Irish would presumably prefer it to be brief. The Danes want no transitional period at all, but consider that they should take part in the UK's agricultural negotiations 'from the very beginning' owing to the decisive impact they will have on vital Danish interests.[14]

[9] Statement made on behalf of the Danish government by Mr. Tyge Dahlgaard, Minister of Commerce and European Market Relations, to the Commission of the Communities, 18 July 1967.
[10] Civil Service Committee's report, p. 227.
[11] Statement to the Dáil.
[12] Opinion, p. 38.
[13] Statement to the Dáil.
[14] Statement made on behalf of the Danish government (see note 9 above).

Index

Printed by
The Camelot Press Ltd
London and Southampton